WISDEN

ON GRACE

AN ANTHOLOGY

EDITED BY
Jonathan Rice

BLOOMSBURY
LONDON · NEW DELHI · NEW YORK · SYDNEY

BY THE SAME AUTHOR

Wisden on India
The Wisden Collector's Guide

John Wisden & Co Ltd
An imprint of Bloomsbury Publishing Plc

50 Bedford Square
London
WC1B 3DP
UK

1385 Broadway
New York
NY 10018
USA

www.bloomsbury.com

WISDEN and the wood-engraving device are trademarks of John Wisden & Company Ltd,
a subsidiary of Bloomsbury Publishing Plc

First published 2015

www.wisden.com
www.wisdenrecords.com
Follow Wisden on Twitter @WisdenAlmanack
and on Facebook at Wisden Sports

British Library Cataloguing-in-Publication Data
A catalogue record for this book is available from the British Library.

Library of Congress Cataloguing-in-Publication data has been applied for

ISBN: HB: 978-1-4729-1163-6
ePub: 978-1-4729-1164-3

2 4 6 8 10 9 7 5 3 1

Typeset in Minion Pro by Newgen Knowledge Works (P) Ltd., Chennai, India
Printed and bound in Great Britain by CPI Group (UK) Ltd, Croydon CR0 4YY

To find out more about our authors and books visit www.wisden.com.
Here you will find extracts, author interviews, details of forthcoming events
and the option to sign up for our newsletters.

A Gloucestershire team photograph from 1877. WG is unmistakeable in the front row, with his elder brother EM on his left. Fred Grace is directly behind WG, while their cousin WR Gilbert is in the back row, third from the left. *Courtesy of The Roger Mann Collection*

CONTENTS

INTRODUCTION
WISDEN ON GRACE

Wisden was first published in 1864, the year in which William Gilbert Grace made his first impact in English cricket, by scoring 170 for South Wales against the Gentlemen of Sussex at Brighton at the age of not quite 16. This innings was big enough to attract the attention of the cricket hierarchy, even if the match was never considered to be truly "first-class" (a distinction that did not exist in 1864). His elder brother, Edward Mills Grace, then aged 23, was already established as "the biggest run-getter in the world" according to Sydney Pardon, and had spent the winter of 1863-64 with George Parr's team touring Australia. In 1864 cricket was divided into two separate but not mutually exclusive camps – the amateurs, as exemplified by the Marylebone Cricket Club (the Earl of Dudley was president of the club in that year), and the professionals, who were grouped in the more northern parts of England, in the teams led by William Clarke and others, who toured the country playing cricket as "All-England", "The United Eleven" and other such catch-all names.

Amateur cricket was, in the 1860s, somewhat in the doldrums. Matches were not played at Lord's during the grouse season, and the quality of the matches played there during the rest of the year was not always high. A new secretary, R. A. Fitzgerald, had been appointed in 1863, and it was his responsibility to restore the club's image, its finances and its position as the arbiter of all matters cricketing. He was starting from a fairly low base. Professional cricketers were not, of course, allowed to be members of the Marylebone Club, but they were employed to bowl in the nets at the members, and they were allowed to play for "MCC and Ground" against all-comers.

John Wisden was a professional cricketer. He finished playing in 1863, but by this time he was already building his sports-equipment business, and it seems that he thought a slim publication looking forward to the cricket season each year would act as a useful advertisement for his company. There were already other publications on cricket – Frederick Lillywhite's *Guide To Cricketers*, for example, had been published regularly since 1849 – so John Wisden was not being original in his venture, but he did manage, perhaps more by luck than good judgment, to hit a nerve with the public, who took to his little book from the outset. His timing turned out to be perfect.

Wisden did not edit the book himself. It was printed by W. H. Crockford in Blackheath, who is also described as "'compiler'", but the main editor from the outset seems to have been W. H. Knight, a journalist with *The Times*, who continued to edit the Almanack until his death in 1879. The contrast between Wisden, the professional cricketer, and Knight, the *Times* journalist, gave their publication an editorial tension that worked. Wisden lived in the world of the professionals, his former colleagues, while Knight – and even more so future editors like Charles and Sydney Pardon – was more closely involved with the upper strata of Victorian society on display at Lord's, the universities and the public schools. In their Almanack, they chronicled all cricket, taking in both amateur and professional, and those who trod the narrow line between the two.

Cricket was changing in mid-Victorian times. Roundarm bowling had been legalised earlier, but in 1864 overarm bowling was officially sanctioned, and by mastering this action bowlers became quicker, more accurate and more devious in their spin. Overs were of only four balls then: it was not until 1889 that they were increased to five balls, an experiment that lasted only a decade. In 1900, they were increased again, this time to the present six balls.

In 1864 there were also no declarations allowed: with the quality of the pitches as poor as they were, few innings lasted long enough for a captain to want to declare them closed. But at about this time, mechanical lawnmowers were coming into common use, which meant that the quality of pitches improved greatly. This led occasionally to farcical periods of cricket when the batsmen were trying to get out and the fielders were trying to keep them in. In 1889, declarations were permitted for the first time, but only on the third day of a match. In 1900, this law was relaxed so that declarations were allowed any time after lunch on the second day. Even though *Wisden* probably did not realise it at the time, cricket was metamorphosing into a sport that could – and would – capture the public imagination. All it needed was a hero.

That hero was, of course, William Gilbert Grace. The man who became known to the world soon enough by his initials only, but still to some of his intimates as "Gilbert", was born into a comfortably middle-class family living in the Gloucestershire countryside. His father was a doctor, and in due course he and his elder brother Edward also became doctors, as would have his younger brother Fred had death not taken him before his 30th birthday. The Graces ranked solidly in the middle of Victorian society, halfway up, neither up nor down.

WG was exactly what cricket needed, and therefore he was exactly what the fledgling *Wisden's Almanack* needed. He was the perfect hero not only for cricket enthusiasts, but also for all Victorians. The Victorian educated middle classes had a certainty about them – an absolute conviction that their way of life was the best of all possible worlds and that the benighted heathen needed to be told that fact often and loudly. "Muscular Christianity", as it was known – the personification of spiritual values through physical activity – was a crucial part of the message of the British Empire, and cricket was perhaps the most important component. Cricket, in the Victorian mind, taught all the values of honesty, integrity and team spirit, as well as the well-thumbed values of "play up, and play the game" (which is a quotation from a poem written in 1892, more than a quarter of a century into WG's career). Cricket is still today the sport most associated with the British Empire.

There is no evidence to suggest that W. G. Grace was any more a keen Empire-builder than the next man, but his dominance of cricket for almost 40 years made him a symbol of British sporting greatness, and a character about whom the British public could never tire of reading. Wisden's Almanack was fortunate to have WG to write about as it grew in authority.

There is, however, a strange equivocation in *Wisden*'s attitude to WG. While his brothers received almost uniformly good reports from *Wisden*'s reporters, their attitude to the Champion, as they quickly began to name him, was grudging in its praise. In the first few years of *Wisden*, and of WG's career, there were no reports, only scorecards, so there was no opportunity for the editors to comment on the style or quantity of the runs scored. But once the editors took the decision to comment on the matches played (a decision almost certainly influenced by the colossal scores WG was racking up each season) it is noticeable that while lesser batsmen may be praised for their "faultless play" or "fine strokes" in making, say, 40, the comments on WG's century in the same innings might be not much more than that he was dropped when he had only scored four.

The early reports, especially of the "great matches" such as Gentlemen v Players and the Canterbury Week, often gave as much space to describing the crowds and their reaction to the play as to the play itself, but WG was always a focus of attention, whether for being successful as usual, or for a much rarer and therefore more remarkable failure. But it was very obvious that for *Wisden* and its readers in the early years of publication, the social aspect of cricket was as important as the scorecards. England was (mostly) a rich country at peace with the world and with itself, and cricket reflected the state of its society. W. G. Grace brought a glamour to cricket which encouraged crowds to flock to see him play. Although the majority of the people cheering him on from the boundary would not have been anything other than working class, *Wisden*'s reports, and those of the newspapers in those more hierarchical days, concentrated on the members of the gentry who were gracing the matches with their presence. If WG had played as a professional, the effect might have been very different.

W. G. Grace was in reality neither professional nor amateur. But he was soon made a member of MCC, and that made him officially an amateur. WG's cricket not only helped build *Wisden's Cricketers' Almanack* into a publishing phenomenon, it also went some way towards saving the reputation and finances of the Marylebone Club, for whom he was selected as often as MCC could manage. For the purposes of the scorecard, he was an amateur, "Mr W. G. Grace" or "W. G. Grace, Esq.", or more occasionally in his later years, "Dr W. G. Grace", rather than "Grace" or "Grace, W. G." For the purposes of his bank account, he was a professional, making far more money out of the game than any professional of his day.

WG's success in the great matches of the day, notably the Gentlemen v Players fixtures, turned cricket on its head. Where previously the professionals had won pretty well every match every year, unless the weather intervened, once WG came on the scene, the amateurs dominated. To be more precise, WG dominated, and ten other amateurs in each team enjoyed the ride. The professional elevens, through whom John Wisden had made his name, disappeared from the scene as public interest waned, and the amateur matches, dominated by MCC but also including Oxford v Cambridge, Eton v Harrow, I Zingari and a host of others, filled up the pages instead. The Gloucestershire county side, it should be remembered, was entirely amateur in its first years of existence, years in which they went unbeaten at home almost entirely thanks to the efforts of the Grace family.

The young WG batted sublimely, for Gloucestershire and for any other side he chose to play for, establishing records that few had thought possible until this astonishingly athletic young man showed it could be done. He dominated the first-class averages throughout the 1860s and '70s, and was not seriously challenged as a batsman until his career was well into its second decade, when players like Arthur Shrewsbury and the Surrey professionals Bobby Abel and Tom Hayward came on the scene. What's more, he also bowled.

Bowling was meant to be what the professionals did. It is clear that *Wisden*, under its early editors, considered bowling to be far less important than batting. Many of the most remarkable bowling performances of the 1860s and '70s were almost completely overlooked by *Wisden*'s reporters, while an innings of 40 containing a couple of elegant strokes was deemed worthy of several lines of obsequious praise. It is not until near the end of his career that *Wisden* even records WG's style of bowling, and certainly the descriptions of fine bowling spells which celebrated the efforts of, say, Verity, Lindwall, Trueman, Holding, Warne, McGrath and many others in later years are entirely absent from the *Wisden* reports during Grace's career. We never get much idea of how the great man bowled, nor indeed how he managed to lure quite so many batsmen to their doom.

While *Wisden* never says so in so many words, at least not until Geoffrey Moorhouse's remarkable piece in the 1998 edition, the Almanack seemed to disapprove of W. G. Grace. Reading between the lines of their reports of his doings over 40 years, there is no warmth in their descriptions of his "hits", and one might almost feel that the editors are looking down their noses at this far-too-successful Gloucestershire lad who was making them have to rewrite the record books with almost every innings. Why, for example, was WG not featured in the "Cricketers of the Season" section - which became "Five Cricketers of the Year" – until his wonderful season of 1895? He was the best batsman, and perhaps the best bowler, for many years before that. True enough, the public loved WG, as several testimonials, not to mention reports of loud cheering and throwing of hats, so amply prove. *Wisden* records all these, but perhaps through slightly gritted teeth.

It is not until his later years, as for example in recording the feats of 1895, that *Wisden* warms towards the man who ensured they had something marvellous to write about every year. Sydney Pardon wrote in 1896 that

"Having known Mr Grace for many years, and seen him make a goodly proportion of his 107 hundreds, I can truthfully say that my feeling of delight when he succeeds, or of disappointment when he fails, has not become less keen with the lapse of time."

This could be interpreted as a slightly two-faced comment in that we are not told how keen Mr Pardon's feelings of delight and disappointment were in the first place, but Lord Harris in the same edition shows no reserve in his praise for the professional amateur with and against whom he played countless times.

"I regard WG as the most prominent exponent there has ever been of the finest and purest game that has ever been played, [and] the old man is the kindest and most sympathetic cricketer I have ever played with."

That is not an opinion that would have received universal acclaim even then, and over the years WG has acquired a reputation for gamesmanship and sharp practice. There is nobody still alive who saw him play (they would have to be almost 110 years old even to have seen him play from their prams), so we cannot say for certain what his manner was like on the field of play. What we do know is that he and his brother EM were among the most competitive cricketers ever to play the game, and that they always played to win.

Wisden 1909 records that:

"Mr E. M. Grace, in all matches in which he has participated during his extraordinary career, has scored 76,705 runs and obtained 11,959 wickets. He was born in 1841, and for the Thornbury Club in 1904, he took 277 wickets. In 1905 he took 303 wickets, and in 1906 as many as 352. In 1907 he obtained 212 wickets for 2382 runs, and had 208 catches missed off his bowling. He did not play in 1908, owing to lameness."

Despite being in his mid-sixties, he still recorded (and no doubt remembered in detail) how many catches were missed off his bowling, and although he did not play in 1908, he did not consider himself retired – yet. This was a competitive man, and his brother was of the same ilk.

By the end of WG's career, after his falling-out with Gloucestershire and his rather odd – but well-paid – attempt to get first-class cricket established at Crystal Palace, *Wisden* acknowledged that this man almost single-handedly raised cricket from a slightly seedy northern professional sport to the national game. Even as the Champion's records were starting to be broken by MacLaren, Fry, Ranji and others, *Wisden* was beginning to realise that there would never be another WG.

W. G. Grace's influence lives on, and his name appears frequently in every Almanack apart from the very first one, as he is still a permanent fixture in the Records section. Over the years, the tributes, assessments and reassessments have totalled several hundreds of thousands of words, not to mention all the pages of statistics that accompany WG wherever he is mentioned. W. G. Grace was perhaps not the first, but is still the greatest, giant of the game, just as John Wisden's little Almanack was not the first, but is still the greatest, record of the game of cricket. Neither Grace nor *Wisden* would have done quite as well without the other.

In this anthology, I have tried to tell the story of W. G. Grace's career, and the careers of other members of his family, as reported by *Wisden*. The focus is inevitably mainly on WG himself, simply because there have probably been more words written about him in the pages of *Wisden* over a century and a half than about any other cricketer, but the deeds of other Graces, which are intertwined with the Champion's, are also included. It is clearly impossible to include match reports of every game WG played in, or even to note *Wisden*'s thoughts on each of his 126 centuries, as that would create a book of vast proportions and massive weight, but the extracts selected have, we hope, covered every significant moment in the cricketing careers of the Graces. We have also included articles which over the years have reflected on the phenomenon and heritage of WG, and which include anecdotes and thoughts of the great man which were not published during his lifetime. The intention is to give a complete picture of the Grace family's impact on cricket as *Wisden* saw it, and to remind ourselves quite what a giant of the game W. G. Grace was.

We are now a century on from the death, at the age of only 67, of W. G. Grace, but his name and face are probably as familiar to cricket lovers today as the names and faces of many current Test players. He dominated cricket as nobody else ever dominated a sport. My guess is that *Wisden* will be recording many thousand more words about the great man over the next century, too.

Jonathan Rice
October 2014

CHAPTER 1

THE GRACE FAMILY STORY BEGINS:
1863 TO 1874

"As wonderful as it is unparalleled"

John Wisden retired from professional cricket at the end of the 1863 season, just as overarm bowling was permitted. This change in the Law, along with advances in the art of pitch preparation and an increasing wealth of both time and money in Victorian Britain, created the right environment for cricket to become ever more popular as a spectator sport. In its early years, Wisden's little Almanack attempted only to give the scores of the major matches (and some minor ones too – the distinction between different standards of cricket were not clear at this stage), without any comment whatsoever. In the very first Almanack, it was WG's elder brother, Edward, who had the honour of being the first member of his family to be mentioned in Wisden.

In the first dozen or so years of its existence, the Almanack gained in confidence and authority, and cricket gained a huge following. County clubs were formed and the County Championship began. In 1864 there were eight counties deemed to be capable of putting out first-class sides (not including Gloucestershire, where there was then no county cricket club in existence). By 1873 there was a full calendar of county matches each summer. The County Championship title was not officially granted until 1890, but in the years before that there was a general acceptance of which county was each season worthy of the title of Champion. The county matches, along with such games as Gentlemen v Players and the University Match, were the focus of public attention, and success in these games often afforded national fame. Test matches did not begin in England until 1880.

The editors of Wisden's Almanack quickly recognised the story of W. G. Grace and his family as the core of public interest, and made sure that their pages were full of their exploits. The transformation of cricket from the bucolic pastime it was in the early years of the 19th century to the professional public entertainment it became by the latter third of the 1800s is discernible in Wisden's reports of the era.

WISDEN 1864

The first mention of any of the Grace family in Wisden *comes in the very first edition, on page 25. WG was only 15 in 1863, but his elder brother, the 21-year-old Edward Mills Grace, was already a famous cricketer.*

"Long Scores"
1862, July 24. Lord's for South Wales v MCC and Ground, Mr E. M. Grace 118.

Also in the first edition, page 81, scorecard of "Gentlemen Under Thirty Years Of Age v Players Under Thirty Years Of Age" at Lord's, July 14 and 15, 1862, E. M. Grace Esq. opened for the Gentlemen and was c Jackson b Wootton 25 in the first innings, and b Tarrant 7 in the second. He took two catches and clean-bowled Wootton in the Players' second innings, but the Players still won by 157 runs.

He featured in matches on the next two pages (Gentlemen v Players at Lord's, June 29 and 30, 1863, and Gentlemen v Players at The Oval on July 2, 3 and 4, 1863), but was on the losing side on both occasions. He took five wickets in the Players' first innings at Lord's and again in their first innings at The Oval, but the Gentlemen lost by eight wickets and nine wickets respectively.

EM was by this time already acknowledged as one of the very best players in England. His younger brother, who had already played big games in his home county, had not yet stepped on to the national stage.

WISDEN 1865

The first mention of WG in Wisden *comes on page 73 of the 1865 edition. WG, just a few days past his 16th birthday, is listed among the players for the South Wales Club versus MCC and Ground at Lord's on July 21 and 22, 1864. He made 50 in the first innings and just two in the second; he took one wicket. He outbatted his older brother EM, who made nought and four, but was outbowled by him. E. M. Grace took five wickets in the MCC and Ground first innings, but the match ended in a draw.*

A week later, Wisden *records the brothers playing for the South Wales Club against I Zingari, again at Lord's. They opened the batting in each innings, with EM making 55 and 18 while WG made 34 and 47 out of team totals of 140 and 159. E. M. Grace took two wickets in the IZ first innings, and WG two in the second, but I Zingari still won by three wickets.*

In the early editions of Wisden, *no comment or commentary was made on the matches it reported. Only the scorecard was published.* Wisden *expressed the view that its readers would have just as expert a view of the skills of the various cricketers as its editor, whose opinion was thus unnecessary.*

E. M. Grace's achievements are dotted throughout the second edition. Opening the batting for England against Thirteen of Kent at Canterbury on August 8 and 9, 1864, he scored 31 as England cruised to a victory by an innings and 83 runs, making this match incidentally the first recorded in Wisden *to feature any member of the Grace family on the winning side. Two days later, still at Canterbury, he is playing for MCC against the Gentlemen of Kent, in which EM's contribution is just 17 and 15, but with four catches and a stumping, he seems to have been making a rare appearance behind the stumps. The Marylebone Club won by 241 runs. For England against Surrey at The Oval on August 15, 16 and 17, EM is recorded as making 78 and 31, but still Surrey won by nine wickets.*

In the English winter of 1863–64, an English Twelve toured Australia and New Zealand, with E. M. Grace a key member of the side. Among his achievements was victory in a single-wicket match, recorded by Wisden:

Grace and Tarrant v Eight of Ballarat
At Ballarat, January 13, 1864

Two of England
E. M. Grace b Wills 11
G. F. Tarrant b Bryant 9
$$\overline{20}$$

Ballarat

W. H. Greaves b Tarrant 2	J. M. Bryant b Tarrant 0
D. Sweeney b Tarrant 0	G. Murray run out 0
A. Phillips b Grace 5	T. W. Wills run out 0
W. Neap b Grace 0	$\overline{11}$
J. Oldham b Tarrant 4	

Grace and Tarrant repeated the feat in New Zealand, playing against Eleven of Otago. At Dunedin on February 15, 1864, Grace and Tarrant v Eleven of Otago ended officially in a draw, but Grace and Tarrant scored eight (Grace seven, Tarrant one) and 16 (Grace ten, Tarrant six) against The Otago Eleven's seven all out (Tarrant taking all 11 wickets), and then Wisden *records that*

"The Eleven did not play their second innings".

At Castlemaine, Grace and Jackson played a single-wicket match against Eleven of Castlemaine, "Tarrant fielding for the two." Grace and Jackson made 14 (Grace 13, Jackson nought, no-balls one), while Eleven of Castlemaine were all out for two, Jackson taking all the wickets.

Great cricketer though he was proving to be, E. M. Grace was not as quick on his feet as his younger brother.

"Having time on hand at Otago, the following foot races were run:

	Distance run	Winner
Mr Grace v Holmes	¼ mile	Holmes won as he liked
Mr Grace v Tarrant	600 yards	Tarrant, by six yards
Mr Wardill v Mr Grace	100 yards	Mr Wardill
	Throwing the cricket ball	Mr Grace won, distance thrown, 101 yards."

Back in Australia, at Maryborough, Tarrant's Eleven, including E. M. Grace, beat Parr's Eleven by 56 runs.

At the conclusion of the grand match, a Single Wicket match was got up, Mr Grace challenging any six of the local players; and going first to the wickets, remained there the rest of the day, hitting away in brilliant style to the tune of 106, and carrying his bat out into the bargain. His play during the afternoon was eagerly watched, and some of his hits were enthusiastically cheered. The bowling was repeatedly changed, but the "great gun" was invulnerable.

WISDEN 1866

The Gentlemen v Players matches had for many years been lopsided affairs, with the Players routinely proving too strong for the Gentlemen. The 1865 match at Lord's proved a turning point. The match at The Oval on July 3 and 4 was won by the Players by 118 runs, despite seven wickets for WG and four for EM, but when the sides met again a week later, the Graces played a major role in the victory:

Gentlemen v Players
At Lords, July 10 and 11, 1865

Players

T. Humphrey c Cooper b E. M. Grace ... 38	c Lyttelton b E. M. Grace	6
J. Smith c V. E. Walker b Evans 33	c Maitland b Evans	18
W. Mortlock c Mitchell b E. M. Grace 4	c Mitchell b E. M. Grace	0
T. Hayward c and b E. M. Grace 9	c and b E. M. Grace	7
R. P. Carpenter c Cooper b Evans 1	b E. M. Grace	0
H. H. Stephenson c Mitchell b E. M. Grace 16	c E. M. Grace b Evans	14
G. Parr c Lyttelton b Evans 13	st Cooper b R. D. Walker	60
G. Bennett c I. D. Walker b E. M. Grace .. 2	c Lyttelton b Maitland	7
J. Grundy c W. G. Grace b Evans 2	b E. M. Grace	3
G. Wootton not out 7	b E. M. Grace	0
A. Shaw c E. M. Grace b Evans 0	not out	17
L-b 3, w 3, n-b 1 7	L-b 1, w 7	8
132		140

Gentlemen

E. M. Grace, Esq., lbw b Grundy	24	Hayward b Wootton	30
W. G. Grace, Esq., run out	3	Smith b Wootton	34
R. D. Walker, Esq., b Grundy	18	not out	1
Hon. C. G. Lyttelton, b Bennett	24		
B. B. Cooper, Esq., c Shaw b Hayward	70		
R. A. H. Mitchell, Esq., not out	44		
C. F. Buller, Esq., b Hayward	0	not out	8
F. R. Evans, Esq., b Wootton	3		
V. E. Walker, Esq., b Wootton	4		
I. D. Walker, Esq., c Carpenter b Hayward	0		
W. F. Maitland, Esq., st Stephenson b Wootton	0		
B 2, l-b 5, w 1	8	B 2, l-b 2	4
	198		77

The Gentlemen winning by eight wickets

When *The South Wales Club played I Zingari at Lord's on July 27 and 28 that year, the Grace influence was as strong as ever. EM made 89 out of 163 in the South Wales first innings, and WG 85 out of 180 in their second. The brothers each took five wickets in the IZ first innings, and EM took seven wickets to WG's two in the second innings. WG took five catches in the match, to his brother's two. Their team won by 104 runs.*

For the Gentlemen of England against the Gentlemen of Middlesex, EM scored 12 and 111 and took three wickets as his team won by four wickets. WG, batting at No. 7, scored 48 and 34. This was a month after he had scored 121 for 18 of the Lansdown Club against The United Eleven. The Eighteen included EM's brothers WG, who made 11, and in a rare appearance in the pages of Wisden, *Henry, who made eight. The Grace brothers took all the wickets between them (EM 10, Henry five and WG 4, with one run-out) as the United England side was crushed by an innings and 113 runs. EM also turned out for 18 of Eashing and District against the United South Eleven at Godalming at the end of July. He was clearly willing to travel all over the south of England for a game of cricket. At the end of September, he even played for Eighteen of the Surrey Club against Eleven Players of the South, top-scoring in both innings with the bat, and taking 13 wickets as his side won by 155 runs. All in all, another successful year for E. M. Grace.*

For the South Wales Club against the Surrey Colts at The Oval on July 31 and August 1, 1865, WG took eight wickets in the Colts' first innings, but the match was drawn.

WISDEN 1867

By now, EM was listed as Dr E. M. Grace, while his younger brother was still W. G. Grace Esq. Playing at Lord's for the Gentlemen against the Players on June 25, 26 and 27, 1866, Wisden's scorecard shows that the Grace brothers took all ten wickets between them in the Players' first innings, six for EM and four for WG, and five more in the second innings (EM three and WG two), but the Gentlemen's batting let them down and the Players won by 38 runs. Thomas Hearne's superb 122 not out in the Players' second innings proved to be the matchwinner.

England v Surrey
At the Oval, July 30, 31 and August 1, 1866

England

Dr. E. M. Grace c Jupp b Humphrey 9	V. E. Walker, Esq., c Jupp b Noble 54
C. Payne b Griffith 86	James Lillywhite, jun. b Jupp 32
G. Wootton b Jupp 19	J. Round, Esq., b Miller 42
T. Hearne c and b Jupp 19	E. Willsher c Miller b Noble 9
W. G. Grace, Esq., not out 224	
C. Coward b Humphrey 9	B 4, l-b 9, w 1 14
G. Bennett c Griffith b Humphrey 4	521

Surrey

T. Humphrey c E. M. Grace b Wootton 0	b Wootton 20
H. Jupp b Wootton 15	c Payne b Bennett 0
H. H. Stephenson c Willsher b Wootton 20	c E. M. Grace b Willsher 34
E. W. Pooley b Willsher 0	c Round b Wootton 13
G. Griffith c Bennett b Willsher 14	c Willsher b Wootton 3
J. Caesar c W. G. Grace b Willsher 0	st Round b Bennett 3
T. Sewell c Walker b Wootton 0	c Bennett b Willsher 6
J. W. Noble, Esq., not out 22	c E. M. Grace b Wootton 14
F. Burbidge, Esq., c Lillywhite b Wootton 6	c Hearne b Bennett 25
E. Dowson, Esq., lbw b Willsher 14	st Round b Willsher 0
F. P. Miller, Esq., c Willsher b Wootton 4	not out 5
B 2, l-b 2 4	B 2, l-b 1 3
99	126

England winning in one innings and 296 runs

This was WG's maiden first-class century, just 12 days past his 18th birthday, and it was by far the largest score at The Oval to that date. After his exhausting innings, during which 431 runs were added to the total and, in those days before boundaries, would have all been run out, he took part of the next day off to compete in the National Olympian Association meeting at Crystal Palace, where he took part in, and won, the 440 yards hurdles race in a time of one minute ten seconds. The modern equivalent, the 400 metres hurdles, is considered perhaps the most exhausting of all track and field events, but WG was back on the cricket field at The Oval in time to help his team complete victory over Surrey.

At Canterbury on August 6, 7 and 8, 1866, South of the Thames played North of the Thames. The South included G. F. Grace, the youngest of the brothers, who thus makes his first appearance in Wisden. Fred was not yet 16 years old, batted at No. 11 and did not appear to bowl. Both teams were, however, very strong, and this was a baptism of fire for the young man. Modern cricket historians do not, incidentally, consider this his first-class debut, whatever it may have been considered by Wisden at the time. That distinction goes to his participation in a match between the Gentlemen of England and Oxford University starting on May 21 that year, but the full scorecard is not included in Wisden.

As soon as his debut match at Canterbury was finished, Fred stayed on and played for the Gentlemen of the South against I Zingari, a 12-a-side match that nevertheless merits a full scorecard in Wisden. All three Grace brothers were playing and between them made 119 of the 310 runs scored by the Gentlemen, and took 14 of the 22 wickets. They also took eight catches. Their team won by 121 runs.

WISDEN 1868

W. G. Grace did not score a first-class hundred in 1867. He played only four first-class games that summer, thanks to a combination of a sprained ankle in May and June, scarlet fever in July and August, and a split finger at the end of the month, but he was still a match-winner with his medium-pace bowling. His 11 wickets for the Gentlemen, including eight for 25 in the Players' second innings, helped him to a season's tally of 39 wickets at an average of 7.51, which would prove to be his best ever. Wisden did not give full bowling analyses in its early years, so this fact is not recorded within its pages.

Gentlemen v Players
At Lord's, July 8, 1867

Players

T. Humphrey c R. D. Walker b Appleby	0	c and b Appleby	13
H. Jupp hit wkt b W. G. Grace	0	b W. G. Grace	0
G. Summers b W. G. Grace	7	b W. G. Grace	7
A. Shaw c Round b Appleby	1	b W. G. Grace	7
E. W. Pooley b W. G. Grace	18	c E. M. Grace b W. G. Grace	7
T. Hearne b Appleby	8	c R. D. Walker b W. G. Grace	8
W. Mortlock c Buller b R. D. Walker	21	c Cooper b W. G. Grace	2
G. Griffith b Appleby	0	b W. G. Grace	13
James Lillywhite, jun. b Appleby	17	(10) b Appleby	0
J. Grundy c W. G. Grace b Appleby	0	(9) c and b W. G. Grace	0
G. Wootton not out	4	not out	0
B 1, l-b 1, w 1	3	B 2, l-b 1, w 1	4
	79		61

Gentlemen

E. M. Grace, Esq., lbw b Wootton	20	b Wootton	1
W. G. Grace, Esq., c Pooley b Griffith	18	(4) not out	37
A. Lubbock, Esq., c Grundy b Griffith	3	not out	12
B. B. Cooper, Esq., b Wootton	9		
R. D. Walker, Esq., b Wootton	18		
C. F. Buller, Esq., c Griffith b Grundy	2		
I. D. Walker, Esq., b Wootton	1	(2) b Wootton	1
W. F. Maitland, Esq., b Grundy	0		
V. E. Walker, Esq., not out	5		
J. Round, Esq., c Pooley b Wootton	0		
A. Appleby, Esq., b Wootton	1		
B 5, l-b 5	10	B 1, l-b 3	4
	87		**55**

The Gentlemen winning by eight wickets

On August 28, 1867, Surrey played The World at The Oval. The match was badly affected by the weather.

Surrey v The World
At The Oval, August 28, 1867

The World

E. M. Grace, Esq., st Lockyer b Southerton	115	E. Willsher st Lockyer b Southerton	0
T. Hearne st Jupp b Lockyer	47	G. Bennett c Pooley b Miller	33
C. Payne c Jupp b Griffith	11	F. Silcock not out	0
James Lillywhite, jun. c Pooley b Southerton	4		
H. Charlwood not out	55	B 2, l-b 1	3
T. A. Mantle st Lockyer b Southerton	6	(7 wkts)	274

J. Payne and W. G. Grace, Esq., did not bat.

Surrey

T. Humphrey, H. Jupp, Rev. C. G. Lane, F. P. Miller, Esq., Julius Caesar, G. Griffith, E. W. Pooley, F. Burbidge, Esq., T. Lockyer, W. Mortlock and J. Southerton.

And that was that. WG's split finger prevented him from batting. Surrey did not have a chance to bat. EM's century for "The World" seems to be the only one ever recorded for a first-class team bearing that name.

WISDEN 1869

On page 34 of the 1869 edition, the first scorecard of a Gloucestershire match is included. At Lord's on June 25 and 26, 1868, Gloucestershire beat a reasonably strong MCC and Ground side by 134 runs. The Grace brothers dominated, especially with the ball. It is the only Gloucestershire county match included in that year's Almanack.

Gloucestershire v MCC and Ground
At Lord's June 25 and 26, 1868

Gloucestershire

E. M. Grace, Esq., c Sutton b Wootton	6	b Farrands	65
L. Abbott, Esq., c Balfour b Farrands	21	b Wootton	11
J. Halford, Esq., hit wkt b Farrands	18	b Biddulph	0
W. G. Grace, Esq., c Price b Wootton	24	c Biddulph b Wootton	13
G. F. Grace, Esq., b Wootton	3	b Farrands	2
W. Wall b Farrands	2	b Farrands	5
T. G. Matthews, Esq., not out	27	b Biddulph	32
F. Baker, Esq., c Wootton b Price	13	b Wootton	4
T. Brindley, Esq., c Biddulph b Price	4	c Biddulph b Farrands	8
W. D. L. Macpherson, Esq., st Biddulph b Farrands	11	b Wootton	0
W. Kelly absent		not out	1
B 3, l-b 2, n-b 1	6	B 14, l-b 3, w 1	18
	135		159

MCC and Ground

W. F. Higgins, Esq., lbw b E. M. Grace	6	b E. M. Grace	7
E. G. G. Sutton, Esq., c Wall b W. G. Grace	2	hit wkt b E. M. Grace	26
R. D. Balfour, Esq., b E. M. Grace	37	st Halford b E. M. Grace	16
W. Price run out	4	c and b E. M. Grace	4
S. Biddulph run out	4	run out	0
Lieut.-Col. F. T. A. Hervey-Bathurst c G. F. Grace b W. G. Grace	1	b E. M. Grace	6
A. B. Coddington, Esq., c G. F. Grace b W. G. Grace	0	c Abbott b E. M. Grace	0
G. Wootton b E. M. Grace	0	b W. G. Grace	15
W. H. Richards, Esq., b E. M. Grace	3	c W. G. Grace b E. M. Grace	3
A. W. Fitzgerald, Esq., c E. M. Grace b W. G. Grace	4	not out	3
F. H. Farrands not out	4	b E. M. Grace	2
B 4	4	B 2, l-b 7	9
	69		91

Gloucestershire won by 134 runs

In the first article ever to be included in the Almanack, editor W. H. Knight writes about "Individual Innings of 200 or more runs".

Of WG, he writes:

"In 1866, as many as four of these innings of 200 runs were played – one of 220 runs by that exceedingly fine batsman, Mr Alfred Lubbock, one of 269 runs by Mr Scobell, one (in a Marlborough College practice match) of 274 runs by Mr Monnington, and one of 224 not out by Mr W. G. Grace, who was then only 18 years old, and who a month later on also played an innings of 173 not out; both matches were played on The Oval, and this playing on one ground in about a week two successive innings of 224 and 173, both not-outs, the first against Surrey, and the second against the Players of the South, is a batting feat as wonderful as it is unparalleled, and it is the more astonishing for being accomplished by one so young (Mr W. G. Grace was born on July 18, 1848).

... But great as had been all these doughty deeds with the bat, vast as had unquestionably been the great scores of Alfred Adams, Mr Ward, Marsden, the two Grace's [sic], Hayward, and others, they were all outdone and put in the shade by the (numerically) greater scores played in 1868, during which very hot and arid season one innings of 404 runs was hit, and five of more than 200 runs – the six innings giving an aggregate of 1543 runs... Mr Tylecote's 404 was made in a Clifton College practice match, and was hit in six hours... The others of these innings hit last season were – one of 228 runs by Mr E. P. Ash, one of 211 not out by Mr Pauncefote (Captain of this year's Oxford Eleven), one of 201 runs by Mr A. N. Hornby, and one of 210 by Mr W. G. Grace (who hit this innings the week following his playing his two great innings of 130 and 102 not out, in one match in Canterbury).

This last sentence is the only comment on WG's remarkable achievement, playing for "South Of The Thames" against "North Of The Thames" at Canterbury on August 3, 4 and 5, when he hit two centuries in the match, the first time this feat had been accomplished since William Lambert in 1817. Incidentally, despite his batting triumph in this match, Grace still came out on the losing side.

EM also featured strongly in the piece:

... In 1862... that bold batsman, dashing hitter and rapid scorer of runs, Mr E. M. Grace, hit his 208 not out, and also his 241 – an extraordinary batting feat to accomplish in one season; but in that season this extraordinary batsman was in extraordinary hitting form, as in addition to this double 200, Mr E. M. Grace at Lord's hit an innings of 118 runs against MCC, and at Canterbury for MCC, he not only played an innings of 192 not out, but with his bowling had all the ten wickets down (it was a 12-a-side match) in the second innings of the Gentlemen of Kent. (In all, Mr E. M. Grace scored 2190 runs in '62, finishing up his hitting that season with 42 and 135 in a match at Bedminster)...

In 1867 there was an innings of... 200 by Dr E. M. Grace (who thus has played more of these innings, and hit therein more runs than any other cricketer living or defunct).

WISDEN 1870

Between 1869 and 1880, W. G. Grace headed the English first-class batting averages ten times in 12 seasons. Only in 1875 and 1878 was he not the leading batsman, beaten in two low-scoring summers by Lord Harris (1875) and John Selby (1878). The 1870s were the years of WG's total dominance as a batsman.

For the first time Wisden *included summaries of matches and of the county clubs' performances in the previous season. It also found space, in the section on the Marylebone Club, to record that:*

In 1868 the New Tavern was erected. Many cricket incidents of interest occurred on Lord's Ground this year, but the following two *must* be chronicled:

In 1868 Mr W. G. Grace played that splendid hitting innings of 134 not out for the Gentlemen v the Players of England, and it was in 1868 that Mr C. I. Thornton, for Eton v Harrow, made his famous straight drive that sent the ball flying high and clear over the Pavilion out of the ground for six.

WG was elected a member of MCC at the beginning of the 1869 season, and success for the new club member was quick to arrive:

MCC and Ground v Oxford University
At Oxford, May 13 and 14, 1869

In this match Mr W. G. Grace not only made a remarkable first appearance as a member of the MCC, but, with his 117 runs, he commenced the most wonderful series of large first-class innings ever played by one man in one season for the old club. The first day's cricket closed with MCC having scored 159 for six wickets, Mr W. Grace (in No. 1) then not out 86. Next day Mr Grace was eighth man out, the score at 203; Mr G's 117 being made by two sixes, one five, four fours, eleven threes &c. This innings was the feature of the match... The match was over at five o'clock on the second day, MCC the winners in one innings by 30 runs.

The return match, at Lord's on June 18 and 19, showed that WG's bowling had tightened considerably.

At one time Grundy bowled 24 overs for 14 runs, and Mr Grace bowled 35 consecutive balls without a run being made from his bowling...

Against Cambridge, the same story was told.

MCC and Ground v Cambridge University
At Lord's June 14 and 15, 1869

Showery weather and dead wickets... To Mr Preston and Mr Money ten successive maiden overs were bowled by Mr Grace and Wootton, every ball of the 40 being "there"... Mr Grace was the hitter of the MCC side; when M.C. [*sic*] had scored 21, Mr Grace had made 20 of the 21 runs...

In this match, WG made 63 of the 143 runs scored off the bat by MCC, and took 11 of the 19 Cambridge wickets to fall. Still, MCC lost by 116 runs.

MCC and Ground v Nottinghamshire
At Lord's, July 5, 6, and 7, 1869

This was the only match at Lord's in 1869 that took three days to play it out. The weather was dry and warm, the wickets and cricket good, and 746 runs were scored in the match...

Wednesday was Mr W. Grace's day. He and Mr Balfour commenced the club's second innings at noon. At 2.30 the MCC score was at 119, four wickets down, and Mr Grace 75 not out (87 overs having then been bowled)... Mr Grace went to the wickets, first man in, at five minutes past 12, he was sixth out at ten minutes past four, his 121 having been hit from the bowling of J. C. Shaw, Wootton, Alfred Shaw, Tinley and others. After Mr Grace left, the end quickly came...

WG's reputation was now so good, and expectations of him were so high, that Wisden's report of the MCC match against Lancashire at Lord's on July 19 and 20 was brief and to the point:

Weather fine, wickets not good. This was a match curious for the facts that Hearne's 20 was the highest individual score; that Mr Grace was out for 6 and 0; that 251 was the aggregate number of runs made in the match; and that although Lancashire made 17 more runs "from the bat" than MCC did, MCC won the match by two wickets. This is another instance of the effect of not keeping the "extras" down.

The Canterbury Week
August 9, 10, 11, 12

"The week" of all weeks in the cricketing season is this, annually held in August on the St Lawrence ground at Canterbury. As a Cricket County gathering of all classes, from Peer to Peasant, it never had an equal, and as a cricket week played out by the most eminent Amateurs and Professionals in the country, it is far away beyond rivalry. There have been weeks of finer weather, but otherwise none so successful as "the week" of 1869. As to the cricket, Fuller Pilch (a good authority), stated "He never saw better cricket played on that ground."

... The batting, after the first day, thoroughly mastered the bowling, as many as 1,678 runs having been scored during the five days and few hours' cricket. Mr W. Grace's 96 and 127 were capital antidotes to his nought on the Monday. His 127 was the highest individual score of the week. His 96, made in one hour and 35 minutes, was hit from some of the best bowling in England, and was a grand display of fine judgment in placing the ball, clean, powerful hitting, and rapid scoring.

WG's 127 was made for MCC in a 12-a-side match against The "County" of Kent.

By now, W. G. Grace's batting and bowling feats were becoming commonplace, so his name crops up on page after page:

Surrey v MCC and Ground
Played on The Oval, July 1 and 2, 1869

"Mr Grace was the only one in it," critically exclaimed a professional when this match was over; and inasmuch as Mr Grace was first man in and took his bat out for 138 (out of a total of 215); as his innings exceeded the total runs in either innings played by the Surrey eleven; as his bowling had eight wickets and he caught out another; the critical pro was about right in his criticism.

MCC won by nine wickets.

Gentlemen of the South v Players of the South
Played on The Oval, July 15, 16, and 17, 1869

In this match 1,136 runs were scored – the greatest number of runs ever scored in a cricket match...

Jupp and Pooley were the players who in both innings scored the runs for the Professionals' first wickets, and Mr W. G. Grace and Mr B. B. Cooper were the Gentlemen who made the 283. That 283 was indeed an extraordinary affair. The innings was commenced at a quarter past two, at a quarter past four the 100 was up, at ten minutes to five the 150 was hoisted, at 25 past five the 200 was scored, and at 20 minutes to seven the 283 runs were made for no wickets down...

The weather was bright and burning hot, and the wickets throughout the matches were in splendid form for batting. Match unfinished.

In this match WG made 180.

South of England v North of England
At Sheffield, July 26, 27, and 28, 1869

Mr W. G. Grace was the prominent man in this match, as he hit an innings of 122 runs (out of a total of 169 from the bat) for the South, and took six out of the ten wickets in the first innings of the North.

For the first time, Wisden *featured a special article on the Grace family's batting achievements:*

THREE BROTHERS' THREE-FIGURE INNINGS IN 1869

Or, 2,022 runs in 15 innings by Messrs. W. G., G. F., and E. M. Grace

Mr W. G. Grace hit innings of 180, 172*, 138*, 127, 122, 121, 117, 111 and 100, or –	1,188
Mr G. F. Grace " " 206*, 153, 150, 112* and 104, or	725
Dr E. M. Grace hit an innings of	109
Total runs in the 15 innings	2,022

Mr W. Grace's 1,188 runs in nine innings (two not-outs) is a wonderful batting exploit, especially when it is borne in mind that in five of these innings he played against such bowling as Freeman's, J. C. Shaw's, Willsher's, Emmett's, Wootton's, Alfred Shaw's, Southerton's, Griffith's, R. C. Tinley's, Bennett's and others. Perhaps it may not be deemed out of place to record here the following incidents in the cricketing career of this great batsman. In 1864, Mr W. G. Grace played his first match at Lord's, i.e. for South Wales Club v I Zingari. In that match he scored an innings of 50 runs, pretty plainly indicating what was "looming in the future" from his bat. His first match at The Oval was also played that season: it was South Wales Club v Surrey Club, wherein he scored 5 and 38 only; but in the following week, at Brighton (for South Wales Club v Gentlemen of Sussex) Mr W. Grace scored 170 and 56 not out, and... he was not quite 16 years old when he played those two innings in one match. The 170 was played without giving a chance, he being out at last by playing the ball on...

Mr G. F. Grace's 725 runs in five innings (two not-outs) is a cricket item quite in character with the hitting form of the family. It is true these runs were made in country matches, but equally true is it that 725 runs in five innings is a great batting exploit for a lad of 18 to accomplish... Mr Grace's 206 not out must have been a fast bit of scoring indeed; he was No. 1 in, and when the other ten were out the total of the innings was 287, of which number 25 were "extras", so Mr Grace actually hit his 206 whilst the other ten were contributing 56 only. But that he is a fast run-getter was evident on The Oval last autumn, when in the rapidly dying daylight he made 60 runs in the hour. His dashing, vigorous hitting and the cool confident way he (at point) put up his hands and – from a very hard cut – made a catch, forcibly recalled to mind the 1863 form of his brother "The Doctor". (Mr G. F. Grace made 1,641 runs in 39 innings in 1869).

Dr E. M. Grace was out of cricket practice in 1869. Had this gentleman been in his 1863 form wherein he hit six innings of three figures, and scored (all told) the enormous total of 3,074 runs – the probability is there would have been a material increase to the 15 three-figure innings made by the three brothers in 1869.

180	caught	Mr W. G. Grace	for Gentlemen v Players of the South	The Oval
172	not out	Mr W. G. Grace	Stapleton v Knole	Stapleton
138	not out	Mr W. G. Grace	MCC and Ground v Surrey	The Oval
127	caught	Mr W. G. Grace	MCC v Kent	Canterbury
122	bowled	Mr W. G. Grace	South v North	Sheffield
121	bowled	Mr W. G. Grace	MCC and Ground v Notts	Lord's
117	caught	Mr W. G. Grace	MCC and Ground v Oxford University	Oxford
111	bowled	Mr W. G. Grace	Stapleton v Swindon	Swindon
100	caught	Mr W. G. Grace	Bedminster v Lansdown	Bath
206	not out	Mr G. F. Grace	Chipping Sodbury v Tetbury	Badminton Park
153	bowled	Mr G. F. Grace	Frenchay v Cold Ashton	Frenchay
150	caught	Mr G. F. Grace	Clifton v Gloucester	Clifton
112	not out	Mr G. F. Grace	Clifton v Cadoxton	Neath
104	caught	Mr G. F. Grace	Frenchay v Schoolmasters	Frenchay

Near upon 160 other cricketers are stated to have hit "one innings" of three figures last season; of those the following will be found the best authenticated, and the most generally interesting. Space could not be spared for all.

109	Dr E. M. Grace

WISDEN 1871

For the first time, Wisden *includes the three Grace brothers in its list of "Births and Deaths Of Celebrated Cricketers", but in age order rather than alphabetical order.*

Grace, Dr E.M. (Glouces) b Nov 7, 1841
Grace, Mr W.G. (Glouces) b July 18, 1848
Grace, Mr G.F. (Glouces) b Dec 15, 1850

The MCC were clearly happy with WG's season's work on their behalf, as Wisden *recorded:*

Two prominent items of MCC cricket in 1870 are:

Mr W. G. Grace having in 15 innings (3 not-outs) scored 666 runs
Average for MCC .... 55 runs per innings

Alfred Shaw having in 12 of the principal MCC and Ground matches bowled for MCC:
775 overs (436 maidens) for 759 runs and 102 wickets

Wisden *sometimes heaped praise on WG where it was due. In the Gentlemen v Players match at Lord's, which the Gentlemen won by 4 runs,* Wisden's *correspondent noted that:*

with the score at 182, Mr W. Grace was bowled (off his legs) for 109, a truly great display of cricket, that included a brilliant on-drive for five, six fours and so many as 47 singles.

On the other hand, Fred Grace's equally important performance with the ball (three for 17 and four for 26) goes largely unrecorded, apart from noting that Hayward was dismissed in the second innings by "a good 'c and b' by Mr F. Grace".
    At the end of the report, the following note appeared:

Mr W. G. Grace's Innings in the Two Gentlemen v Players Matches of 1870
On The Oval   6 and 215   At Lord's   109 and 11   Average 85 per innings and one over

The calculation of the average – "and one over" – became more precise in later years when Wisden *began to use the decimal point.*
    WG also enjoyed the MCC bowling when he came up against it:

MCC and Ground v Gloucestershire
At Lord's, August 1 and 2, 1870

The storm that broke over and swamped the ground, and the great hitting by Mr W. Grace, will have vividly impressed this match on the memories of those who were up at Lord's on the 1st of last August. Mr W. Grace and Mr Gordon began the batting; in one hour they had made the score 73 (Mr Grace 47 not out, and Mr Gordon 23 not out), then a fierce storm of lightning, thunder and heavy rain stopped play until five minutes to five, when, on wickets of mud and sawdust, they resumed their hitting, rapidly scoring runs for the Shire until a quarter to six, when Price bowled Mr Gordon, the score being then 139 for one wicket! Mr Gordon's innings of 53 was an innings of careful, good defence, clean, hard cutting, and excellent cricket. No other Gloucestershire man "stayed" that day with Mr Grace, play ceasing with the Shire having lost five wickets for 208 runs, Mr W. Grace not out 133.

At 20 past 12 the following day the innings was resumed; the sixth, seventh and the eighth wickets each fell with Mr Grace still in, and in he stayed until the score was 276 when a clean, clever, and hot one-hand catch by Wootton at cover point settled the great batsman for an innings of 172 runs. Mr Grace was nearly had at cover point when he had made 21 only; nevertheless, his innings for successful defence, correct timing the ball, and fine batting, was a great one. First man in, Mr Grace was ninth out; when the score was 100 he had made 63; when it was 200, he had made 126; when it was 240, he had made 150; and when it was 276, he had made 172. His hits included three fives, seven fours, and 59 singles. No run was scored after Mr Grace left, the innings ending at 20 to two for 276...

... In the two Gloucestershire matches played on London grounds in 1870, Mr W. G. Grace scored 143 v Surrey and 172 v MCC and Ground; or 315 runs in two innings!

And WG had another week in east Kent to enjoy, but despite the glorious setting and large crowds, he did not have much success, at least not by his standards.

The Canterbury Week
August 8, 9, 10, 11, 12 and 13, at Canterbury, 1870

Of late years each succeeding cricket week at Canterbury has topped its predecessor in interest and popularity. The reappearance of Carpenter and Hayward in the match to be played by the two strongest batting elevens that could well be got together added to the interest felt among cricketers in the week of 1870, and the increased popularity of the gathering among the general public was attested by the facts that on the two great days of the week (Tuesday and Thursday), more admission money was taken than was ever before taken on those days at the gate in the old Dover Road. Barring a few light rainfalls on Monday, and the frequent and heavy showers on Wednesday, the weather was pleasantly fine; brilliantly so on Thursday, the Ladies' Day, when a bright, hot sun beamed on one of the most charmingly gay and animated cricketing scenes possible to witness. On that day some 7,000 visitors and 300 well-filled and fairly freighted vehicles (conveying the cream of Kentish society), passed the gates, and on no other cricket ground in England has been witnessed a sight that surpassed in beauty and interest, that seen about 4pm of the 11th of last August on the St Lawrence Ground at Canterbury.

... Mr W. Grace was more than once during the week caught out from a skier, but he was in form in MCC's second innings, his 46 being a fine display of punishing leg-hitting; by one hit to leg (the finest leg-hit made in the week's cricket), the ball was sent bounding down the next field to near the entrance gate.

In less than one hour Mr W. Grace and Mr I. D. Walker hit the MCC score from three for one wicket to the required 84 to win.

It was not all WG, though.

THE GREAT RUN-GETTING MATCH IN 1870.

1,141 RUNS FOR 31 WICKETS!!

Gentlemen of the South v Gentlemen of the North
At Beeston in Notts, August 18, 19 and 20, 1870

The Beeston ground is famous for true wickets – this match will materially enhance that fame. 769 runs had been scored when the match had been just half played out, three men having then made 471 runs. Mr A. N. Hornby was first man in, he was eighth out, the score at 243, he having made 103; his innings included 17 four's. Mr W. G. Grace was first man in, and third out with the score at 136. Mr I. D. Walker went in two wickets down with the score at 14, he was fourth out with the score at 424; Mr Walker was batting six hours and a half, his 179 included one five and 25 fours. Mr G. F. Grace went in when his brother was out, i.e. at three wickets down for 136, so 346 runs were made during Mr G. F. Grace's stay at the wickets for his 189 not out – made by 29 singles, six twos, four threes and 34 fours. The South wanted 39 runs to win when they were compelled to leave to catch the up train on the Saturday evening.

This was the highest score of Fred Grace's brief career.

For the first time in 1870 Gloucestershire put out a team, even if it was not yet officially established as a county side.

The Shire played a brief but brilliant cricket season in 1870, winning every match the Eleven played. There was no county club for Gloucestershire then in existence, the matches being arranged by, and played under, the management of Mr W. G. Grace; however there is very little doubt that in 1871 a County Cricket Club for Gloucestershire will be established on a firm basis; and just prior to this going to press (in November), we learnt that there was a great probability of Gloucestershire playing MCC and Ground, Yorkshire, Nottinghamshire, Surrey and Lancashire in 1871, which season thus early bids fair to be an especially busy one in county cricket.

The matches played in 1870 by Gloucestershire were three in number, i.e. two v Surrey and one v MCC and Ground... In each of the three matches, Gloucestershire played all amateurs, who won the first match by 51 runs; the second by an innings and 129 runs; and the third by an innings and 88 runs – that is to say Gloucestershire won three matches in four innings, having an aggregate of 268 runs to spare. The following summaries will tell how the Gloucestershire gentlemen bowled… and hit in those three matches:

Gloucestershire Bowling

	Overs Bowled	Maiden Overs	Runs	Wides	No bls	Total wkts taken	Wkts bowled
Mr W. G. Grace	157–2	78	212	3	–	23	5
Mr G. F. Grace	137	76	163	2	–	10	5
Mr R. F. Miles	136–1	52	208	2	–	24	5
Dr E. M. Grace	5	3	2	–	–	–	–

Gloucestershire Batting

887 runs were scored in the four innings played by Gloucestershire. Of that number, Mr W. G. Grace contributed 366 by innings of 26, 25, 143 and 172 runs; Mr G. F. Grace scored 16, 15, 33 and 9;… Dr E. M. Grace 2 and 18.

Gloucestershire also played Glamorganshire, described by Wisden *as an "amateur match". Mr W. G. Grace made 197 out of 418, with other major contributions coming from Mr F. Townsend (105), Dr E. M. Grace (30) and Mr G. F. Grace (24).*

Glamorganshire scored 104 and (two or 2 absent) 46. Barring the run-outs, all the Glamorganshire wickets fell to the bowling of the two brothers Grace, Mr G. F. had nine and Dr E. M. seven.

If this innings be added to the other three it will make 1,305 runs scored in four innings by the Gloucestershire Amateurs, 563 of which were contributed by Mr W. G. Grace. This will give an average of 326 runs per innings to the Eleven, and 140 per innings to Mr W. G. Grace. Prodigious scoring, this.

The 1871 Wisden *lists nine scores of 100 or more by WG during the season, for six different teams. There is little differentiation between the top-class matches, such as Gentlemen v Players at The Oval, when WG made 215, and the less important games, for instance U.S.E.E. v 22 of Sleaford, in which match he scored 115. It was not until much later that the attempt to separate the first-class scores from the lesser innings was made, by the* Wisden *statistician F. S. Ashley-Cooper and his successors, which began a controversy which has still not been satisfactorily settled to this day.*

WISDEN 1872

W. G. Grace was still only 22 at the start of the 1871 season, but Wisden *already described him routinely if grudgingly as a "great batsman", commenting more on his surprising failures than his inevitable triumphs. In fact, the 1871 season turned out to be perhaps his most dominant of all, in terms of comparison with other batsmen. As Neville Cardus would point out in* Wisden 1963,

"In the summer of 1871 his aggregate of runs was 2,739, average 78.25. The next-best batsman that year was Richard Daft, average 37."

WG was always keen to turn out for or against any opposition in any conditions if it suited him. The season at Lord's in 1871, a summer of terrible weather, began with

MCC and Ground v Fifteen who had never played at Lord's
At Lord's, May 8, 9 and 10, 1871

This was the opening match of the 85th season of the Marylebone Club and the weather at this opening match too truly foretold what was looming in the future for the Club's 85th season. On the first day there was a violent storm of lightning, thunder, wind and rain; on the second day frequent showers fell, and a cold north wind blew; and on the third day it was so nippingly cold as to be more suggestive of February and football than May and maiden overs…

… In his first innings Mr Grace was missed at slip from Clayton's bowling when he had scored three runs only… The most "effective" bit of bowling was that by young Grundy on the second day; he commenced and continued bowling maiden overs to Mr W. G. Grace, who the young Notts man clean bowled in his fifth over… Grundy's bowling was subsequently hit a bit, and on the third day his bowling was severely thumped; but Grundy deserved Mr Grace's second wicket, as from the third ball he bowled that day Mr Grace was missed at short leg; indeed, had the first chances given in each innings by Mr Grace been secured, the great batsman would have made only three runs in this match.

In the next match at Lord's, against Surrey, Grace scored 181.

There was some superb batting by both Mr W. Grace and Jupp; in fact, it is the opinion of many that the 181 by Mr Grace and the 85 by Jupp in this match are their most skillful and perfect displays on London grounds in 1871. Mr Grace was first man in at 12.10; when the score was at 164 for four wickets Mr Grace had made exactly 100 runs; when he had made 123 he gave a hot – a very hot – chance to short square leg, but he gave no other chance; he was much hurt by a ball bowled by Skinner when he had made 180, and at 181 Southerton bowled him, he being fifth man out with the score at 280. Mr Grace's "timing" and "placing" the ball in this innings was truly wonderful cricket; he appeared to hit "all round" just where he chose to, and placing the field for his hit was as useless as were the bowler's efforts to bowl him. Mr Grace's hits included a great on-drive past the pavilion for six, four fives (all big drives), and 11 fours… Surrey tried a bowling colt, Skinner, whose fate it was to commence his bowling at

Lord's to the great batsman of the period, and that too at a time when Mr Grace was well set.

For The South against The North at Lord's over the Whitsun holiday, WG was joined by his brother Fred. When two batsmen were in partnership, Wisden and other journals used the word 'faced' where now we would say 'joined', as in "Mr. G. F. Grace faced his brother." Today a batsman faces a bowler: then two batsmen faced each other.

Mr W. Grace and Jupp opened the South's innings to the bowling of the two Shaws; they had freely and finely hit the score to 78, when long-stop settled Jupp for 22. Wootton then summarily settled Mr Green and Pooley, whereupon, with the score at 91 for three wickets, Mr G. F. Grace faced his brother – the time 20 minutes past one. At eight minutes to two Mr W. Grace had made his 100 (the score then at 143 for three wickets), and at lunchtime, 2.30, the score was 189, Mr W. Grace 135 not out and Mr G. F. Grace 23 not out. At 3.15 they went at it again; in five minutes the 200 was up (only three wickets down), Mr W. Grace then 148; these figures he increased by two fours and a five in one over of Mr J.C. Shaw's, but after making 17 more runs, he skied one that Plumb easily secured, and the great batsman was out for one of the grandest "hitting" innings played in '71... an innings that brought out such a long succession of hearty, ringing cheers (it was Whit Monday) as were never before or since heard at Lord's...

   ... Mr G. F. Grace, who had gone in three wickets down with the score at 91, stayed whilst six wickets went and 237 runs were added to the score, and was last man out for 83, showing especially fine defence and hitting against most of the best bowling of the North.

When Surrey played Gloucestershire at The Oval, the home side was undone by the three brothers. Even though WG and EM scored only four runs between them, the batting of young Fred (69) and the bowling and fielding of all three gave Gloucestershire victory by an innings and 60 runs.

This was a match of contrasts. Those two days of "leafy June" were as nippingly cold as five months further on were the similar dates of "leafless November". Two Surrey men made 175 runs in the match, the other nine made 69 only. Mr W. G. Grace was out for one run, yet his side scored 315, and won with an innings and 60 runs in hand...

   ...A splendidly hit 69 by Mr G. F. Grace revenged the early closing movement of the two elder Graces... The fielding of G. F. Grace at leg and long field, of Mr W. G. nearly "all over the field", and of Doctor G. at point, was glorious cricket. The Doctor's catches that settled the colt (Clifford) and the veteran (H. H. Stephenson) were marvellous bits of fielding.

Surrey v Gloucestershire
At The Oval, June 8-9, 1871

Surrey

H. Jupp b Strachan	70	c E. M. Grace b W. G. Grace	45
R. Humphrey b Miles	7	b E. M. Grace	8
C. W. Potter, Esq., b W. G. Grace	3	c G. F. Grace b E. M. Grace	5
E. W. Pooley b Strachan	51	b E. M. Grace	9
J. C. Gregory, Esq., b E. M. Grace	11	b W. G. Grace	10
T. Humphrey b Strachan	0	not out	0
H. H. Stephenson c and b E. M. Grace	5	c and b E. M. Grace	1
G. Griffith st Bush b Strachan	0	c Strachan b W. G. Grace	7
G. Clifford b Strachan	0	c E. M. Grace b W. G. Grace	2
James Street not out	6	c G. F. Grace b E. M. Grace	0
W. G. Marten st Bush b E. M. Grace	3	c G. F. Grace b E. M. Grace	1
B 2, l-b 3	5	B 5, w 1	6
	161		**94**

Gloucestershire

W. G. Grace, Esq., c R. Humphrey b Street	1	H. Grace, Esq., b Street	0
Dr. E. M. Grace run out	3	T. G. Matthews, Esq., c Griffith b Street	23
C. S. Gordon, Esq., c Pooley b Street	68	R. F. Miles, Esq., b Marten	79
C. R. Filgate, Esq., c Griffith b Street	21	W. D. L. Macpherson, Esq., not out	0
G. F. Grace, Esq., b Marten	69		
G. Strachan, Esq., c Marten b Street	24	B 10, l-b 13, w 1	24
J. A. Bush, Esq., b Street	3		**315**

Gloucestershire won by an innings and 60 runs

WG also turned out for Single v Married at Lord's, a match staged for the benefit of one of the greatest early professionals, Edgar Willsher of Kent.

Married v Single of England, played at Lord's last July for Willsher's benefit, was unfortunate as regards weather. On the first day it was bright and pleasant up to luncheon time; soon after rain fell and frequently stopped play. Throughout that night rain fell heavily and unceasingly, and continued so to fall up to midday on Tuesday, preventing any play that day. On the Wednesday, frequent showers interrupted the cricket, but for all that the match was finished, and the Single won by an innings and 73 runs – a result due to the extraordinary batting of Mr W. G. Grace, who accomplished the rare batting feat of commencing the innings and taking his bat out for 189 (out of a total of 310 – 304 from the bat), and this too against the bowling of J. C. Shaw, Hewitt, Alfred Shaw, Southerton, Iddison and Mr Kelson… a truly great innings, the latter part of it being played in a bad light and on wickets beaten out of all form by rain.

Wisden felt that a list of WG's innings at Lord's that wet and cold summer was called for:

Mr W. G. Grace's Innings for MCC in 1871

v The Fifteen	at Lord's	b Grundy jun.	44	b Buttress	31
v Surrey	"	b Southerton	181		
v Yorkshire	"	b Clayton	23	run out	98
v Middlesex	"	b Howitt	88	caught	10
v Cambridge University	"	caught	4	caught	4
v Oxford University	"	caught	15		
v Kent	"	b Lipscomb	51		
v Sussex	"	stumped	59		
v Surrey	at The Oval	caught	146	caught	21
v Kent	at Canterbury	caught	117		
Total runs scored in 1871 "for MCC"			892		
Average per innings			59 and 7 over		

Other Innings played "at Lord's" by Mr W. G. Grace in 1871

For South v North	caught	178		
For Gloucestershire v MCC & Ground	"lbw"	49	not out	34
For Gentlemen v Players	caught	50	caught	37
For Single v Married (first man in)	not out	189		
Total runs scored "at Lord's"		1,145		
Average per innings "at Lord's"		71 and 9 over		

Even so, this list excluded his two biggest innings that summer, 268 for South v North at The Oval, and 217 for Gentlemen of England v Players of England at Brighton.

Of his innings at The Oval, in a match for the benefit of H. H. Stephenson, Wisden recorded that:

The weather was bright throughout, and the company present so numerous that the attendance averaged 6,000 per day, and those present the three days witnessed Mr Grace out from the first ball bowled in the match, and subsequently play the largest innings ever scored by a cricketer on The Oval, his two innings forming the sensational contrast of 0 and 268...

Mr Grace was eighth out at five minutes to four on the Wednesday, as many as 426 runs were made during his stay; his score was 268; his hitting all round was masterly, and his skill and success in "placing" the ball so wonderful that throughout that long innings the only chance he gave was to the wicketkeeper when he had made 152.

His innings at Brighton two weeks later, in another benefit match, this time for John Lillywhite, was remarkable in that here too he was dismissed first ball in the first innings, and hit a double-century in the second.

Under a bright hot sun the match was commenced... Mr W. G. Grace and Mr Dale starting the batting, and J. C. Shaw and McIntyre the bowling. Shaw began to Mr Dale, who got the second ball away for a single, but the third ball – a breakback – clean bowled the off stump of Mr Grace's wicket, and to the manifest astonishment of all present (and subsequent comers that day) the great batsman was out for 0...

The Gentlemen's second innings was commenced at five minutes to three by Mr W. G. Grace and Mr Dale... Then, at 25 minutes past three, Mr G. F. Grace went to the wickets and commenced that memorably brilliant hitting display that was not ended until "the brothers" had – against the Players of England bowling – in two hours and a half put on the extraordinarily large number of 240 runs for a wicket... When, at five minutes to six, Hayward bowled Mr G. F. Grace for 98, the score stood at 275 for two wickets. Mr Grace's 98 was a remarkable display of brilliant driving, and included so many as '17 fours. A hearty, ringing, deserved cheer greeted the young gentleman's return to the pavilion, and for years to come many a cricketer then present will tell you how magnificently young Mr Grace helped his brother to increase by 240 runs the Gentlemen of England's score at Brighton in 1871...

Mr W. Grace was first man in at five minutes to three on the Tuesday; when he had made 21 runs he was missed (from J. C. Shaw's bowling) at mid-off by Daft, and when he had made 86 he was missed (from Lillywhite's bowling) at wicket by Phillips. He then hit away in grand form, sent a slow from Daft clear out of the ground for six, made two fours and a single from an over of McIntyre's, and when stumps were drawn at a quarter to seven that day, he had made exactly 200 runs. The next morning he increased his score by 17 runs, and was then out by the wicketkeeper running to short leg and there cleverly catching the ball.

The apparent inconsistency in the use of initials when Wisden refers to cricketers of the time is not really very inconsistent. W. G. Grace is almost always given both initials, with the prefix 'Mr" denoting his amateur status, although in the passage above they merely call him "'Mr W. Grace"'. Amateurs were designated by "'Mr'" or "'Dr" or other title, followed by their full initials, while professionals were merely referred to by their surname. Scorecards sometimes printed their names with the initials following the surname. Occasionally initials were used to distinguish two professionals with the same surname, as for example with J. C. Shaw and A. Shaw, both of whom came up against the Graces many times.

Despite his huge scores, there does not seem to be the same affection for WG that comes through the pages for, for example, young Fred Grace. Words like "masterly" and "grand" are used for WG, but it's "magnificent" for a lesser score by Fred. Already, Wisden's contributors are perhaps wondering whether WG is just too good.

In 1871, the Gloucestershire County Cricket Club was formed. Among its officials were "Treasurer: The late Henry Mills Grace Esq."

This is WG's father, who died during the year. Wisden greeted the newly formed club enthusiastically.

The formation in 1871 of a County Club for Gloucestershire is a most important addition to the C C C.'s which, after all is said, written and done, are the real mainstays of the popularity of the game; are productive of the best all-round cricket; are the first to produce to public notice most of the skilled cricketers of the country; and by their "return" matches keep alive those pleasant, popular gatherings of all classes for which the county contests of our national game are so famous.

That Gloucestershire should be enrolled among the C. C. C.'s of the country received an additional welcome from the fact that the Shire's return matches would give opportunities to many of witnessing the great batting abilities of Mr W. G. Grace, who would otherwise perhaps never see him play. Thousands of Nottingham people enjoyed that opportunity in '71, and this year Yorkshire and Sussex people will have the same chance of witnessing their county cricketers enjoy an outing against the great batsman and his ten amateur confreres.

On the final page of the 1872 Almanack, Wisden lists all "Mr W. G. Grace's Innings on The Oval". The list is 41 innings long, includes three double-centuries and five other scores of over 100, and as a footnote, Wisden records that:

Mr John Walker is the only cricketer that has bowled Mr Grace out in both innings of one match on The Oval. James Lillywhite has bowled him twice on The Oval, and so has Alfred Shaw. Those who have only once hit his stumps there are Willsher, the late T. Sewell Jun., Luke Greenwood and Southerton. Of the 41 innings played by Mr W. G. Grace on The Oval, five were not-outs, representing 598 runs. He had been ten times bowled, 23 times caught out, once stumped, once run out, and once (to that memorable first ball of J. C. Shaw's) lbw.

In 1871 Mr W. G. Grace made (all matches told) 3,696 runs

In 1863 Dr E. M. Grace made (all matches told) 3,074 runs.

WISDEN 1873

On the opening page of the 1873 edition, the editor admits to a mistake.

Erratum – On page 82 the two concluding lines respecting Mr W. Grace's innings at Lord's should read:

"All told Mr W. Grace played 18 innings *(3 not-outs)*, and scored 880 runs at Lord's in 1872 – average per innings at Lord's 48–16."

(The error arose through the compiler inadvertently calculating the two innings played at Chorleywood).

Wisden *was already taking itself seriously as the most accurate and reliable record of cricket scores, and since admitting its first mistakes in the 1870 edition, would own up thereafter to even the most minor of errors.*

Today, the average would read differently, as 880 runs in 15 completed innings gives an average of 58.66. 880 runs divided by eighteen innings gives an average of 48 and 16 left over, given in Wisden as "48–16", with a hyphen rather than a decimal point.

From the MCC report:

Mr W. G. Grace, the monarch of all MCC (and other batsmen), notwithstanding the wet and slow wickets that prevailed in the early part of last season, again contributed very largely to the Club's success on several occasions, for out of the gross total of 1,556 runs made for MCC in the 15 innings Mr Grace played for the Club, he made 528, or more than one-third; his MCC average for 1872 being 40–8 runs per innings.

Even without the monarch of all cricketers, Gloucestershire had other members of the family to come to their rescue.

Gloucestershire v Nottinghamshire
At Clifton College, August 22, 23 and 24, 1872

As Mr W. G. Grace was in Canada when this match was played, and neither Mr Strachan, Mr Filgate nor Mr Brice were able to play, it was thought by many that Gloucestershire would suffer an emphatic defeat. Not so, for when play, in those memorable three days at Clifton, had become part of cricket history, the Gloucestershire men had made 484 runs for the loss of 14 wickets, and had much the best of the drawn match, wherein 723 runs had been scored with only 24 of the 40 wickets down...

The Doctor and Mr Matthews had made 68 runs (Dr Grace 42) when luncheon was called – no wicket down; but from the second ball afterwards delivered Mr Matthews was had at wicket. Mr Townsend made 15 whilst the Doctor done [*sic*] the rest of the work in hitting the score to 129, when Mr Townsend played on; then it was Mr G. F. Grace faced his brother, and the score was rapidly hit to 170, when Dr Grace was smartly caught out at the wicket for 108, the result of two hours and 20 minutes hitting... Mr E.K. Browne and Mr G. F. Grace continued the fast scoring up to 214, when the Cheltenham captain was captured at the wicket and at 216 Wyld also had Mr Fewings… When stumps were drawn for the day, at 6.30, the Gloucestershire innings wore this shape:

Six wickets down, 264 runs scored. Mr G. F. Grace, not out 77, Mr Lang, not out 6.

On Friday play was resumed about noon… and when Harness had bowled Mr Miles the innings was finished at 1.25 for 317 runs; Mr G. F. Grace not out 115, a fine innings that was made by 24 singles, five twos, seven threes and 15 fours; Mr F. G. made 115 of the 188 runs scored whilst he was at wickets…

Notts having just escaped following on, the Gloucestershire second innings was commenced at 3.10. Dr Grace made 40 runs in 60 minutes, when he was had at long-field, the score at 59. Mr G. F. Grace then went in, but at 63 a capital catch settled Mr Matthews… Mr Bush and Mr G. F. Grace stayed until the stumps were drawn at six o'clock; the match drawn, Mr Bush not out 13, and the scorebook showing the following wonderfully successful batting exploit:

Mr G. F. Grace not out 115, and not out 72.

The Three Brothers Grace on the August 22, 1872

A coincidence worthy of record here is, that on the day the above match was commenced – August 22 – all the three brothers Grace scored largely, thus:

At Clifton, Dr Grace scored 108; At Clifton Mr G. F. Grace scored 77 not out (a portion of his innings of 115 runs); In Canada Mr W. G. Grace scored 81.

In the next match, Fred Grace scored 1 and 44, and took seven for 43 in Sussex's second innings, to secure a win for Gloucestershire by 60 runs.

The Gloucestershire county averages for 1872 show the three brothers being the three top-scorers with the three best averages, and the only players who scored a century for Gloucestershire during that summer. They were also the three who bowled the most overs.

Gloucestershire Batting in 1872

	Matches Played	Inns commenced	Times not out	Times bowled	Largest innings	Total runs scored	Average per inns.
Mr W. G. Grace	5	6	-	2	150	284	47– 2
Mr G. F. Grace	7	10	2	5	115*	306	38 – 2
Dr E. M. Grace	5	7	-	2	108	244	34 – 6

Gloucestershire Bowling in 1872

	Overs Bowled	Maiden overs	Runs scored from	Wide balls	Caught from bowling	Wkts bowled	Total wkts taken
Mr W. G. Grace	284	113	406	1	28	6	40
Mr G. F. Grace	256	99	346	8	1	12	14
Dr E. M. Grace	174	64	226	5	3	5	8

No bowling average, as we know it today, is published, but for the record, WG's average was 10.15; Fred's was 24.71, and the Doctor's 28.25.

The best bowling average among the Gloucestershire players was Mr E. Brice's. He took 12 wickets for 69 runs, at an average of 5.75.

In all matches in the 1872 season, W. G. Grace took 62 wickets at 11.87 each, the second-best seasonal bowling average of his career, but his tally of wickets was far inferior to James Southerton of Surrey, who took 169 at 13.07.

Summary of Mr W. G. Grace's Innings in 1872

Mr Grace played 61 innings... Was four times not out
    Played eight innings of more than 100 runs... Was four times out for 0
    SCORED 2,571 RUNS
    Was 19 times bowled out; 33 times caught out; four times lbw; *and* once stumped.
    His eight largest innings were 170 *not out*, 150, 142, 117, 114, 114, 112, and 101; or 1,020 runs in eight innings – *one not out.*

The four 0's were thus registered: one at Chorleywood, where he was bowled by Hughes for 0; one at Lord's, where he was lbw to Southerton for 0; one on The Oval, where Lillywhite bowled him for 0; and one in Canada, where Mr A. N. Hornby stumped him for 0.

    In England, Southerton bowled Mr Grace three times (*twice in one match*); J. C. Shaw bowled him three times; Howitt bowled him twice; and Mr Powys, Hill, Lillywhite, Iddison, Alfred Shaw, Hughes and Bishop each bowled him once.

    In Canada, Mr Grace was bowled by Boothroyd and by Wright.

    In America, Mr Grace was bowled by Newhall and by Eastwood.

WISDEN 1874

GLOUCESTERSHIRE IN 1873

Of the 2,239 runs scored from the bat for Gloucestershire in 1873, the three Graces made 1,140, or more than half; nevertheless there are other fine batsmen in the ranks of their shire, and so long as the Graces keep up their '73 form, and the shire can recruit among the Clifton Collegians, the Gloucestershire team will be a hot lot for any county.

All the Graces contributed heavily, once again, to Gloucestershire's success.

Gloucestershire v Yorkshire
The Return – at Clifton College, August 14, 15 and 16, 1873

Gloucestershire 404 (G. F. Grace 165*; Hill 6–132) and 69–5
(W. G. Grace 25; Rowbotham 3–37); Yorkshire 182 (Lockwood 55; Miles 5–50)
and 287 (Emmett 104; W. G. Grace 4–88).

This match was largely and fashionably attended, and was played on wickets so excellent for batting that ... the large number of 942 runs were made for the 35 wickets down, averaging nearly 27 runs per wicket.

The Graces commenced the batting; Dr Grace was missed at wicket when he had scored only one run, and Hill clean bowled Mr W. Grace when the score was at 36. Dr Grace was second wicket down, the score at 137; Mr G. F. Grace went in with the score at 140 for three wickets; he had made 120 when the stumps were pulled up for the day, the score at 344 for eight wickets. Mr G. F. Grace was the *not out* man when the innings was over at a quarter past one the following day, of which number the three brothers had made 250. Mr G. F. Grace's 165 *not out* was made by two fives, 23 fours, four threes, nine twos and 33 singles. *Bell's Life* termed this "a magnificent exhibition of all-round cricket". *The Sportsman* described it as "a masterly innings of four hours' duration"...

Yorkshire's first innings included..... a magnificent catch by Mr W. Grace (Rowbotham the victim).

Wisden was already beginning to modify its praise for WG with comments about perceived shortcomings, and with fulsome praise for lesser innings. WG's innings of 48 against Surrey included a six which was described as "a by no means difficult hit for six." Yet Swann's 25 was "excellent cricket" and Humphrey reminded spectators of "his old days" in making 27. Was WG just too good for unstinting praise? Were Wisden's *reporters beginning to hope that the Champion would fail? From this distance it is impossible to be sure, but there is a change in the way* Wisden *reports WG's achievements as he reaches his cricketing apogee.*

Gloucestershire v Surrey
The Return – at Clifton, August 25, 26 and 27, 1873

Gloucestershire 172 (W. G. Grace 48; Southerton 6–40) and 281–2
(W. G. Grace 160*, Knapp 90*); Surrey 134 (Humphrey 27; W. G. Grace 4–19).
Match drawn.

A fine first day was unpleasantly backed up by rain on the second and third days; nevertheless, the attendances were numerous and fashionable. The Graces began the batting, but before a run had been scored, Southerton drove Dr Grace on to his wicket, and later on, Southerton served Mr W. Grace the same way; Mr W. G. hitting his wicket so hard as to knock a stump out of the ground. Mr W. Grace's 48 included a hit out of the ground for six... but one report stated "the fence was only 60 yards from the wicket, a by no means difficult hit for six.".... In gloomy unpleasant weather, the Surrey batting was commenced by Freeman and Swann; the former was bowled before a run was scored, but the four following batsmen knocked up over 100 runs between them, the two Humphreys doing their full share of that century, Thomas Humphrey having hit in a style reminding the spectators of "his old days"; Richard Humphrey "played good cricket", his 27 included a hit for six. Swann made 25 "by excellent cricket", Caffyn 25 "by patient and careful cricket"... In the Shire's second innings, Dr Grace skied one to the long-stop, who very properly held it, and Mr Townsend was bowled with the score at 26; thereupon Mr Knapp faced Mr W. G. Grace, and despite dull weather, frequent showers, wet wickets and eight bowling changes, *these two gentlemen increased the score from 26 to 281*, when "time" was up, and the match drawn materially in favour of Gloucestershire, Mr W. G. Grace *not out* 160, described as "a magnificent innings, the chief hits being four sixes, one five and 12 fours"; and Mr Knapp *not out* 90, reported "a carefully played innings, containing five fours, one three, and seven twos." Furthermore the reports stated that "Mr Grace ought to have been caught by Mr Burls at point early in the innings"; that "at a later period, Mr Knapp sent a hot one to Mr Boult at point, which might have been taken"; but that "the feat they accomplished in putting on 225 runs without the loss of a wicket, entitles them to undying praise."

Against Sussex at Brighton, the Graces had mixed fortunes. Gloucestershire won by 9 runs, but
    Fillery was handy in getting rid of Mr W. G. Grace for 6 and 1 – the crack's two briefest innings in a County match last season. Mr G. F. Grace was "paired off" comfortably for Sussex, but Dr Grace physicked the South Coast bowling (principally Fillery's) so effectively that he made two fives and eight fours in his second innings of 76 runs [*out of the 109 made by his side*].

The bowling efforts of the Graces are not mentioned in the report, but Fred took 4 for 51 and 4 for 32, WG took 3 for 45 and 4 for 25, while EM, who only bowled 16 overs for 19 runs, took two catches to add to his 89 runs in a low-scoring match.

SUMMARY OF MR W. G. GRACE'S BATTING IN FIRST-CLASS MATCHES IN 1873

Matches Played in, 23   Innings Commenced, 37   Times Not Out, 7
Total Runs Scored, 2102   Average per Innings, 70–2

In those 37 first-class matches [*sic*] – played against the best bowling in England –
Mr W. G. Grace made the following splendid series of innings of over 50 runs:
192 *not out*, 163 *c and b*, 160 *not out*, 158 *bowled*, 152 *caught*, 145 *caught*, 134
caught, 98 *bowled*, 83 *caught*, 79 *caught*, 70 *caught*, 69 *not out*, 68 *run out*, 67
caught, 57 *not out* and 51 *caught*

MR W. G. GRACE'S INNINGS AGAINST TWENTY-TWO'S IN 1873

These innings were played for the United South Eleven. So far as a careful look over
the newspapers permits, we find that Mr W. G. Grace commenced 32 innings, and
scored 872 runs; his highest score being 91, made close by Nunhead Cemetery, his
lowest was 0 and 8 at Leicester, being bowled in both innings by F. Randon (the
new bowler at Lord's in 1874).

THREE SIXES – ONE 140 YARDS FROM HIT TO PITCH

Mr W. G. Grace – In an "extra" match between the U. S. E. E. and 18 Gentlemen
of Edinburgh, last May, Mr W. G. Grace scored 47 runs, making "three splendid
hits out of the ground for six each – one pitching 140 yards."

*Wisden, reflecting the enthusiasm for cricket at all levels, rarely distinguished
between what we would now call first-class matches and others. Thus the list of
"Individual Innings of Three Figures Hit in 1871" (quite obviously a misprint for
"1873") begins with five double-centuries, all of which were made in club or minor
games.*

The 200's. – There were five innings of over 200 hit in 1873. Dr E. M. Grace's
259 not out was the highest score of the season; the Doctor's hits in that innings
were: 36 singles; nine twos; seven threes; 25 fours (no fives), and the very large
number of 14 sixes; *Dr Grace scored those 259 runs in less than 100 minutes, so for
nearly 1¾ hours the Doctor made runs at the rate of 2½ per minute.*

*The innings in question was played for Thornbury at Thornbury. The name of the
opposition is not recorded.*

WISDEN 1875

It was not until Wisden *reached its 12th edition that its editors decided to devote an article to "THE THREE ENGLISH TWELVES WHO HAVE VISITED AUSTRALIA", the first being H. H. Stephenson's team of 1861–62, the second being George Parr's side of 1863–64, which included Dr E. M. Grace, and the third being*

MR W. G. GRACE'S TEAM – Time of Visit 1873–74.

Mr W. G. Grace (Capt.)	Mr G. F. Grace	James Lillywhite
Mr F. H. Boult	Andrew Greenwood	Martin McIntyre
Mr J. A. Bush	Richard Humphrey	William Oscroft
Mr W. Gilbert	Henry Jupp	James Southerton

This mixed team were the third and last lot of English Cricketers who left England to play the game in Australia. They left Southampton on October 23, 1873, and landed at Melbourne on December 13. They commenced match playing on December 26, and played 15 matches, winning ten, losing three and leaving two unfinished; a fairly successful tour, considering the undoubted improvement made by Australian cricketers since the visit of Parr's team, and the generally admitted fact that Mr Grace's team did not nearly represent the full cricketing strength of the old country. But notwithstanding these drawbacks, the Englishmen made at Ballarat the largest innings (470 runs) ever scored by a side in Australia, and in that innings Mr W. Grace made 126, and Mr F. Grace 112. Moreover, in the match at Hobart Town, Mr F. Grace hit an innings of 154 runs, the largest score ever made against 22 in the field. They left Adelaide for home on March 29, and arrived at Southampton on Monday, May 18.

SOME BITS OF ENGLISH BOWLING – BY MR W. GRACE'S TEAM

Mr W. G. Grace's bowling had ten wickets in the first match played by the team in Australia.

Lillywhite all the wickets, Mr W. Grace all the runs. – In the single-wicket match between seven English and 12 New South Wales men, the Englishmen won without losing a wicket: Lillywhite's bowling got all the NSW men out for 29, and Mr W. G. Grace scored 28 not out; two byes made the winning total 30.

Back in England, WG enjoyed a very successful summer in 1874.

Sussex v Gloucestershire
At Brighton, June 11 and 12, 1874

Gloucestershire **381** (W. G. Grace 179; Lillywhite 6–113); **Sussex 231**
(Fillery 87; W. G. Grace 5–76) and **148** (W. G. Grace 7–82).
Gloucestershire won by an innings and two runs.

Splendid weather and large attendances favoured this match... Mr W. Grace won choice, and with Mr Matthews commenced batting to the bowling of Fillery and Lillywhite. Mr Grace started with a capital cut for four; then he lifted one that – "owing to a misunderstanding" – neither mid-off nor cover point secured, and then, as is his wont on such occasions, Mr Grace laid on to the bowling with great severity, and eventually brought off one of his famous and fine three-figure innings... From one over of Skinner's Mr Grace made two fours (drives) and "a magnificent leg hit for six"; and by such hitting was the score enlarged.. (until) the big bat was at last done with by "lbw" for 179, and so – reported *Bell's Life* – "one of the finest innings ever played by Mr Grace was brought to a close".

WG took the opportunity to play against all levels of opposition. Playing for MCC and Ground against Herefordshire at Lord's on June 18 and 19, 1874, Wisden records that

The Herefordshire Eleven were considerably overweighted in this match. In their two innings they made only 110 runs – 93 from the bat... In MCC's innings only one wicket was bowled; Mr W. G. Grace made 109 and Mr F. J. Crooke 121; these two gentlemen increased the Club score from 89 for two wickets, to 292 for 3. Mr Grace was caught out at mid-on; his hits were four fives, seven fours, nine threes, eight two's and 18 singles... Not only did Mr Grace score 109, but his bowling had 12 wickets – four bowled. MCC won by an innings and 223 runs.

WG took four for 16 in the Herefordshire first innings, and eight for 29 in the second.

Wisden's account of the Gentlemen of the South v the Players of the South not only features yet another large score by WG, but also indicates how different playing conditions were almost a century and a half ago. It is also interesting to note that once again Wisden comments favourably on the play of the lesser player, but leaves WG's statistics to speak for themselves.

Gentlemen of the South v Players of the South
At The Oval, June 26 and 27, 1874

Wet weather; consequently queer wickets and a ridiculously easy win by the Gentlemen were the features of this once famous great run-getting match. The eleven Players scored two innings of 77 and 163 runs. Per contra, Mr Fryer hit an innings of 72 runs and Mr W. Grace one of 150, and thereby the Players were defeated by an innings and 40 runs! Pooley was the only player really in it; he got rid of four of the ten Gentlemen's wickets and scored 92 runs; his 80 not out was commenced with the score at 17 for five wickets, and finished in a drenching downpour of rain…

Mr W. Grace's 150 was the result of 3½ hours' batting, his hits being one five, 11 fours, six threes, 19 two's and 45 singles… Mr Fryer played – as he invariably does when well set – great cricket.

A "drenching downpour" would these days certainly take the players off the field, leaving even a "great run-getting match" as a draw. That Pooley and his team-mates played on in a rainstorm when all was lost possibly shows a greater regard for the spirit of cricket than is sometimes shown today. But then, although there were no central contracts riding on the result of Gentlemen v Players, Pooley himself, an inveterate gambler, might perhaps have had an interest in playing on through the rain. Whether the spectators were happy to sit watching them play in a downpour is another matter altogether.

W. G. Grace was his usual prolific self during Canterbury Week, and this time Wisden gives credit where credit is due:

The Canterbury Week of 1874 was reported to have been the most successful "week" yet played. The weather on the two most important days – Monday and Thursday – was most fortunately favourable, and the attendances numerous and brilliant beyond precedent. The new match – Kent and Gloucestershire v The Rest of England – that formed the prominent item in the cricket programme has (it was stated) by its success "become a great fact". The two county balls were crowdedly patronised by the beauty, rank and fashion of the county. "The great concomitant of cricket in the Canterbury Week", The Old Stager's Theatricals, were "blazes of triumphs", and beyond and above all, the great star of the cricketing world, the most wonderful batsman of all times, shone with unwonted batting brilliancy, for, as the journals of the period eloquently recorded, in the only three innings he played in the Canterbury Week of 1874,

Mr W. G. Grace scored 94, 121 and 123!!!

KENT AND GLOUCESTERSHIRE V THE REST OF ENGLAND

In pleasant weather, and in the presence of a large company, "the Counties" commenced the batting with Mr W. G. Grace and Mr Thornton, to the bowling of Alfred Shaw and Morley… The feature of the innings was Mr W. G. Grace's 94, which was described as "a faultless innings" and "one of the best displays ever given us by the great Gloucestershire batsman". First man in, Mr W. Grace was sixth out, the score at 179, of which number Mr Grace had made 94.

... The second innings of the Counties was... commenced by Mr W. G. Grace and Lord Harris, who so thoroughly mastered the bowling of "The Rest" that, despite Alfred Shaw, Morley, Lillywhite, Reynolds and Morley (again) bowled, they made 115 runs before the first wicket fell, Lord Harris then being c and b by Morley for 33. Several more wickets fell before the score reached 200, when Mr Thornton faced Mr W. G. Grace, who, however, was shortly after had at slip by Mr Walker for 121, the only three-figure innings hit in the match... *Bell's Life* described this 121 of Mr Grace's as "a fine innings, during which he had not given a chance." (And the old "Bell" in ringing its praises of the great batsman, might have added, that the 94 and 121 of "Mr WG's" in this match was a batting feat that had only once been surpassed at Canterbury, and that was when Mr W. G. Grace scored 130 and 102 not out in the 1868 match).

... Mr W. G. Grace in this match made 215 runs, had ten wickets with his bowling and caught out two others.

WG's 123 was made for The Gentlemen of MCC against The County of Kent, a 12-a-side match that nevertheless received a full write-up in Wisden. *His 123 was made out of total of 174 when he was third man out. His bowling in this match was equally effective, five for 82 in the first innings and six for 47 in the second, as MCC won by an innings and 53 runs.*

WG's reputation for stretching the laws of cricket to their limits found its way into Wisden *for the first time in the 1875 edition. The umpiring also clearly was far short of impartial:*

Gentlemen v Players
At Prince's Ground, July 23, 24 and 25, 1874

Gentlemen **222** (G. F. Grace 93*; A. Shaw 6–58) and **209** (W. G. Grace 110; Morley 6–62); **Players 243** (Charlwood 85; W. Gilbert 4–54) and **128** (W. G. Grace 7–58, G. F. Grace 3–23).

... Mr F. Grace went to wickets at seven minutes past one, when the score was 41 for two wickets; he was batting for about three hours and a quarter, played his share of 120 overs, saw eight men come and go, and 181 runs scored, 93 of which he himself made by eight fours, five threes, seven twos and 32 singles, that comparatively large array of singles, testifying to the careful, steady cricket Mr F. Grace had played; he was earnestly and deservedly cheered.

... The Gentlemen's second innings was commenced by Mr W. Grace and Mr Gilbert... and Morley's first over should have cost the Gentlemen their great wicket, for in that over Mr W. Grace played a ball to leg, which, had Humphrey seen, and taken three steps back, he would in all probability have secured; but he could not have seen the ball, for on being shouted at he paced forward three or four steps and so lost all chance of making the catch. Later on that evening the Players had another upset. When the second wicket (120 runs scored) had fallen, Mr F. Grace faced his brother, and before Mr F. G. had scored he played the ball back to the bowler, Lillywhite, who could easily have caught it, had not Mr W. G. Grace been "palpably in the way". Lillywhite appealed to both umpires as to Mr Grace having obstructed the field, each umpire answered "Not out", decisions that were received with marked dissatisfaction by the Players, whose misfortune in this match was that nearly every appeal made by the Gentlemen was decided affirmatively, and the Players' appeals were mainly met with "Not out".

WG always seemed to do particularly well against Yorkshire:

Yorkshire v Gloucestershire
At Sheffield, July 27, 28 and 29, 1874

Gloucestershire 314 (W. G. Grace 167, Townsend 66; Clayton 5–91, Ulyett 5–126); Yorkshire 117 (G. F. Grace 4–53, W. G. Grace 4–57) and 103 (W. G. Grace 7–44). Gloucestershire won by an innings and 94 runs.

Mr W. G. Grace and Mr Knapp commenced the hitting on "splendid wickets" and to the intense gratification of the thousands of Yorkshiremen present, Mr W. G. Grace stayed and hit one of his familiarly fine three-figure innings... at 303, Mr W. G. Grace lifted one to long-on, whereat Mr Monkland (fielding for Hill) watched for the ball in capital form, and making a clever catch, Mr W. Grace was out for 167.

Gloucestershire v Yorkshire
At Clifton, August 14, 15 and 16, 1874

Although stormy weather marred the attendances, the pleasure, and the wickets so carefully prepared for this match, it did not mar the hitting of the three brothers, who contributed 259 of the 303 runs from the bat scored for Gloucestershire; Mr W. G. Grace making 127 runs, Mr G. F. Grace 81, and Dr E. M. Grace 51. Mr W. G. Grace and Dr Grace commenced the Gloucestershire innings; they scored 137 runs before a wicket fell, the Doctor being then out for 51; and when the score was at 216, Mr W. G. Grace was held at slip for 127 – an innings reported as "chanceless and splendid". More than 290 runs had been scored when

Mr G. F. Grace was c and b for 81, another innings that won high praise from the "cricket critics". The brothers were also chronicled to have fielded very finely, especially Dr E. M. at point.

Although Wisden's reporter does not mention it, WG and GF between them took 15 of the 18 wickets to fall (Yorkshire could only muster ten men for this match). They also took five catches between them.

CHAPTER 2

THE GRACE FAMILY AT ITS PEAK:
1875 TO 1880

*"Mr Grace's play was acknowledged to be such
as they never before witnessed"*

Throughout the 1870s, the Grace brothers were probably the three best all-round cricketers in England. By the second half of the decade, GF had joined his two elder brothers in the top rank of English cricketers, and between them they carried Gloucestershire to the unofficial title of county champions three times during these years. Gloucestershire have never been champions since. WG, it must be admitted, had four or five comparatively fallow summers between 1878 and 1882, but these were years when he was qualifying as a doctor and building up his practice, which limited his appearances. In 1876 he set a record which still stands, in making 839 runs in ten days, including two triple-centuries, at an average of 419.50. His 344 for MCC against Kent at Canterbury remains the highest score ever made by an MCC player, and the highest score ever made at Canterbury. His 318 not out for Gloucestershire against Yorkshire remained the highest score for the county until 2004.

WISDEN 1876

In summarising Gloucestershire's season, Wisden *noted:*

The soft slow-wicket season of 1875 does not appear to have nicked well with the play of several of the Gloucestershire batsmen, most of whom are known to like the ball "to come along well", the faster the preferable to them so long as wickets are true. 1874 was an exceptionally great run-getting season for Gloucestershire, and the 84–6 per innings made by Mr W. G. Grace that year an exceptionally large County average; hence his past season's doings for his shire appear, by contrast, small; but considering he hit an innings of 119 runs against Notts; made 111 and 43 in a match against Yorkshire, and 36 and 77 in a Sussex match, it cannot be said Mr W. Grace did so badly for Gloucestershire on the soft slow wickets of

1875. Mr G. F. Grace's average in '75 is also less than in '74, but his 25 and 56 against Yorkshire, his 31 not out against Notts, and his famous 180 not out against Surrey on the Clifton ground, evidence he still retains that very fine hitting form that brought off his splendid and famous 98 at poor John Lillywhite's benefit at Brighton in 1871. Dr E. M. Grace came well to the front in Gloucestershire's return matches of 1875, scoring 0, 23, 27, 28, 65, and 71 in the four matches he played, the 65 and 71 being top scores in the two Gloucestershire innings against Sussex. Dr Grace increased his average from 26–2 in 1874 to 35–4 in 1875...

The Gloucestershire bowling summary will show a curiously large proportion of wickets caught out, and men lbw, to Mr W. Grace's bowling... Mr G. F. Grace bowled down 14 of the 22 wickets credited to him; and in putting the figures together it will be found that Dr E. M. Grace's 102 overs for 147 runs and 15 wickets was the least expensive and most successful bowling of the lot.

North v South of England
At Prince's, May 27, 28 and 29, 1875 (for the benefit of The Cricketers' Fund Friendly Society).

Among the thousands on Prince's Ground on the opening day of this match there was one manly form and cheery voice missing that had never been missing at previous "Fund" matches; it was the form and voice of him whose earnest staunch advocacy obtained permission for the "Fund Match" to be annually played at Prince's; all present who knew him spoke respectfully of the man, and regretfully of the death of John Lillywhite...

At 12.15 on the day after the Derby, Mr W. Grace and Mr I. D. Walker commenced the South batting to the bowling of Hill and Mr Laidlay; 46 runs had been scored from 25 overs when Hill bowled Mr Walker for 15, and 50 was up when Mr Buller was had at long-on from the slows; then Mr F. Grace faced his brother, and so great a stand was made that the score was at 138 when Mr W. Grace was lbw for 82, an innings that included seven fours and 21 singles. But a still more effective stand was made when Mr Fryer went to Mr F. Grace's aid, as those gentlemen increased the score from 138 to 248, when a catch at point settled Mr F. Grace for 103, the largest innings in the match, and an exceedingly fine display of driving. Mr F. G.'s hits were one five (drive from Hill), ten fours, nine threes, nine twos and 13 singles. (Of the 248 runs then scored, the brothers had made 185!)

The Gentlemen v The Players of England
At Lord's, July 5, 6 and 7, 1875

Gentlemen **152** (Longman 70; Morley 6–36) and **444** (W. G. Grace 152, Webbe 65; Morley 5–135); **Players 169** (Greenwood 51; W. G. Grace 7–64) and **165** (Lockwood 67; W. G. Grace 5–61).
Gentlemen won by 262 runs

... With the first half of the match so evenly played, expectation was general of a close and exciting finish, but on Mr W. G. Grace and Mr Webbe commencing the Gentlemen's second innings at 1.33 those hopes were gradually, finely, and surely scattered, so fine, so great, so wonderful, and so unprecedented (at Lord's) a stand did those Gentlemen make against the Players of England's bowling. It is true that an accident to his foot deprived the Players of Alfred Shaw's services after dinner – a great loss indeed; nevertheless the batting was simply splendid, and thoroughly beat the bowling, the careful, skillful defence of the young hand, and the wonderful hard play, the fine hitting, and masterly power of placing the ball displayed by the old hand, affording the lookers-on a batting treat of the highest and most enjoyable form, cheers repeated again and again, and still again, markedly telling how highly such batting was appreciated... Mr Webbe was on his defence, and Mr Grace in his very best hitting form... Dinner was called with the score at 60, no wicket down, Mr W. Grace 45 not out, Mr Webbe 12 not out, extras three. At 3.15 the innings was resumed to the bowling of McIntyre and Lockwood (Wyld fielding for Alfred Shaw). The batsmen kept up their before-dinner form in superb style... and at 20 minutes to five the 200 was hoisted on the boards, no wicket down, the lusty and prolonged cheering that greeted this unprecedented opening of an innings at Lord's testifying to the thorough pleasure felt by the thousands of spectators; but when three more runs were made, a loud "How's that?" and toss-up of the ball by Pooley told all that Mr Webbe was at last out, the scoreboards then shewing the wonderful figures (in such a match) of 203 for one wicket... Mr Webbe's 65 included five fours (three of them to leg), five threes and six twos; he was earnestly cheered by all on the ground, the players heartily applauding him, Richard Daft pointedly paying his tribute of praise to the young Oxonian's batting, a high compliment this, but one highly merited. Mr Longman then went to the aid of Mr W. Grace, and the heavy scoring was continued, the figures rapidly rising to 242, when a splendid bit of fielding between Hill and Pooley fairly and clearly run out Mr W. Grace for one of the, if not the, best innings he had ever played. Mr Grace began his batting at 1.33; he was out at 5.25 for 152 runs, the score at 242 for two wickets; the exact time Mr Grace was batting was three hours and seven minutes, and the bowlers used against him were Alfred Shaw (for a time), Morley, Hill, Martin McIntyre, Lockwood, and Oscroft, most of them on more than once. Mr W. Grace's hits were a sharp snick for five (the second hit he made), nine four's, ten three's, 14 twos and 53 singles. The features of this truly great innings were the fine hard form in which he played and scored runs from balls which other (and good) batsmen would have thought themselves clever to have simply stopped, and that old, wonderful, unique power of "placing the ball out of danger", which has rendered his batting career so famous and so successful. The only chance the compiler of this book witnessed was when he had made 137, when

Daft just got hold of the ball close to the people sitting by the pavilion, but overbalancing himself in the effort Daft slipped, fell, and dropped it... On Mr Grace's retirement, he was lustily and justly cheered.

... In cricket history the innings, numerically great though it be, will be most celebrated for the splendid and effective stand made by Mr W. G. Grace and Mr A. J. Webbe before a wicket fell.

... Mr W. G. Grace's bowling was very successful – 12 wickets for 125 runs.

WG's cricket – or at least his batting – was by now generally recognised as something marvellous. Although described as an "old hand" in comparison to Mr A. J. Webbe, WG was still a few days short of his 27th birthday when he played this innings. Webbe was then a 20-year-old Oxford undergraduate.

The Yorkshire match against Gloucestershire that year was for the benefit of John Thewlis, a long-serving professional. Wisden's opening paragraph of its match report sums up the attitudes which held cricket, and society at large, together in the latter part of the 19th century. "Good conduct", as the fate of Bobby Peel a few years later was to show when he was sacked by Yorkshire for drunkenness, was rated more highly in professional cricketers than "skilled exertions".

Yorkshire v Gloucestershire
At Sheffield, July 26, 27, and 28, 1875

Gloucestershire **194** (W. G. Grace 111) and **107** (W. G. Grace 43; Hill 6–38);
Yorkshire **211** (Lockwood 74; W. G. Grace 5–64) and **93–3** (Lockwood 39*).
Yorkshire won by seven wickets

Yorkshire cricket officials of the present day repay their professionals' good conduct and skilled exertions with marked consideration and liberality. All are well paid for playing, special notice being taken of markedly good bowling or batting; and since 1871 no season has been allowed to pass away without the Committee setting aside the most attractive match in their programme for the benefit of some old and faithful cricketer who has played years of good yeoman service on the cricket field for his shire... Last season the match was played to benefit old John Thewlis, an unobtrusive, civil fellow, and – as a batsman and long-stop – about as good a cricketer as ever put on flannel for Yorkshire. All wished old John a good benefit, and the weather being favourable he had one.

On the Monday, about 12.40, the match was commenced by Mr W. Grace and Mr Matthews batting to the bowling of Hill and Lockwood... Wickets then fell fast, five having fallen when only 73 runs had been scored; but Mr W. Grace was still there, batting his best, to the evident delight of thousands of cricket-loving Yorkshiremen... Mr W. Grace was first man in and seventh out; he was about three hours at wickets, and his innings of three ones was described as having been "made in his best form without a chance".

THE CANTERBURY WEEK

Despite WG.'s bowling proving much more successful in 1875 than in any previous season, there is little comment in Wisden *about it: he is still regarded by* Wisden *as a great batsman rather than a great all-rounder. The bowler of the season was probably Alfred Shaw of Nottinghamshire, who took well over 100 wickets during the summer, at an average of around nine runs apiece.* Wisden's *eventual obituary of Shaw stated that "from 1872 to 1880 he was, beyond all question, the best slow bowler in England." Grace, who would at this time be more correctly described as a medium-pace bowler, took only 54 wickets for Gloucestershire in 1875, but his final first-class tally for all teams was 191 wickets at 12.92 runs apiece, the most victims of any season of his career. Shaw took 160 wickets that summer, at 9.34 runs each. These figures would have been very hard to calculate from the pages of* Wisden, *who gave little information about bowling at this time.*

Kent and Gloucestershire v England

August 2 and 3, 1875

England 220 (Greenwood 54; W. G. Grace 5–82) and **68** (W. G. Grace 6–35);
Kent and Gloucestershire 248 (Renny-Tailyour 54; Morley 6–100) and **44–4**
(Foord-Kelcey 16).
Kent and Gloucestershire won by six wickets

Inasmuch as neither Mr A. N. Hornby, Mr Longman, Mr J. M. Cotterill, Mr W. H. Hadow, Mr A. P. Lucas, Richard Daft, Ephraim Lockwood, nor William Oscroft played, it cannot be fairly stated "England" was thoroughly represented. The combined Counties' Eleven were all amateurs, and a rare team of fine hitters they were. But the England Eleven comprised seven professionals. Mr Webbe and Jupp commenced the batting to the bowling of Mr W. Grace and Mr Kelcey…

… After dinner "England" commenced a second innings so brief in its duration, and so surprising in its ineffectiveness, that in one hour and 20 minutes they were all out for 68 runs.

The Counties then required but 41 runs to win the match. Mr Wyatt was run out at 18; Mr Kelcey and Mr F. Penn bowled at 26; and Mr Townsend bowled ("off his body") at 28. Mr W. Grace then went in and the match was quickly won for "The Counties" by six wickets; thereupon play ceased for the day. Mr Bush stumped five and caught out another "Englander"; smart wicketkeeping this. Mr W. Grace's bowling had 11 England wickets for 117 runs, very successful bowling that won him high praise from the cricket critics.

The third day was dry but breezy, and a stiff breeze from the N. E. up at St Lawrence is no joke to those out pleasuring on that famous old ground. At noon play for the day commenced with the 12-a-side match

GENTLEMEN OF MCC V THE COUNTY OF KENT

The Club began the batting with Mr W. G. Grace and Mr A. J. Webbe, and, wrote the chronicler, "a sad disappointment occurred to the spectators when Mr Grace was finely caught (left hand) low down by Mr Yardley at mid-on ere he had made a run". But such is cricket, and even Mr W. G. Grace, like other batsmen, must have his 0's as well as his 100's.

The reports of Gloucestershire's home matches in August make consistent reading:

Gloucestershire v Yorkshire
August 12, 13 and 14, 1875

The three brothers Grace made 158 of the 288 runs scored from the bat for Gloucestershire in this match, and two of the brothers' bowling had 17 of the Yorkshire wickets, Mr "G F" making 81 of the runs, and Mr "WG" taking 13 of the wickets...

Gloucestershire v Nottinghamshire
August 16, 17 and 18, 1875

Mr W. G. Grace was in three-figure form in this match, scoring 119 runs in the only innings his side played, and as Dr E. M. made 27, Mr G. F. 31 not out, and the brothers' bowling had six of the 11 Notts wickets down, it may be fairly stated the old form of the family was ably maintained in this match, though others played a prominent part for Gloucestershire...

Gloucestershire v Sussex
August 23, 24 and 25, 1875

Dr E. M. Grace was front-rank man for Gloucestershire in this match, for "The Doctor" scored 65 and 71, had five wickets with his bowling, and caught out another.

In this match, WG caught the eye in another way – a further mention in Wisden *of what might be considered his sharp practice on the field. This has metamorphosed into a long-lasting reputation for unsportsmanlike behaviour (see* Wisden *2005) which has little foundation in truth, if the pages of* Wisden *during WG's playing days are to be believed.*

... and, wrote a critic in the *Sportsman*, "the Gloucestershire fielding was very smart", for, continued the critic, "WG now took up a very unusual position, confronting Mr Smith, and not more than four yards from him, just out of the bowler's line, a circumstance calculated to intimidate and embarrass a batsman. He gave Phillips a wider berth." *Bell's Life* also noticed the same "incident", stating, "Mr W. G. Grace had been fielding right in front of the batsman in a most unusual way." However, and for all that, Phillips and Mr Smith increased the score to 120, when Mr G. F. Grace at cover point caught out Phillips; so Gloucestershire won the match by 40 runs.

WG also played four matches for United South v United North. Wisden's reports are brief, and there are no complete scorecards published.

Under this popular but somewhat abused title, matches were played at the back end of last season at Huddersfield, Tunbridge Wells, Hull and Loughborough.

The Huddersfield match was a remarkable one... Only 25 wickets fell but so many as 756 runs were scored. Mr W. G. Grace made 92 and 73; Mr A. N. Hornby 71; Charlwood 3 and 117; James Lillywhite 2 and 32 not out; and Mr G. F. Grace 36 and 147 not out. Of the 158 runs made in the South's first, the two Graces made 128, the next-highest (!) scorer being Fillery with 8...

The Tunbridge Wells match was a thorough contrast to that at Huddersfield. In Allen Hill's first over, Mr W. G. Grace was had at point for 0, Charlwood was bowled for 0, and Mr F. Grace was had at mid-off for 0, and yet these three men made 468 runs at Huddersfield. There were eight 0's in the South's two innings; and 31 by Lillywhite, 19 by Mr W. Grace (his second innings) and 17 by Charlwood were the only double figures made by the Southerners...

The Hull match was won by the South by 23 runs (Mr Hornby absent in the North's second). Mr Hornby made 48; Mr W. G. Grace 29 and 37... In the South's first innings, Emmett had eight wickets (five bowled) for 54 runs.

The Loughborough match was remarkable for the South being out for a first innings of 38 runs (Mr W. G. Grace 20). Richard Daft with 25 and 26 was the highest scorer in the match. Mycroft's bowling had 14 South wickets for 38 runs and one no-ball. Mr W. G. Grace's bowling had 14 North wickets for 148 runs.

Wisden's analysis of WG's season shows that he scored 1,605 runs in 48 completed innings, with three centuries and a highest score of 152, at an average of "33 per innings and 21 over", and concluded with the comment:

There was much weeping and wailing among a certain set about "the falling off of Mr Grace's average," but surely the above series of innings are "good enough" for any cricketer to have played in one season.

INDIVIDUAL INNINGS OF THREE FIGURES HIT
IN 1875 – THE 200'S

Dr E. M. GRACE 235, 235 and 214 not out. Dr Grace's 235 against Lansdown was hit at Thornbury on the 17th of June; the hits that made that 235 were two sixe's, one five, 35 fours (140 runs in fourers!), five three's, 14 two's and 35 singles. At one time Dr Grace made the following consecutive hits – 2, 4, 4, 6, 4, 4, 4, 4, 4, 3, 4, 2; and at another period of his innings he made the following successive hits – 4, 2, 4, 4, 4, 3, 2, 3, 5, 4; no single in either batch. (Dr Grace was eighth wicket out, the score at 336). Dr Grace's 235 against Sneyd Park was hit at Thornbury on the 20th of August. The last man was in and the score was at 333 when the Doctor was bowled for 235; his hits were one six, 29 four's, four three's, 24 twos and 53 singles. Dr Grace's 214 not out against Cotham was hit on May 29 at Thornbury; his hits were two sixe's, one five, 27 fours, two threes, 15 two's and 53 singles. Thornbury's total was 316. When the first wicket fell at 108, Dr Grace had made 58, and when the third wicket fell at 160 he had made 80 only, so whilst the last seven wickets were making 22 runs, Dr Grace made 134.

WISDEN 1877

WG had an astonishing year in 1876, even by his own standards. The review of Gloucestershire's season noted that:

Of their eight matches commenced they won five, and three were unfinished, the draws being the three last matches played. They began 14 innings, lost 110 wickets, and scored 2,850 runs, 2,735 from the bat. Of those 2,735 runs, 890 were made by Mr W. Grace; 297 by Mr F. Grace; 274 by Mr Gilbert; 271 by Mr Townsend; 245 by Mr Moberly; and 152 each by Dr E. M. Grace and Mr Filgate.

In other words, WG made 32.5% of the side's runs, and together with his two brothers accounted for 49% of their runs. If we add in their cousin Mr Gilbert, the four men made 59% of Gloucestershire's runs in 1876.

The 11 largest individual innings hit being 63 by Dr E. M. Grace; 86 by Mr W. Gilbert; 88 by Mr Townsend; 93 by Mr Filgate; 103 by Mr Moberly; and the following by Mr W. G. Grace: 318 not out, 177, 104, 78, 60, 57. Mr W. Grace's 78 and 104 were made from Sussex bowling; and his 57 and 318 not out from Yorkshire bowling. But the most curious feature in the great batsman's County hitting of 1876 is that from the weakest bowling Eleven – Surrey – that Gloucestershire played against, Mr W. Grace scored only 1 and 29. His 318 not out against Yorkshire is a truly marvellous affair, look at it in what way you will; it is the largest innings ever hit in a County v County match, and it is the main reason why his county average for 1876 reaches the huge figures of 80–10, or more than double his average in 1875. As a means of ready reference, a record is here made of Mr W. Grace's last five seasons' averages for Gloucestershire, as they are chronicled in "*Wisden's*":

In 1872	In 1873	In 1874	In 1875	In 1876
47–2	62–1	84–6	38–9	80–10

Gloucestershire bowling captured 126 wickets last season, at a cost of 2,014 runs. Of those 126 wickets Mr W. Grace's bowling had 43 (only six bowled) for 659 runs. Mr F. Grace's bowling had 39 (20 bowled) for 502 runs.

Wisden *still reported regularly on minor matches. Under the heading "278 RUNS FOR ONE WICKET",* Wisden *published this scorecard:*

Thornbury v St George's
At Thornbury, June 3, 1876

St George's played an innings of 48 runs; Thornbury then went in, and when rain put a stop to the play at ten minutes to four o'clock the score was:

Thornbury

G. F. Grace, Esq., not out	192
C. Turrin, Esq., b Vealer	11
J. Bernard, Esq., not out	69
Extras	6
	278

Three weeks later, Fred Grace was playing at The Oval, but Wisden *was unimpressed.*

Gentlemen of the South v Players of the South
At The Oval, June 22 and 23, 1876

Notwithstanding Mr W. G. Grace was not in the Gentlemen's Eleven (he was playing for MCC v Oxford at Lord's), the Players had so much the worst of the struggle when this match was drawn at the end of the second day's play, that the Gentlemen had seven wickets to fall and but 22 runs to win. The match was uninteresting, unattractive and undecided. Score as follows:

Players 147 (Pooley 45; G. F. Grace 5–27) and **160** (Pooley 30; Hadow 4–32);
Gentlemen 246 (Blacker 86; Lillywhite 5–62) and **40–3** (Wallroth 27; Lillywhite 2–13).

Fred Grace was out for 0 in both innings, as he would be in his only Test match.

The second Gentlemen v Players match of the season caused Wisden *to rhapsodise about WG's batting.*

Gentlemen v Players of England
At Lord's, July 3, 4 and 5, 1876

Gentlemen 449 (W. G. Grace 169; Morley 6 for 73)
Players 219 (Oscroft 58; Appleby 6 for 96) and **132** (Daft 39*; W. G. Grace 6 for 41)
Gentlemen won by an innings and 98 runs.

When the luncheon bell rang at 2.30, the Gentlemen's score was:-

One wicket down........174 runs scored.
Mr. W. G. Grace, not out 119......... Mr. Webbe, not out 14.

They went at it again at 12 past 3, and by 25 minutes to 4 they had made *the 200 with only one wicket down,* the delighted thousands present giving vent to their pleasure in a roar of cheers when those three figures were hoisted – cheers that were vigorously renewed again and again, and still again, when, shortly after, *Mr. W. G. Grace drove the first ball of an over grandly to the on past the skeleton stand for 6, and* – with a terrific smack – *drove the third ball of the same over as far as it could go past the little chestnut trees for 7.* Ah, that 7 *was* a hit! The ring of it tingles in this compiler's ears whenever he recalls it to mind. Truly wonderful hitting was those 13 runs from two balls of one over. Emmett was then (very properly) rested…

At 262, another capital catch at slip – this time by Hill – settled Mr. W. G. Grace for 169 – one of the very best innings the great batsman ever played – wonderful as much for its powerful hitting as for that old, marvellous, unrivalled skill in placing the ball out of danger, for which his batting has ever been, and ever will be, famous.

A TRULY "GREAT" BIT OF BATTING BY MR W. G. GRACE

United South of England Eleven v United North of England Eleven
At Hull, August 3, 4 and 5, 1876

In this match, Mr W. G. Grace made 126 and 82. His 126 was part of a total of 159 – 154 from the bat; and when it is considered that Mr Grace made those 126 runs against such bowling as Alfred Shaw's, Hill's, Morley's, Tye's and Oscroft's, and that the other ten good batsmen could only make 28 between them, it becomes a question whether this is not (for merit) the best bit of batting played by Mr W. Grace in 1876. Ephraim Lockwood was also in very fine batting form; he went in with one wicket down, the score at 26, and took his bat out for a splendid, chanceless 108. The match was not finished.

United North of England Eleven v United South of England Eleven
At Hull, August 3, 4 and 5, 1876

United South of England Eleven

W. G. Grace, Esq., hit wkt b Shaw	126	c Greenwood b Lockwood	82
H. Jupp b Shaw	1	c Lockwood b Shaw	12
W. R. Gilbert, Esq., run out	0	c and b Oscroft	37
G. F. Grace, Esq., c Hill b Morley	0	b Shaw	23
E. W. Pooley c Shaw b Tye	14	b Oscroft	17
R. Humphrey b Oscroft	3	b Hill	10
George. Elliott c Morley b Oscroft	4	c Hill b Morley	9
Frank Silcock c Tye b Shaw	1	b Shaw	1
W. T. Jupp c Hill b Oscroft	0	c and b Shaw	2
E. Henty not out	1	not out	0
J. Southerton b Hill	4	c Morley b Oscroft	1
B 3, l-b 2	5	B 3, l-b 7, w 3	13
	159		**207**

United North of England Eleven

W. Oscroft c W. G. Grace b Gilbert	51		
A. Shrewsbury c Pooley b W. G. Grace	8	not out	8
E. Lockwood not out	108		
R. Daft st Pooley b Gilbert	4		
A. Greenwood c Humphrey b Gilbert	37	not out	4
R. P. Smith, Esq., b Southerton	0		
A. Shaw b Southerton	0		
R. Butler, Esq., b Gilbert	3	b Gilbert	19
A. Hill st Pooley b Gilbert	10		
J. Tye c Humphrey b Gilbert	14		
F. Morley c Humphrey b Gilbert	5		
B 1, l-b 1	2		
	242		**31**

Match drawn

Wisden's *report of the Canterbury Week (August 7–11) was somewhat over-egged, but as the highest score yet recorded in a first-class match occurred here, it was perhaps not surprising. 139 years on, Grace's 344 is still the highest score, and the only triple-hundred, ever made at Canterbury. That it was made in a 12-a-side match did not detract from the fact that it was then, and still is now, considered a first-class match.*

Wisden resorted to the use of capital letters, bold type and exclamation marks from time to time in the early years, most especially for its reports on the happenings during Canterbury Week, then one of the highlights of the cricket season, and of the social season.

THE CHARGE OF ONE SHILLING ADMISSION TO THE GROUND ON EACH OF THE SIX DAYS; SPLENDID SUNNY SUMMER WEATHER FROM MONDAY MORN TO SATURDAY EVE; LARGE AND BRILLIANT ASSEMBLAGES ON THE CRICKET GROUND; WICKETS ROLLED TO UNSURPASSABLE SMOOTHNESS BY A STEAM ROLLER(!); INNINGS BY SIDES OF 557 (for nine wickets) – 473 – 355 – 345 – 226 – 206 (for eight wickets) – AND 144 RUNS; INDIVIDUAL SCORES OF 344(!) – 154 – 143 – 109 – 91 – 84 – 63 – 58 – 57 not out – AND 52 RUNS; TWO THOUSAND THREE HUNDRED AND TWENTY-EIGHT RUNS SCORED, BUT NO MATCH FINISHED, AND THE OLD I ZINGARI MATCH NOT EVEN COMMENCED, are the facts and features that will render THE CANTERBURY CRICKET WEEK OF 1876 the most famous yet played.

... The cricket programme for The Week was: KENT AND GLOUCESTERSHIRE v ENGLAND, GENTLEMEN OF MCC v THE COUNTY OF KENT, and GENTLEMEN OF KENT v I ZINGARI; but committees propose and batsmen (aided by steamrolled wickets) dispose of these matters; and unprecedentedly large scoring not only prevented either of the two matches commenced being concluded, but wholly pushed the old IZ match out of the programme.

The wickets and grounds were as smooth as a carpet, for – said the *Kent Herald* – for months past industrious workmen had been busily engaged in preparing turf for the purposes of cricket; and the wickets were pitched upon turf as true as a billiard table.

MONDAY, THE FIRST DAY: BANK HOLIDAY was a superb day for cricket and its enjoyment; and the attendance up on the pleasant old ground at St Lawrence was large. The week's cricket was set to commence with the unmeaning, uninteresting match entitled:

KENT AND GLOUCESTERSHIRE V ENGLAND

But, as neither Mr Hornby, Mr I. D. Walker, Mr Ridley, Mr W. H. Hadow, Mr Longman, Richard Daft, Jupp, Pinder, Pooley, H. Phillips, Oscroft, or Barlow played, the full strength of England was not opposed to the Eleven strong batting team of Amateurs of the two counties, who won choice of innings, and at a quarter to one (delay caused by holiday trains) the week's cricket was commenced by Mr W. G. Grace and Mr Gilbert batting... Mr W. Grace had made nine (all the runs then scored) when he was captured at slip, his early retirement (said the *Kent*

Herald) as usual meeting with hearty applause. But though the crack collapsed so suddenly, Mr Gilbert stayed so effectively that he was four hours and 50 minutes at wickets, saw six men go, made 143 runs, and was not got out until 330 had been scored; then he was lbw to Shaw. His hits included 17 fours, four threes, 11 twos, and 41 singles; and (said the *Kent Herald*) Mr Gilbert was very heartily cheered for his very fine cricket, and rightly so.

The "Rest of England" (as Wisden *also named the team) finished their first innings 119 runs behind Kent and Gloucestershire.*

At 5 o'clock England followed on, the brothers Webbe starting the innings to the bowling of Mr Kelcey and Mr Absolom. The younger brother was well caught out at wicket with the score at 10; but the elder stayed and played splendidly, and, with Mr Lucas, evidenced to the delighted spectators the high form University batting had attained in 1876. Bowlers were changed and changed in vain – Mr Kelcey bowled, Mr Absolom bowled, Mr W. Grace bowled, Mr Gilbert bowled, Mr G. F. Grace bowled, and Mr Absolom bowled again; but at five minutes past six the 100 runs had been made. Then more bowling changes were tried, and at 121 one of Mr Townsend's lobs bowled Mr Lucas for 48, so many as 111 runs having been put on by the Oxford and Cambridge cracks since the fall of the first wicket. Lockwood then went in, but no more wickets fell that day…

WEDNESDAY'S weather was truly splendid. They resumed cricket at a quarter to 12, and by a quarter to four the Englanders had added nearly 200 runs to their Tuesday's runs. Mr A. J. Webbe and Lockwood increased the score from the overnight's 159 to 204, when a catch at wicket settled Mr Webbe for 109 – a fine leg-hitting innings… The innings was over at a quarter to four for 355 runs…

The Counties' second innings was commenced at five minutes past four; between then and 6.45 they had to score 237 runs to win. Mr W. Grace and Mr Yardley began the batting, to the bowling of Emmett and Alfred Shaw. They started the hitting at so clipping a pace that 40 runs were made in 20 minutes, and when Davey at wicket caught out Mr Yardley he – by five fours, &c. – had made 32 of the 52 runs then scored. Mr W. Grace was then faced by another hard hitter and rapid scorer – Mr Townsend – and again was the score so busily increased that by 5.30 the 100 was hoisted. Hill then bowled v. Alfred Shaw, and Morley v. Ulyett, but still the score rose, and when 152 runs were made Ulyett was tried again; that change settled Mr Townsend for 28. Lord Harris then went in, and hit in Lord Harris's best form; he scored fast, the bowling was frequently changed, and runs were rapidly run up, but no wicket went down until Shaw was once more tried; he forthwith clean bowled Mr W. Grace for 91 – a fine innings made by a six, a five, ten fours, a three, eight twos, and 21 singles… There were… 31 runs to score to win and four wickets to fall, and the excitement as to whether The Counties, England, or old Time would win being great – excitement that was heightened as Alfred Shaw first bowled Mr Penn and then Mr G. F. Grace, the three last wickets down all falling at 206; but then 6.45 was at hand, the stumps were pulled up, and this great run-getting and grandly-contested match ended in A Draw, The Counties wanting 31 runs to win with two wickets to fall, their 206 runs having been made from 76 overs and two balls, bowled by five of the best professional bowlers of The North.

Kent and Gloucestershire 345 (W. Gilbert 143; A. Shaw 5–78) and **206–8**
(W. G. Grace 91; A. Shaw 5–61); **England 226** (Lockwood 63; Kelcey 4–49) and **355**
(A. J. Webbe 109; Gilbert 3–63).

There were 14 different bowlers tried; 513 overs and one ball bowled; 38 wickets fell, and 1,132 runs scored in this unfinished match, which makes the second of more than 1,000 runs played in The Canterbury Weeks up at St Lawrence; the other thousand-runs' match being NORTH OF THE THAMES v SOUTH OF THE THAMES, played in 1868, when 1,018 runs were scored, Mr W. G. Grace making 130 and 102 not out; the Rev. J. McCormick 137 and 27, and Mr R. A. H. Mitchell 22 and 90.

In this match, W. G. Grace bowled 43 overs for 107 runs and no wickets.

THURSDAY (THE LADIES' DAY) was – as a ladies' day should be – bright and beautiful; and the scene presented on the historically famous old ground must have been magnificent... On the slope at the upper side of the ground, under the famous "Tree", the ladies mustered in greater force than ever, and at this spot the spectators were six and seven deep. Splendid weather, the large expanse of ground, in every part occupied by an appreciative assemblage, in which were some of the fairest and comeliest faces to be seen at any event during the cricket season...

And so on, in those polite and pretty phrases so natural to cricket critics, did other special correspondents sing high praises of The Ladies' Day of 1876. The cricket played on that day commenced with the 12-a-side match:

THE COUNTY OF KENT V THE GENTLEMEN OF MCC

A marvellous run-getting match, which – like its predecessor – three days of splendid cricketing weather was insufficient to play out. Kent commenced the batting in this wonderful match at noon, and when the stumps were drawn at ten minutes to seven the Kent batsmen were still pegging away at the MCC bowling... But Kent's hero on that ladies' day was Lord Harris, who went to wickets with the score at 70 runs for three wickets, stayed until 304 had been scored, and then was caught out at mid-off for 154 – the longest score, wrote the chroniclers, the Kentish Captain has yet made in a first-class match… Doubtless his innings was a brilliant display, for assuredly Lord Harris was never in finer hitting form than he was throughout the great scoring season – 1876. That day of hard hitting closed with Kent having scored 453 runs and lost ten wickets; George Hearne, not out 51; Henty, not out six.

FRIDAY was as lovely as had been the Thursday, but the attendance was slack. Play was resumed at ten to 12. In ten minutes the innings was over… MCC batting was commenced at 12.25; by 4.20 their innings was over for 144 runs…

With the large lot of 329 runs to hit off ere they could make a start from Kent's first innings, the MCC men commenced their follow-on at five minutes to five with Mr W. Grace and Mr Lucas. With the score at seven only Mr Lucas was out, and the previously seeming hopeless task appeared still more hopeless; but then Mr Grace started his wonderful hitting in such form, that he made 20 runs from two successive overs of Hearne's; had brought the score to 100 in 45 minutes; and when the stumps were drawn at 6.45 he (by hitting almost unexampled in its brilliant severity) had in 110 minutes raised the score to the following hopeful phase:-

Mr W. G. Grace not out 133
Mr A. P. Lucas c Thomson, b Hearne 7
Mr H. N. Tennent c Penn, b Absolom 12
Mr G. Bird b Foord Kelcey 13
Mr L. S. Howell c Shaw, b Thornton 30
Mr P. Crutchley not out 5
            Extras 17
                    For 4 wickets   217

(Mr Grace and Mr Howell had increased the score from 125 for three wickets, to 203 for four.)

SATURDAY was the last day of the Week, and Mr GRACE"S DAY; for on that day he completed the largest innings ever played for MCC, made three-fifths of the runs in the largest innings ever scored on the Canterbury ground, and had – according to the *Kent Herald* – "completely settled the Kentish Twelve".

The day was intensely hot, and so was the hitting of the MCC two – Mr W. Grace and Mr Crutchley – who resumed their innings at noon, and were not parted until late in the afternoon when they had increased the score by 227 runs! as Mr Crutchley went to wickets with the score at 203, and was out for 84 with it at 430. There were then five wickets down at an average of 86 runs per wicket, and Mr Grace as full of fine hitting as he had been at any phase of this great display, and he kept on hitting, scoring, and fagging the field until near the end, for he was not out until 546 runs had been scored, and play finally ceased when the score was at 557, nine wickets having then fallen. Then time was up for the Canterbury Week of 1876; and this stupendous run-getting match was drawn; 19 different bowlers having bowled therein; 1,999 balls bowled; 1,099 runs from the bat, and 75 extra scored, and 31 wickets having fallen.

Mr W. Grace commenced MCC's second innings; he was six hours and 20 minutes at wickets, and had scored 344 runs out of the 540 booked, when he was caught out at mid-off, *Bell's Life* stating – "He scored those 344 runs without positively giving a chance". His hits consisted of 76 singles, 20 twos, eight threes, and 51 fours (204 runs by fourers in one innings!).

But WG, who had earlier in the season scored 400 against 22 of Grimsby, had not finished yet. His next match was back at home starting two days after he had finished laying waste the bowling at Canterbury.

Gloucestershire v Nottinghamshire
At Clifton, August 14, 15 and 16, 1876

Gloucestershire 400 (W. G. Grace 177, G. F. Grace 78; A. Shaw 5–116) and **33–0;**
Nottinghamshire 265 (Oscroft 84; G. F. Grace 5–55) and **165** (Tye 48; W. G. Grace 8–69).

This was the first of the famous Gloucestershire returns of 1876 – matches that will form chapters of wondering interest in the history of the game so long as the game be played. Splendid weather, splendid wickets, splendid assemblages, and some splendid hitting befriended this match. Mr W. Grace and Dr Grace began the batting; the Doctor left for 16 when 54 runs were scored; Mr Gilbert was out for 13 when 105 was booked, and Mr Townsend for 25 at 205; then Mr F. Grace faced his brother and the hitting of the two told so effectively that 262 was scored when Mr W. Grace was caught out at long field for 177 – made by 31 singles, nine twos, four threes, 23 fours (92 by fourers!), a cut for five from Shaw and two sixes (leg hit from Clark and drive out of the ground from Oscroft), and one seven (a fierce smack to square leg from Tye). Mr W. Grace was three hours and ten minutes at wickets; when 70 had been scored he had made 50; at lunchtime the score was 122, Mr "WG" 83; and when the third wicket went at 205 Mr W. Grace had made 142. So it may readily be believed that the great batsman was greeted with "a complete ovation on his retirement". That day's play ceased with Gloucestershire's score at 339 for four wickets, Mr F. Grace not out 66, Mr Moberly not out 28.

Next day Mr Moberly was out at 356, and at 362 a smart catch at wicket by Sherwin settled Mr F. Grace for 78 – an innings made by a seven to square leg from Selby, two fives, five fours, four threes, &c.

… The day's play closed with the Notts score at 212 for three wickets down, Selby not out 13, Mr Tolley not out ten.

On the following day one hour and 25 minutes play used up the innings for 265 runs. Notts followed on at 1.30; Daft and Oscroft made 32 before the first wicket (Oscroft's) fell. Daft and Shrewsbury increased the score to 57, when Daft was c and b by Mr W. Grace for 23 – including a great hit to square leg from Mr Gilbert for seven. Then wickets rapidly succumbed, and at 4.30 the innings was over for 165, the highest scorer being Tye with 48. The 31 runs required by Gloucestershire to win were made in 25 minutes by Dr Grace and Mr G. Grace, the latter winning the match in great "Grace" form with a fine, hard square leg hit for six from Tye. Gloucestershire won by ten wickets, the three brothers Grace having made 304 runs, and had a hand in the downfall of 17 of the 20 Notts wickets.

The fact that WG took eight of those wickets in the Notts second innings is not mentioned by Wisden – perhaps they had run out of superlatives describing his batting. His match figures were 177 runs, nine wickets for 138 runs and four catches. Fred scored 98 runs, took six wickets for 80 runs and held two catches. "The Doctor" E. M. Grace (not yet "The Coroner") scored 29 runs, took no wickets for 28, and held four catches.

The very next day, WG was up against the side against whom he always seemed to score runs – Yorkshire.

Gloucestershire v Yorkshire
At Cheltenham August 17, 18 and 19, 1876

Gloucestershire 528 (W. G. Grace 318*, Moberly 103); **Yorkshire 127–6** (Myers 46*).
Match drawn.

"A Best on Record" was made by Mr W. G. Grace in this match; that is to say his 318 not out is the largest score ever hit in a County v County contest. The match was commenced at 12.30 by Mr W. G. Grace and Dr E. M. Grace starting the Gloucestershire innings to the bowling of Hill and Armitage. Dr Grace left at 29; Mr Gilbert at 160; Mr Townsend at 167; and Mr G. F. Grace at 168. Then Mr Moberly and Mr W. G. Grace stayed and hit so grandly that when "time" was up that day the Gloucestershire score stood in this form:

Mr W. G. Grace, not out	216
Dr E. M. Grace, caught out	5
Mr W. Gilbert, bowled	40
Mr F. Townsend, stumped	0
Mr G. F. Grace, bowled	0
Mr W. O. Moberly, not out	73
Extras	19
for 4 wickets	353

On the second day rain fell, preventing play commencing until one o'clock; then the two not outs increased the score to 429 when cover point caught out Mr Moberly for 103, *so many as 261 runs having been added to the score since the fall of the preceding wicket.* The sixth, seventh, eighth and ninth wickets fell quickly; but Mr J. A. Bush, the last man in, was so troublesome that he and Mr W. Grace hit the score from 466 to 528 before the end came by Ulyett bowling Mr Bush for 32.

Mr W. G. Grace commenced the innings at 12.30 on the Thursday; when the innings finished, at ten minutes to four on the Friday, Mr W. G. Grace was the not-out man, having made 318 out of 528 (504 from the bat) runs scored. He was timed to have been about eight hours batting; he ran 524 times between wickets, and the hits he made were 76 singles, 30 twos, 12 threes, 28 fours (*112 by fourers*), three fives, two sixes and a seven. One critic described this 318 [as] "a wonderful innings"; and another as "played in his very best style with only one chance, and that was when he had made 201."

After his marathon innings, Grace bowled 36 (four-ball) overs, taking 2 for 48, as well as holding one catch.

Five days later, Grace and Gloucestershire were back at Clifton, but Grace failed to hit a century, and in the second innings was overshadowed by his two brothers and his cousin.

Gloucestershire v Sussex
At Clifton, August 24, 25 and 26, 1876

Gloucestershire 342 (Filgate 93, W. G. Grace 78) and **172–6** wickets (E. M. Grace 63; A. Smith 4–53); **Sussex 281** (Greenfield 126, W. G. Grace 6–93). **Match drawn**.

Mr W. Grace commenced the innings, and was fourth out, the score at 127; his 78 included two fives and eight fours and – it was stated – "he retired amidst the loud cheers of the large assembly"…

The Saturday was a damp and cold day. The Friday-afternoon form of the two Sussex gentlemen was not maintained, as at 246 both were out – Mr Cotterill through a magnificent left-hand catch by Mr W. Grace from his own bowling, and Mr Greenfield through a ball bowled by Mr F. Grace knocking down the middle stump of his wicket…

Gloucestershire's second was commenced at 1.30 by Mr W. Grace and Dr E. M. Grace. When only 22 runs had been scored Mr Greenfield – standing deep at point – caught out Mr W. Grace for seven; but the Doctor and Mr Gilbert hit so freely and effectively that the score was at 105 when wicket No. 2 went by Mr Gilbert being out for 43. At 106 Mr Townsend was out, and at 119 Dr Grace was lbw for 63. Mr F. Grace stayed up to 172, when, at six o'clock, the match was drawn, Gloucestershire 233 runs to the good with four wickets to fall. Dr Grace was reported to have hit "with all his old freedom and vigour"; no doubt he did, for his hits included three threes, three fours, a hit to leg for six, and a square-leg hit for seven. Mr Gilbert's 43 included five fours and a drive for six, and Mr F. Grace's 41 four fours.

Gloucestershire Bowling in 1876

	Matches Bowled	No. of overs bowled	Maiden overs	Runs Scored	Wide Balls	Caught from bowling	Wickets bowled down	Total wickets taken
Mr W. Grace	8	490.2	218	659	–	29	6	43
Mr F. Grace	7	422	203	502	2	17	20	39

From Mr W. Grace's bowling six were lbw, one was stumped, and one hit wicket. From Mr F. Grace's bowling two were lbw.

The bowling figures show that WG's bowling, while very successful, was clearly not as accurate as his brother's. He bowled no wides all summer, but took only about 28% of his wickets bowled or lbw, as compared with 51% of Fred's. Their respective averages for the county (not calculated by Wisden*) were 15.33 for WG, and 12.87 for Fred. In the batting statistics, however, WG was unrivalled.*

Gloucestershire Batting In 1876

	Matches Batted In	Innings commenced	Times not out	Times bowled	Times caught	Largest innings	Total runs scored	Average per innings
Mr W. Grace	8	12	1	2	9	318*	890	80–10
Mr W. O. Moberly	5	7	1	2	3	103	245	40–5

His average was double the next man's, and his tally of runs one short of three times the next highest total, Fred Grace's 297 runs at "24 and 9 over", as averages were expressed in Wisden *then.*

A full page of statistics devoted to WG's season showed that he scored 2,622 runs in 11-a-side matches and a further 1,047 in matches against odds, that is to say, a team of 11 men playing against a team of more than 11. This was common practice among the professional teams of the 1850s and '60s who went around the country playing against XVI's or XXII's, or sometimes even more. His 344 in a 12-a-side match is listed among the 11-a-side statistics, as it was not "against odds".

A note under the list of scores against odds reveals the drawing power of WG in his prime:

"A third innings was allowed Mr Grace (against 22 of Stockport), who had been bowled out after scoring 13 in their second innings, but subsequently, when eight wickets had fallen for 77 runs, he was asked to go in again, and made 133." – *Sportsman*, September 5.

(This is the reason why Mr Grace is credited with 13 and not 133 in the above table).

THE ABOVE DISSECTED In Eleven-A-Side matches

Seven innings of more than 100 runs were scored, i.e. 344, 318 not out, 177, 169, 126, 114 not out, and 104 – or 1,352 runs in seven innings, two not-outs! The 344 is the highest innings ever hit in a first-class 11-a-side match [*sic*], and consequently is the largest innings ever hit for MCC.

The 318 not out is the largest innings ever hit in a County match.

For MCC, 494 runs in seven innings.......... Average 70½ per innings

For Gentlemen v Players of England, 309 runs in five innings........... Average 61 per innings and four over

For South v North, 474 runs in ten innings (three not-outs).......... Average 67 per innings and five over

For Gloucestershire (excluding the match at Canterbury),

890 runs in 12 innings (one not out) ..... Average 80 per innings and ten over

For The United South Eleven, 242 runs in six innings........ Average 40 per innings and two over

Total in Eleven-A-Side Matches

2,622 runs in 46 innings (four not-outs)....... Average 62 per innings and 18 over

In Matches Against Odds

1,047 runs in 22 innings (one not out)...... Average 49 per innings and 18 over

The 400 not out (!) is a long way the largest innings ever hit against a Twenty-two (or any other odds) in the field; and it is the second-largest innings ever hit in any match. (Mr E. F. S. Tylecote's 404 not out is the largest.)

Mr W. G. GRACE IN 1876 PLAYED IN 38 MATCHES; COMMENCED 68 INNINGS; WAS FIVE TIMES NOT OUT; AND

SCORED 3,669 RUNS.......... AVERAGE 58 PER INNINGS AND 15 OVER.

Only capital letters would do for so stupendous an achievement.

Wisden *also noted that on August 11 and 12, while WG was compiling his 344, GF was playing for Knole Park, Sevenoaks, and scoring 213 against the Incogniti. It also noted that Dr E. M. Grace hit 327* for Thornbury during the summer.*

A further note on WG's 400 not out:

Respecting this wonderful innings a correspondent sent the following particulars to *Bell's Life*: "Mr W. G. Grace's score was made as follows: four sixes, 21 fours, six threes, 58 twos and 158 singles. The bowling was up to the average, the wickets perfection; but Mr Grace's play was acknowledged by all present (including the members of the South team) to be such as they never before witnessed. He gave no chance whatever on the first and second days. On the third day he gave two easy chances – one to short slip, the other to long leg; but he had then scored 350 runs. Altogether he was at the wickets about 13½ hours, and had no less than 15 bowlers opposed to him."

At the end of the summer, James Lillywhite took a team of 12 players to Australia, who achieved cricket immortality when they played what became accepted as the first two Test matches in cricket's longest-running international rivalry (U.S.A v Canada always excepted). WG was not available – he was busy studying for his medical examinations – so he had the chance to rest a little, with his wife and two infant children, the second, Henry, having been born during his father's quadruple-century against Grimsby.

WISDEN 1878

WG began his summer with a remarkable match bowling analysis of 23 for 104, but this was not mentioned in the report.

MCC and Ground (11) v 22 Colts of England, with a captain
At Lord's May 7 and 8, 1877

The Colts of England 114 (Hind 31; Mycroft 11–50) and **131** (Thewlis 24; W. G. Grace 13–52); **MCC and Ground 93** (W. G. Grace 23; Freeman 6–19) and **131** (W. G. Grace 54; Freeman 4–23).
Colts of England won by 21 runs.

Wintry winds were hereabouts succeeded by balmy breezes, and this match was played out in as sunny, summer-like weather as cricketer could desire, but for all that, and notwithstanding Mr W. G. Grace played, the attendance was scant, the absence of the public pointedly proclaiming their distaste to those abominations mistermed "matches" of Elevens v Twenty-Twos, which ought never to find a home at Lord's.

… Young Flowers' four wickets (three bowled, one "WG") for 30 runs in the Club's second innings materially helped him to a place in the Notts' Eleven, and that too, notwithstanding, in one of his overs Mr Grace hit a six and a four, the sixer being a huge on-drive high over the Grand Stand, the ball pitching near the poplar tree that o'er tops all other trees at the rear of the G. S. Mr Grace's 54 was commenced with 11 singles, and he was 2½ hours making his 54; in fact the Colts' bowling and fielding fairly put the crack on his defence, and it is doubtful if ever Mr W. Grace played as much cricket at Lord's for 50 runs as he did in this match against the Colts of England.

By the end of May, he was in prime form:

North v South of England
At Prince's, May 31, June 1 and 2, 1877

South 459 (W. G. Grace 261; Eastwood 6–69); **North** 143 (Lockwood 46;
W. G. Grace 5–62) and **154** (Lockwood 36; W. G. Grace 6–77).
South won by an innings and 162 runs.

On really splendid wickets, the match was commenced at 12.30 by Mr W. G. Grace and Mr Gilbert… Mr Grace opened his memorable innings with a single to square leg from Morley; he then made two fours from one over of Tye's and when 27 runs had been made from seven overs and one ball, Mr W. G. ran out Mr Gilbert for seven. Then it was Mr Cotterill faced Mr Grace and these two splendid bats made the stand – the superb stand – of 281 runs against the North bowling and fielding. After Mr Cotterill went in, Tye's bowling suffered so frightfully that 27 runs were made from three overs and one ball, so he was shunted for Clayton; later on Morley was put on one side for Lockwood, who, farther on, was shifted for Oscroft, but for all that the score rose, and when at 20 minutes to two the 100 was hoisted there had been 46 overs bowled, and Mr W. Grace had made 77. Runs then came less rapidly, and the call to luncheon at two o'clock found the score at 119 for one wicket down,

Mr W. G. Grace, 90, not out…… Mr J.M. Cotterill, 20, not out.

They resumed play about 3 o'clock. When the score had been hit to 135, Mr Grace had made his 100. Then Mr Cotterill took up the run-getting, and when at a quarter past four they had hoisted the 200, Mr Grace had made 130, and Mr Cotterill 62. And so they went on playing and hitting the varied bowling tried against them in such masterly form that at 5.30 the scoreboards showed the wonderful phase of 300 runs for the loss of one wicket only, Mr Grace then having made 202! But then the parting was at hand, for when eight more runs only had been, Mr Cotterill was stumped from a lob. Only think of a man staying while 281 runs were scored from some of the best bowling in England and then to be licked by a lob!... Then Mr G. F. Grace faced his brother, and despite the bowling of Morley, Pinder, Oscroft, Eastwood, Tye and Mr Tolley, there the brothers stayed until time was called at 6.30... During that memorable day's hitting, there had been eight different bowlers tried, four of them on at both ends; there had been 16 bowling changes, and 165 overs bowled for 385 runs and two wickets.

On the Friday a strong wind and heavy rain caused the attendance to be slack, the wickets soaked, and commencement of play deferred until ten minutes to one, when the brothers went on with their innings... Eastwood failed to bring off a c and b chance given by the big batsman, who, however, shortly after skied one from Morley high, and a patiently-waited-for, well-judged catch by Mr Tolley at mid-on (the wind blowing strong at the time) ended Mr W. Grace's innings for 261 runs, made by 24 fours, eleven threes, 31 two's, and 70 singles. One of Mr Grace's two dozen fourers was a truly grand on-drive that sent the ball over the tress on to the rink, but the innings was far more remarkable for his old, skilled, and successful placing the ball, than for big things in hitting. Anyhow, this 261 of his was not only a marvellous display of batting, but it eventuated in being the largest innings hit in 1877.

Even though WG took 11 wickets for 139 in 103 four-ball overs, Wisden *failed to mention his bowling in their report. Earlier in the season, he had taken seven for 98 for Gentlemen of the South against Players of the North at The Oval, but once again* Wisden *failed to mention his bowling. For* Wisden *in the 1870s, cricket was a batsman's game.*

THE THREE GENTLEMEN V PLAYERS OF ENGLAND
MATCHES IN 1877

The resolve of the secretaries in 1875 that in future there should be nine consecutive cricketing days of Gentlemen v Players of England Matches on the London grounds was duly carried out in 1877, when on June 28, 29 and 30 (Sunday then intervening), and July 2, 3, 4, 5, 6 and 7, Gentlemen v Players cricket was in full swing at The Oval, at Lord's, and at Prince's.

The weather during these nine days was of extraordinary variety, and those present at the three grounds will not easily forget the glorious sunshine at The Oval, the vivid lightning flash, loud thunderclap, and furious rain-pour at Lord's or that remarkable hailstorm that burst over Prince's, and for 20 minutes gave that ground the appearance of being topped by hoar-frost.

As to the nine days' cricket the batting and fielding will long retain a bright spot in the memories of those who witnessed the play, and when beardless and hearty youngsters of the present day have grown grey and feeble, they will have many a tale to tell the cricketers of the future how, in one of the 1877 matches, Mr W. G. Grace was bowled out for a one-hit (a three) innings; how perfect was the cricket played by young Arthur Shrewsbury for his 78; how Mr I. D. Walker in one match went twice to the wickets, received but one ball in that match, and that ball bowled him; how unsurpassably splendid Mr J. M. Cotterill hit for his 59 and 92, and what a grand seven, all run out, he made at Lord's; how daringly Mr A. N. Hornby hit, and how daringly he ran for his 144 (the largest innings hit in the three matches); – with what care, patience, skill, and success Mr W. W. Read played for his 72; how very finely Mr G. F. Grace hit for his 134, and his brother, Mr W. G. did ditto for his 41... and how very finely the Gentlemen finished off the glorious match by Mr G. F. Grace and Mr W. S. Patterson making the requisite 46 runs for the last wicket.

In these three matches, W. G. Grace scored 29, 18, 41 and 3, a total of 91 runs. His bowling analyses were one for 93 and five for 67; one for 52 and two for 66; and three for 55 and none for none, a total of 12 wickets for 333 runs. He made five catches. By his standards, these were poor figures. Nevertheless, the Gentlemen won two of the matches and the third was left drawn.

Fred Grace, by contrast, scored 18, 2, 23* and 134. He bowled in only two matches, taking no wickets for 70 runs, and took one catch. Two of his innings, however, merited the attention of Wisden's *correspondent, who described the action in florid style, even calling his 134 "truly great".*

Gentlemen v Players of England
The Second Match, at Lord's July 2, 3 and 4, 1877

Players 192 (Daft 64; Patterson 7–58) and **148** (Jupp 41; Lucas 4–12); **Gentlemen 198** (Cotterill 92; Watson 5–60) and **143–9** (W. G. Grace 41; Ulyett 4–39).
Gentlemen won by one wicket.

...On the third day bright hot sunshine shone pleasantly on the now famous last round in the fight for victory between the Gentlemen and Players – a struggle that has rightly earned for this contest the title of "The Glorious Match"...

It was one o'clock when the Players' innings finished, leaving the Gentlemen 143 to score to win. "A certainty" and "One of the greatest cricket morals ever known" pompously exclaimed one who should know as much as man can know of these matters; but there were those who fancied the old ground would not play better the dryer it became, and who did not clearly see the "certainty". At 1.30 Mr W. Grace and Mr I. D. Walker commenced the memorable innings; Watson started the bowling to Mr Grace who played the third ball away for a single, but the fourth ball bowled Mr Walker, who thus received but one ball in the match, and that ball bowled him. [*Walker, the Gentlemen's captain, had batted at No. 11 in the first innings and did not face a ball.*] Mr Lyttelton was next man in; Mr "WG" appeared full of hitting, played the game in great form, and when two o'clock stayed play for luncheon, the score stood at 31 for one wicket... They went at it again at 2.37... but at 64 Ulyett clean bowled Mr Lyttelton for a most valuable 20, and ere another run was made a real good left-hand c and b by Morley settled Mr Grace for 41, an innings that included a splendid straight drive for five, and a couple of fours. Getting rid of the big bat thus (comparatively) cheaply, made the look-out a promising one for the Players, and stirred the onlookers to exuberant excitement, especially when 11 runs further on Ulyett, in successive overs, bowled Mr Cotterill for ten, and Mr Hornby for nought, the spectators' delight at this finding vent in roars of cheers. Then Mr Lucas and Mr Ridley made the runs 80, when a catch at point, by Barlow (who fielded out-and-out well) settled Mr Lucas for two, the result of half an hour's batting – a proof this of the difficulty of making runs, and of the good out-cricket shown by the Players, who thereabouts fielded like cats after mice. Six wickets were then down, with the runs 63 short of a win, so the Players were justly hopeful of success, the more so when a sample of real smart fielding run out Mr Ridley at 87. Lord Harris then made a leg hit for four, and a cut for three, when Morley bowled him, and when, three runs later on, Shrewsbury caught out Mr Webbe, and left the score at 46 to win, and one wicket to fall, the applause for the players was loud, long, lusty and deserved, the sympathy of the majority of those present being evidently with the Pros, for "It's their turn!" cried out one elated looker-on, and, "They deserve to win," said another. Then the last of the Gentlemen, Mr Patterson, faced Mr G. F. Grace, and 35 minutes of cricket was played that will be enjoyably remembered and pleasantly talked of for ever so many seasons to come; Mr Patterson started with a square-leg hit for four making the score 101, and causing a hearty shout to ring out from the Pavilion men; this hit was followed by a three from the same bat, and that was backed up by a two and a four by Mr F. Grace, the hoisting of the 110 being welcomed by a ringing cheer, repeated again, and still again with increased vigour, when Mr "F. G." drove two successive balls for four and five. Watson and Mycroft then bowled v Morley and Ulyett, but the wicket, so much desired by the Players, did not come, although the runs so earnestly wanted by the Gentlemen did, as the first ball bowled by Mycroft was driven to the off by Mr F. Grace for five, the announce boards telling of 120 runs scored, being welcomed by great cheering. The cricket, all round, just then, was superb, Watson especially bowling in fine form; the batsmen playing with care and skill, and the Players fielding quite up to Players of England form. The excitement was top class with the spectators, who watched every ball bowled, played and fielded with an excitement that was at times too intense for expression. It was either side's match, and either side deserved to win, so well were both sides playing;

but fortune was then full against the Players, who frequently bowled the ball as near as a sixpence's thickness to the wicket but failed to hit the sticks, and so the score gradually neared the winning numbers until a four to square leg by Mr F. Grace made the tie, and, at 25 to five, a single from the same bat won this "rare match" for the Gentlemen by one wicket. Then the excitement, so long pent up among the spectators, found relief in one loud, long, hoarse shout that did a man real good to participate in and hear; and so with the members at the pavilion upstanding and cheering like Britons, and with the rushing, shouting, and (nearly) maddened hundreds following the two victorious not-outs from the wickets, did an end come to, what hereafter will always be known as THE GLORIOUS MATCH.

Gentlemen v Players of England
The Third Match, At Prince's, July 5, 6 and 7, 1877.

Gentlemen 400 (G. F. Grace 134; Mycroft 3–86) and **16–1; Players 181** (Ulyett 53; Buckland 5–34) and **234** (Ulyett 118; Gilbert 6–93).
The Gentlemen won by nine wickets.

The 1s. admission charge and adverse weather led to comparatively slack attendances at this match, throughout which there were several indications that the London cricketing public did not take kindly to the nine successive days' doses of Gentlemen v Players matches in one season, especially with six of the nine at the cost of 1s. per day.

The weather during the match was something frightful. A dull, murky, mucky afternoon on the first day culminated at evening in "the storm of the season" when the lightning blazed, the air thundered, and the clouds poured down their water in a grand and awful storm; and for one hour and a half London was drenched by the most furious rainstorm that fell over the big city in 1877. And who present at Prince's on the afternoon of the second day will readily forget that fierce outlet of lightning, thunder, rain and hail that raged o'er the ground from 2.30 until three, so thickly topping the turf with pea-sized hailstones as to give it the appearance of being coated with hoar-frost. The splendidly prepared wickets suffered materially from all this; nevertheless, one man played a rare good innings of 72 runs, another hit grandly for 134, a third scored 53 and 118…

… When the score was 48 for two wickets, and the time one o'clock, Mr F. Grace commenced one of the finest hitting innings he has ever played. He and Mr Read so successfully played the bowling of Southerton, Mycroft, Hill, Ulyett and Lillywhite, that at luncheon the score was 123 for two wickets – Mr Read not out 59, Mr F. Grace not out 28… On going at it again they hit the score to 157, when a clever left-hand catch at point by Hill finished Mr Read's score for 72 – a careful innings played without a chance, and including three fours (leg-hit and drives) and eight threes… Mr F. Grace and Mr Buckland then made it troublesome times for the Players, but [they] could not change the batsmen until the score had been rapidly and finely hit from 157 to 236… Further on, Mr F. Grace was clean bowled (middle stump) by Mycroft, who had then bowled the centre stump of both brothers' wickets. Mr F. Grace was batting whilst the score was increased from 48 to 359. His hitting was very fine – nearly as fine as his 98 in John Lillywhite's G. and P. match at Brighton in 1871, and higher praise than this cannot well be given to Mr F. G.'s 134, which was made by 18 fours (72 by fourers!), six threes, eight twos, and 28 singles. This truly great innings was deservedly greeted with great applause.

Gloucestershire and Yorkshire v The Rest of England
At Lord's July 17 and 18, 1877

Gloucestershire and Yorkshire 199 (W. G. Grace 52; Lillywhite 3–35) and **231** (W. G. Grace 110; Lillywhite 3 for 39); **The Rest of England 213** (Hornby 105; W. G. Grace 4–73) and **62–1** (Hornby 33*). Match drawn.

The catch of the season, made by Mr I. D. Walker, a grand hit for six into Dark's garden by Mr G. W. Grace [sic], 52 and 110 by the same batsman, a magnificent catch by Mr G. F. Grace, 105 and 33 not out by Mr A. N. Hornby and weather so wretchedly wet as to preclude any cricket being played on the Monday, are little matters that must mark this novel match as "memorable" in the chronicle of cricket played at headquarters in 1877.

… Mr W. Grace and Mr Gilbert started the Counties' batting fortunately and successfully – "fortunately" because Mr Gilbert ought to have been run out by Barnes before he scored, and Mr "W. G." was missed by Selby when he had made 27, and "successfully" because they made 93 runs before the first wicket fell of Mr W. Grace being caught out by cover point for 52, made by one six, five fours, one three, &c. It was shortly after being missed that Mr Grace made his six – a grand on-drive from Watson, the ball flying over the garden wall by the armoury and pitching in the garden, about three yards from the wall, in St. John's Wood Road. How the spectators did roar out their cheers at that hit, and well they might, for it was indeed – both in timing and power – a splendid blow and one worthy of the fame of the great batsman of the South… Mr F. Grace went in, and he and Lockwood rattled the score up to 152, when Mr I. D. Walker, at long-off, rushed at the ball, and with his left hand low down, caught and held it in grand form. Surprise at this superb bit of fielding held the spectators mute for a moment; but then they gave tongue, three distinct and lusty cheers testifying their delight at witnessing this great "catch of the season" that settled Mr F. Grace for a finely hit 21…

A little later in the match, Fred had his revenge.

Shrewsbury was splendidly caught out at short square leg by Mr F. Grace, who had to run from the top of the ground full 30 yards to get to the ball, which he just clutched and held when stooping forward, and thereby gloriously earned the shout of cheers that so lustily rang out from the few hundreds present. It is rare indeed that one match is made famous by two such superb catches as those made in this by Mr I. D. Walker and Mr F. Grace…

…The second innings of the Counties was commenced at 1.35 by Mr W. Grace and Mr Gilbert; the latter made two, and was then had at slip before Mr W. G. had scored, but who, it was remarked, was "bound to do something that day, because it was his 29th birthday," and he did "do something" for he drove one ball from Watson on to the top of the pavilion for four; one from Morley he drove past the telegraph van for five, and when, at five o'clock, the score was at 200, Mr W. Grace had made 110 by one five, seven fours, seven threes, 13 twos and 30 singles. The "something" having been thus accomplished, cheers, loud and protracted, greeted the big batsman's return to the pavilion, and those present at Lord's on that July 18 will long remember with pleasure the splendid characteristic form in which Mr W. Grace celebrated his 29th birthday. Mr F. Grace also specially marked that day by making two great drives for five each in his 26…

WG was there for Canterbury Week, as ever, but this time not only did he have rather less success with the bat than usual, but also he appeared for Kent, as well as against them.

The Canterbury Week
August 6, 7, 8, 9 and 10, 1877.

The published programme gave KENT (with two given men) v ENGLAND as the opening match, to be followed by KENT v and GROUND, and finished with GENTLEMEN OF KENT v I ZINGARI – an excellent match selection, appropriately providing a week's cricket that should have been contested by the very best talent for England and Kent. But the contingencies of the game again pushed from position the time-honoured IZ match; and other reasons prevented Mr A. N. Hornby, Mr J. M. Cotterill, Richard Daft, Jupp, Pooley, Pinder, and others playing for England.

The most successful bit of bowling during the week was

	Overs	Maidens	Runs	Wickets
Mr W. G. Grace's	27–1	20	11	6

bowled after luncheon on the Thursday, against Kent.

… Monday, the first day, Bank Holiday, was a first-class fine day for cricket, and the attendance was large to witness the week fairly started with

Kent, with Mr W. G. Grace and Mr A.W. Ridley, v England.

Kent 229 (W. G. Grace 50; Mycroft 6–42) and **342** (Penn 135; Emmett 4–89);
England 209 (Lockwood 63; Absolom 4–14) and **32–2**.
Match drawn.

Bank holiday emergencies prevented the Railway men coming up to time at Canterbury that morning, and when at 12.25 Kent began the batting, Mr W. Grace, Watson, and others had not arrived. Mr Ridley and Mr MacKinnon first used the bat to the bowling of Lockwood and Mycroft. With the score at 28, Mr MacKinnon was bowled; at 52, Mr Ridley was caught out; and at 55, Mr Penn was out from a splendid one-hand catch by Shrewsbury. Then a hearty Kentish cheer greeted Mr W. Grace's walk to the wickets, but who – so the critics chronicled – had a narrow escape from lbw the first ball he received. This escape he shortly after squared up by making ten runs (two fours and a two) from one over of Ulyett's; and he and Lord Harris hit the score from 55 to 138, when his Lordship left for 35; and at 151 Mr W. Grace was clean bowled by Emmett for 50, an innings that the critics refused to grant a first-class certificate to... The innings ended at 20 minutes to five, the 229 runs having been made from 118 overs and three balls, W. Mycroft's bowling having settled six wickets.

England batting commenced at five o'clock, Mr I. D. Walker and Mr A. J. Webbe starting to the bowling of Mr W. Grace and Mr Foord-Kelcey... When time was called at seven o'clock, the score stood at 105 for three wickets down, Lockwood, not out, 28; Mr G. F. Grace, not out, 7.

Tuesday was a wet day. They commenced play at 11.20. Lockwood and Mr G. F. Grace made the score to 110, when Mr G. F. Grace was had at the wicket for 12. Shrewsbury was lbw at 133, but Wyld stayed until 162 were booked, when Mr Foord-Kelcey bowled him for 24, including ten (by two fours and a two) from one over of Mr W. Grace's... At 25 minutes to two, the England innings ended for 209 runs, made from 142 Kent overs. Rain then set in, and, hopelessly continuing, the stumps were pulled up at about 3.45, and so ended the second day's play.

On Wednesday, at 11.20, Kent's second innings was begun by Mr W. G. Grace and Mr MacKinnon, to the bowling of Mycroft and Mr Lucas, the wicket being kept by Watson. When 12 runs were scored, Mr MacKinnon was bowled, and at 30, Mr Ridley was caught out at slip. Mr Grace and Mr Penn then hit the score to 111, when Mr Grace was caught out (some yards from the wicket) for 58, well done, and made by eight fours, two threes, &c. Lord Harris was next man in, and by free, fine, and fast hitting the score was moved up to 148, when a clipping catch at mid-off by Mr I. D. Walker got rid of his Lordship for 16. Bad times for England's XI then came, as on Mr Yardley facing Mr Penn, the true Kent hitting was so truly fine, that, notwithstanding Ulyett, Mr Lucas, Mycroft, Emmett, Mr W. Grace, and Watson took a bowling turn at them, they increased the score from 148 to 255, when Mr Yardley was easily caught out at cover point for 61 – a freely and finely hit innings, made by ten fours, two threes, four twos, and seven singles (more fourers than singles); 107 runs were put on the score whilst Mr Yardley was batting. Mr Penn and Mr Foord-Kelcey then hit the score to 301, when Ulyett bowled Mr Penn for 135 – the largest score made in the week's cricket, an especially fine batting display, both of hit and defence, and the unquestionably best played innings of the week... At 25 minutes past five the second innings of Kent ended for 342 runs, made from 178 England overs.

When the clock stood at 5.45 England's second innings was commenced by Mr G. F. Grace and Mr Lucas to the bowling of Mr W. G. Grace and Mr Absolom. They had not been long at work before a delightful little bit of cricket was enjoyed by the spectators in witnessing Mr F. Grace make three fours from one over of his big brother's; all three hits were spanking drives, two of them sending the ball over the boundary; but in Mr W. G.'s next over Mr G. F.'s little game was ended by a catch at long-field, and so fell the first wicket for 18 runs, 14 of which had been made by Mr F. Grace. They worked on to 6.25; then a rainstorm put an end to the play, and the match was left drawn, largely in favour of Kent. 466 overs and 3 balls had been bowled, 32 wickets captured, and 812 runs scored in the three days' cricket.

In the next match WG played against Kent. Yet again, his bowling success was under-reported.

The County of Kent v MCC and Ground (12-A-Side Match)

Kent 177 (MacKinnon 34; Rylott 3–46) and 74 (W. G. Grace 6–19);
MCC and Ground 178 (Crutchley 37; G. Hearne, jun. 5–34) and 74–1 (W. G. Grace 49*).
MCC and Ground won by ten wickets.

... Mr Absolom and McCanlis started Kent's second innings to the bowling of Mr Grace and Morley. They commenced so successfully that that when they went to luncheon 30 runs had been scored, but no wicket had fallen; but after luncheon the Kent men came and left in surprisingly rapid form; at 31 Mr Absolom was caught out at wicket; at 40 Mr Penn was also had by the wicketkeeper, who at 47 stumped McCanlis, all three wickets then down being due to Captain Kingscote's excellent wicketkeeping. But even then the Captain was not done with the Kent men, for after Mr Yardley had been bowled at 50 and Mr MacKinnon c and b at 52, Captain Kingscote, at 54, caught out Mr Kelcey, at 63 he caught out young Hearne, and at 74 he finished the innings by smartly throwing out Mr Cunliffe; so really Captain Kingscote had captured six wickets that innings – a successful sample of wicketkeeping that is worth a record in every chronicle of cricket in 1877… Both Mr Grace and Mr Bray bowled well, but that does not wholly account for so brief an innings; so the result must be credited to that ancient bearer of most cricket mishaps, "The Glorious Uncertainty" &c.

MCC then had 74 to score to win. Mr W. Grace and Mr Anstruther commenced the innings. Mr Grace gave a fair chance at long-on to McCanlis, who had the lowering sun in his eyes, and never saw the ball, so Mr Grace went on hitting away, and the end was that at six o'clock MCC had won the match by ten wickets, Mr W. G. Grace, not out, 49, out of 69 from the bat.

It is not until the Almanack reviews Gloucestershire's season that WG's bowling is given its due:

Mr W. G. Grace is at the top of the tree in all three important batting columns for Gloucestershire; his 110 v England at Lord's, total of 529 runs, and average of 37–11, being the highest all round. But it was the bowling of Mr W. Grace that came so attractively to the front last season, insomuch as of the 180 opposition wickets that succumbed to Gloucestershire's attack, 92 were due to Mr "W. G.'s" bowling, which sums up thus:

Overs	Maidens	Runs	Wickets
834	375	960	92

Those 92 wickets were captured in this way: 22 were bowled, 59 caught out, six stumped, three lbw, and two hit wkt. Dr E. M. Grace ran his brother hard for pride of place in the batting average column, the Doctor's 89 against Notts, 60 against Sussex, and 52, not out, against the Yorkshiremen, giving him a splendid second place; indeed, when it is considered how successful Dr Grace was with some of his old sort of pointing, his Gloucestershire cricket certificate for 1877 should be second to none… Mr G. F. Grace was in fine batting and fielding form in '77, and doubtless there were good reasons, unknown to us outsiders, why he was not in his usual excellent bowling form.

It was also in 1877 that WG's team management style created a radical change within the Gloucestershire ranks:

Hitherto the genuine Gloucestershire team has been wholly composed of amateurs, but in 1877 they played a professional in W. Midwinter from Australia, but who is stated to be Gloucestershire born…

Midwinter, who had already appeared in Test cricket for Australia against England, was indeed Gloucestershire-born, and it was WG who persuaded him to come to England to play for Gloucestershire. His pay as a professional may well still have been less than WG's as an amateur. Billy Midwinter went on to play over 50 matches for Gloucestershire over the next six seasons.

Gloucestershire v Nottinghamshire
At Cheltenham, August 13, 14 and 15, 1877

Gloucestershire 235 (G. F. Grace 83; Morley 5–63); **Nottinghamshire 111**
(Shrewsbury 35; W. G. Grace 9–55) and **79** (Shrewsbury 32; W. G. Grace 8–34).
Gloucestershire won by an innings and 45 runs.

… The run-getting was so slow that it is chronicled, "Mr W. Grace was at one time 40 minutes scoring six runs." However that was made all right by the splendid innings of 83 runs hit by Mr F. Grace, who by a grand off-drive from Morley for six, a five, and seven fours made 39 runs in nine hits. Mr F. G. and Dr Grace increased the score from 125 to 195. The Doctor was out at 203, his 43 including two fours and a single from one over of Morley's, and a very fine hit to leg from Tye for six…

Mr W. Grace in the match bowled 76 overs (36 maidens) for 89 runs and 17 wickets – nine in one innings, eight in the other. In commenting on the extraordinary finish to Notts' second innings on the Wednesday morning, *Bell's Life* stated: "Mr W. Grace's bowling was remarkable; he shared the attack with Midwinter, and his ten overs and one ball were trundled for seven wickets and one run. The seven wickets, however, were really obtained by his last 17 balls for no run."

BATS V BROOMSTICKS

The abrupt and early termination of the match on the third day was the cause of a fill-up-the-time match being arranged for the Gloucester Eleven with broomsticks, to play the Eleven of Cheltenham with bats. The broomsticks made a first innings of 290 runs; of these runs Dr E. M. Grace made 103, and Midwinter 58.

The batsmen had lost two wickets and scored 50 runs, when time was up.

THE GRACE TESTIMONIAL FUND

Despite his amateur status, the success that WG had enjoyed in 1876 prompted the public, led by several august members of the social hierarchy, to set up a Testimonial Fund in his honour.

Gloucestershire v Yorkshire
At Clifton, August 16, 17 and 18, 1877

"The Grace Testimonial Fund" was – according to arrangements made at the meeting in the spring of 1877 – to receive the proceeds of this match…

"The Grace Testimonial Fund"

On February 7, 1877, a public meeting was held in Berkeley Castle, Gloucestershire, for the purpose of making the necessary preliminary arrangements for the formation of a "Grace Testimonial Fund" in recognition of the great and wonderful all-round cricketing abilities displayed by Mr W. G. Grace throughout his extraordinary career. An influential meeting was presided over by Lord Fitzhardinge, to whom is due, we believe, the honour of originating this movement. The committee was (it was understood) formed; Lord Fitzhardinge was appointed Treasurer; a subscription was started, which was headed with £25 by Lord Fitzhardinge...

At one of the MCC Committee Meetings, held in May, at Lord's, the following resolution was unanimously carried:

"That taking into consideration the extraordinary play of Mr W. G. Grace, and his great services to cricket, the Committee of the MCC are of the opinion that the proposal of the President (The Duke of Beaufort) to present a national testimonial to Mr Grace ought to be supported, and that the Secretary of MCC should communicate with the various County and other cricket clubs, and endeavour to bring together representatives from each, who may confer with the MCC Committee as to the best means of carrying out the object in view."

Whether the sensible suggestion of the Duke of Beaufort will be acted upon or not, or what has been the result of the above, this compiler does not know at present time of writing (Oct. 10, '77); in fact, but little was then known by outsiders as to the progress of the fund...

In the end, the testimonial raised £1,458, over £60,000 in today's terms.

At the very end of the 1878 Almanack, the compiler lists all the high scores of the season, including:

200 not out.... Dr E. M. Grace for Thornbury v Kingswood at Alveston

Dr E. M. Grace's 200 was a characteristic bit of batting, inasmuch as it is part of 286 runs – 268 from the bat – scored for the loss of five wickets, the five men out having made only 40 runs between them. Dr A. Grace made 28, not out, there were 18 extras, and Dr E. M. Grace made the remaining 200 runs, not out. A doctor at the beginning, and a doctor at the end. Such is life.

WISDEN 1879

1878 was not WG's most prolific year. He still stood head and shoulders above his Gloucestershire team-mates and above other batsmen in England, but did not score

as heavily in the year he turned 30 as he had done before. He also came up against the Australians in England for the first time.

GLOUCESTERSHIRE IN 1878

Gloucestershire's pride of place as the undefeated county of 1876 and '77 was lost in 1878, when the West Country Eleven were defeated by Yorkshire, Surrey, England and Australia; but were successful over Notts, Lancashire and Sussex (twice)...

Of the old hands, the Captain – W. G. Grace – was where a Captain always should be – bang in front of his men – for he not only took 39 more wickets with his bowling than did any other bowler, but in batting he is at the head of all, as hitter of the largest innings, as scorer of the greatest number of runs, and as highest average man. Mr G. F. Grace is second-highest in the three principal batting columns; and the veteran, "Dr E. M." is well up with his two younger brothers, the three Graces having played in all the 13 matches and made 1,411 of the 2,966 runs scored by the 21 batsmen who went to wickets in 1878 for Gloucestershire. Mr Gilbert was second successful bowler for the Shire with 44 wickets... Mr G. F. Grace did not bowl more than 130 overs for the Shire in 1878. Although "The Doctor" bowled fewer than 100 overs, he took 11 wickets at a cost of 11 runs per wicket.

For Gloucestershire in 1878, WG scored 605 runs at an average of 30–5, with a highest score of 116, making him the only man to score a century for the county that year. He took 83 wickets for 1228 runs, an average of 14.8 runs per wicket.

The Australians v MCC and Ground
At Lord's, May 27, 1878

MCC and Ground 33 (Hornby 19; Spofforth 6–4) and **19** (Flowers 11; Boyle 5–3, Spofforth 5–16); **Australians 41** (Midwinter 10; A. Shaw 5–10) and **12–1**.
Australians won by nine wickets

This, one of the most remarkable matches ever played at Lord's, was commenced at three minutes past 12, and concluded at 20 minutes past six the same day. Only 128 overs and two balls were bowled, and but 101 runs, from the bat, scored in the match. One Australian bowler (Allan) got the crack bat of England caught out from the second ball delivered in the match. Another Australian bowler (Spofforth) clean bowled the said crack for 0 in the second innings... The decisive victory of the Australians was earnestly applauded by the members of MCC and tumultuously so by the thousands of other Englishmen present, whose bones will have mouldered to dust long, long before cricketers of the future – Colonial and English – cease to gossip about the marvellous short-time match played by the Australians at Lord's on May 27, 1878…

MCC won choice, and started the batting (!) with W. G. Grace and Hornby, to the bowling of Allan and Boyle, two excellent head bowlers of medium-pace. Allan began; the first ball he delivered Grace hit to leg for four, the second got Grace easily caught out at short square leg, and thereupon out rang lusty cheers, and shouts of "Bravo, Allan" and "Well done Australia."

… At three minutes to four the second innings of MCC was commenced; at ten minutes to five that innings was over for 19 runs! The bowlers were Spofforth and Boyle. Spofforth commenced in a form that roused the thousands looking on to a frenzy of excitement; from the first ball he delivered, W. Grace ought to have been had at wicket, the second ball thoroughly beat and clean bowled the crack, and the third ball as surely bowled A. J. Webbe; these two great and scientific bats going down before a run was scored, brought out loud and continuing applause, but when (with only one run scored) Boyle in his first over bowled, with successive balls, Booth and Ridley, the cheering was tumultuous, and such as is but rarely heard at Lord's…

… The Australians then had but 12 runs to score to win… At 20 minutes to six this memorable match of 4½ hours actual cricket was won by the Australians…. the members of the MCC keenly joining in the applause of that "maddened crowd" who shouted themselves hoarse before they left to scatter far and wide that evening the news that in one day the Australians had so easily defeated one of the strongest MCC elevens that had ever played for the famous old club.

For South v North at Lord's on June 10, 11 and 12, Grace's all-round cricket dominated the match but failed to force a victory, the North winning by three wickets.

It would be bad form of the compiler if he closed this notice without specially certifying to the very fine all-round cricket played by Mr W. Grace, who made 122 of the 387 runs from the bat scored by his side; whose bowling had nine North wickets, and whose wonderfully active and efficient fielding saved an incalculable number of runs.

All three Grace brothers played for the Gentlemen of England when they challenged the Australians, and this time the results were better for the Englishmen. Even so, the unorthodox reporting style of Wisden's *team was clearly evident.*

The Australians v The Gentlemen of England
At Prince's, June 17 and 18, 1878

The Australians 75 (C. Bannerman 28; W. G. Grace 4–25) and 63 (Midwinter 26;
Steel 7–35); Gentlemen of England 139 (W. G. Grace 25; Boyle 7–48).
The Gentlemen of England won by an innings and 1 run.

Rain fell as A. Bannerman walked to the wicket, and the hundreds of upraised open umbrellas around the ground was not only a curious sight, but those put up in front of the little press hut shut out all view of the play from the reporters, and all that could thenceforth be noted was that at a few minutes past four the Australians' innings closed for 75 runs, only one of the Eleven having been bowled. At 25 past four W. Grace and W. Gilbert commenced England's batting to the bowling of Spofforth and Allen [*sic*]. The Englishmen made runs at a faster pace than had the Australians, and... still the score rose, and many hoped the Englishmen would equal, and pass, the Australians' total without losing a wicket; but not so, for at 43 a loud shout greeted Boyle clean-bowling W. Grace for 25 – the largest English score made.

Sussex v Gloucestershire
At Brighton, June 24 and 25, 1878

Sussex 93 (Phillips 40; Miles 5–22) and 71 (Tester 29; W. G. Grace 4–13);
Gloucestershire 231 (G. F. Grace 71; Skinner 3–28).
Gloucestershire won by an innings and 67 runs.

Although Fillery enjoyed the great satisfaction of catching out Mr W. G. Grace for nought, the Sussex men never had the ghost of a chance of winning this match... nine runs had been made by Midwinter when a left-hand catch low down by Fillery at point settled Mr W. Grace for nought, and brought out roars of Sussex cheering. But if "Mr W. G." did not score, other members of the family did, to the extent of 178 runs, as Mr F. Grace made 71, Dr E. M. Grace 53 and Mr Gilbert 54.

Gentlemen v Players of England
Played on The Oval, July 4 and 5, 1878

Gentlemen 76 (W. G. Grace 40; A. Shaw 5–45) and 202 (W. G. Grace 63; A. Shaw 6–62);
Players 122 (Shrewsbury 34; Steel 6–60) and 101 (Shrewsbury 27; W. G. Grace 3–20).
Gentlemen won by 55 runs.

It is certain that Mr W. G. Grace had not "lost form" when this match was played, for in the Gentlemen's first innings he made 40 runs out of 76, in their second he made 63 out of 202, his bowling captured five Players' wickets, and his fielding settled another good batsman.

... The Gentlemen's first innings was commenced at 12.15 by Mr W. G. Grace and Mr A. P. Lucas; at two o'clock that innings was over for 76 runs, made from 61 overs and two balls, Mr W. Grace being last man out (caught out at leg) for 40 – an innings described as having been played "without anything like a chance".

... (In the second innings) Mr G. F. Grace faced his brother and (as they frequently have done before) made a good stand, fairly getting hold of the bowling, and despite Mycroft, Alfred Shaw, Ulyett, Morley, Mycroft again, Midwinter, Morley again and Barlow bowled, the brothers increased the score from 45 to 134, when Mr W. Grace was lbw for 63 – the largest innings hit in the match... Morley bowled Mr G. F. Grace with a ball that sent one of the bails flying very many yards from the wicket.

WG's innings of 90 as the Gentlemen beat the Players at Lord's on July 8, 9 and 10 was duly praised by Wisden:

It is doubtful if there was ever so much first-class batting played in a Gentlemen v Players of England or any other match, as was played in this of 1,066 runs at Lord's in 1878... A remarkably fine left-hand catch at slip by Alfred Shaw got rid of Mr W. Grace for 90. Mr Grace had been two hours and a quarter at wickets; he commenced with a cut for four from Emmett (the first hit made in this famous match); later on he made... the following fine string of consecutive hits – 4, 4, 4, 2, 3, 3, 4, and 4. When the 100 was hoisted Mr W. Grace had made 61, and of his 90 (out of 151) it is only truth to record that for correct timing and safe placing the ball, clean hitting, and first-class defence, this innings of Mr Grace's was one of the best he ever played.

He came to Canterbury once again for The Week, but played only two matches, neither of them 11-a-side. For Eleven of England against Thirteen of Kent, he scored 21 and 14 and had match figures of 6 for 93. For Twelve of MCC and Ground against Twelve of Kent, he made just nought and one.

Hearne clean-bowled Mr W. Grace for nought whereat wrote one of the chroniclers, "There was a universal outburst of applause!" No doubt there was, and there can be no question that at that particular moment the little bantam cricketer was the most popular man in Kent.

There was also a special fundraising match in September that year, which elicited from Wisden *as high praise for Fred Grace's play as ever his brother had earned. As* Wisden *explained:*

On September 3… a fearful calamity occurred on the River Thames, that overwhelmed England with sorrow. Two steamers came into collision; one ("The Princess Alice", a pleasure boat) was cut in twain and over 700 lives – then in the fullness of joy and pleasure – were sacrificed with awful suddenness, and very many families sadly and seriously bereaved.

The Thames Calamity Fund Match
North v South – played on The Oval, September 17, 18 and 19, 1878.

Those who know who's who in the cricketing world, and will cast their eyes over the names forming these two fine Elevens, will be surprised to find that not only did the South eleven (fairly worth 200 runs at any time) go out for two innings of 64 and 116 runs in the match, but in playing a third innings in a fill-up-the-time match on the Saturday, they were (one man short it is true) actually settled for 58; in fact, in the match, there was only one Southerner who batted up to known form; he was:

Mr F. Grace, who scored 22, not out, and 54, not out.

And when the dead wickets, and the really splendid bowling and fielding of the Northmen is duly considered, it cannot be doubted but that Mr F. Grace's batting in this match was equal to the very best Grace form ever played.

Fred Grace also took four wickets for 33 runs, two of which were caught and bowled, as the South went down by an innings and 123 runs.

WISDEN 1880

Wisden's editor W. H. Knight died in August 1879, and so the 1880 edition was edited by George West.

The summer of 1879 was a particularly wet one, and it followed on from an immensely cold winter of 1878–79, when games of cricket were played on the ice across the country, and reported on in Wisden. No batsman really prospered under the cold and wet conditions of that dreadful summer, but WG kept ahead of the pack, as always. He was the only man to score as many as three centuries that year, but Wisden's reports were more of the weather than the cricket for much of the season.

Surrey v Gloucestershire
At The Oval, June 5, 6 and 7, 1879

It was the first experience we had of really cricket weather; but the previous heavy rains had made the ground dead… Gloucestershire proved to be in fine batting form... On the second day (Friday) Mr W. G. Grace and his brother Mr G. F. Grace (both not out on the previous evening) kept on their way triumphantly. In fact the former made his innings of the season, as it was not until he had accumulated 133 that he was clean bowled by the Surrey captain, having just previously been let off at point. Among his hits were one six (square leg), one five, ten fours, and 14 twos. The only other Gloucestershire batsman who made anything of a stand was Mr G. F. Grace, in whose 57 there were three fours, two threes and eight twos.

The Gentlemen v Players match at Lord's on July 7 and 8 was more typical of the summer:

The wintry clad umpires were at their posts ready for the commencement of the Gentlemen's second innings when a long-threatened storm burst o'er the ground with pitiless fury; rain fell in torrents, the ground was covered with hailstones as large as boys' "Tawny Marbles", and to heap up the misery, half a gale of wind blew across the ground. This storm lasted 25 minutes, and the ground, the long-suffering ground, was in a pitiable state. No more cricket could be played that day, and as more rain fell in the course of that night, and another tremendous downpour at 11.15 the following morning again drenched the ground, no play could possibly take place on the Wednesday, so the match was drawn.

The Testimonial Fund created at the end of the 1876 season came to fruition in 1879.

Over Thirty v Under Thirty
At Lord's, July 22 and 23, 1879

It is admitted beyond all dispute that Mr W. G. Grace is the greatest cricketer "the world e'er saw." Whatever may be the prejudices of those whose memories carry them back to the heroes of the last generation, even they give way, and yield the palm to the Gloucestershire captain. This being so, and considering the impetus which his reputation has given to the game, it was only natural that his admirers should wish to pay him a tribute more substantial than mere praise. Subscriptions were, therefore, invited in the season of 1877, and the outcome of this was the presentation of a testimonial, and a sum of money, to which were to be added the proceeds of the above match... A disappointment, however, had befallen Shaw on account of the weather being so unfavourable on the occasion of his benefit match – North v South – earlier in the season, and with a generosity which met with hearty approval on all hands, Mr Grace asked that the match intended for himself should be devoted to Shaw. But alas! The elements were even more perverse on the days intended for the Over Thirty v Under Thirty match than they had been on the occasion of North v South, and so far as Shaw was concerned little benefit was reaped from it.

PRESENTATION TO MR W. G. GRACE

The presentation to which allusion has been made above took place at the most appropriate spot which could have been selected – viz., in front of the pavilion at Lord's. It consisted of a sum of money and a marble clock, bearing this inscription: "Presented to W. G. Grace, on July 22, 1879, on the occasion of the match Over Thirty v Under Thirty, played in his honour at Lord's," and two bronze ornaments representing Egyptian obelisks.

Lord Fitzhardinge, who had kindly undertaken to make the presentation, regretted his inability to control the weather, as he thought there were few such interesting occasions as that which brought them together. Referring to the testimonial, his Lordship said that the original idea had been to purchase a practice for Mr Grace; but he had talked the matter over with the Duke of Beaufort, and they thought that Mr Grace was old enough and strong enough to take care of himself – (laughter and cheers) – and they would leave him to choose a practice for himself. The total amount, deducting expenses, which would be placed to Mr Grace's credit, including the value of the clock and the ornaments, was about £1,400 (cheers). He had, accordingly, great pleasure in presenting this testimonial to Mr Grace, and he could only say, on behalf of the people of Gloucestershire, that they wished him as much success in his profession as he had reaped in the cricket field (loud cheers).

Mr W. G. Grace, after stating he was not a speech-maker, made a short and appropriate reply, in which he thanked them all for the manner in which they had got up the testimonial. It had far exceeded his expectations, and whenever he looked at the clock he should remember the occasion on which it was presented to him.

Lord Charles Russell, who had been asked as one of the oldest members of the Marylebone Club to say a few words on the occasion, said, "he was not satisfied with the amount. He thought £1,400 was an odd sum to present to any one, and he pledged his word it would be £1,500 before they were done with it. He was an old cricketer, and the enjoyment he had had in the cricket field for many years past was in seeing Mr Grace play cricket. He looked upon cricket as the sport of the people, from the prince to the peasant, and he was delighted to see that it was increasing in popularity year by year… More than agility was wanted in playing cricket. The game must be played with head and heart, and in that respect Mr Grace was eminently prominent… In playing a ball, Mr Grace put every muscle into it, from the sole of his foot to the crown of his head (laughter); and just as he played one ball so he played cricket. He was heart and soul in it. He had never heard a bell ring for cricketers to go into the field, but Mr Grace was in first.

And that was a great matter of cricket playing. The game was a game of laws and regulations. If they relaxed these, then it became merely a pastime fit for young men who had nothing else to do, or some middle-aged men who wanted to get an appetite. (Laughter and cheers.) The Marylebone Cricket Club held its ground for the practice and promotion of good sound cricket, and it was for that reason they had such great delight in taking part in this testimonial to Mr Grace, who was in every respect of the word a thorough cricketer. (Loud cheers.) Allusion had been made to HRH the Prince of Wales having joined the subscribers; it might be presumption in him to speculate on His Royal Highness's motives for doing so, but he must hazard an opinion that HRH was grateful to Mr Grace for affording him an opportunity of showing his respect for the one great game of the people, requiring in those who play it the national essentials of patience, fortitude, and pluck, and fostering the respect for law and love of fair play which are characteristics of us English people. (Loud cheers.)

Against Nottinghamshire at Trent Bridge on August 1 and 2, Wisden's *comment on* WG's *score of 102 out of 197 was typical of the expectations that accompanied the "crack" to the wicket every time he batted:*

Mr W. G. Grace hit away with such vigour that the remainder of his side fell away into insignificance. Altogether he occupied the wicket for four hours and five minutes, and compiled his second-largest innings of the season. It included 11 fours, four threes, 13 twos and 20 singles. After his downfall the rest of the side offered but a feeble resistance.

WG was supposed to be studying for his medical qualifications during 1879, and approaching his final examinations, but he still found time to enjoy another Canterbury Week, from August 4 to 9:

Kent v All England
At Canterbury, August 4, 5 and 6, 1879

Kent 142 (Penn 31; W. G. Grace 5–38) and 174 (Jones 40; Morley 4–44);
All England 72 (Oscroft 15; Bray 4–27) and 246–6 (Flowers 72*, W. G. Grace 63*;
Foord-Kelcey 2–38),
All England won by four wickets.

When England entered on their second attempt, they had 245 runs to get to win… Wednesday dawned most unpromisingly. Heavy clouds fringed the horizon, and a little before noon a terrific storm of rain burst over the ground… In the afternoon, however, the prospect brightened (but) the rain had made the ground soft, and the bowlers could not get any break on the ball. Mr Grace kept triumphantly on, and by free hitting soon altered the aspect of affairs... The batsmen kept steadily on, and defied all the combinations that could be brought against them. The "200" was signalled a little before five o'clock and half-an-hour later Mr Grace made the winning hit.

Wisden's scorecard for Gloucestershire v Middlesex (August 14–16) lists WG as "W. G. Grace, Esq." but two days later, on the card for Gloucestershire v Yorkshire (August 18–20), he appears as "Dr W. G. Grace". Yet against Lancashire at Old Trafford at the end of July that year, the card listed him as Dr W. G. Grace, and there is some continuing inconsistency, as the scorecards for home matches against Lancashire and Surrey at the end of the month list him as "W. G. Grace, Esq." Nevertheless, by the end of the dreadful summer, WG was definitely a qualified doctor, although hardly a practising one. Throughout his subsequent career, he seems to have been referred to as "Dr Grace" or "Mr Grace" in equal amounts. His elder brother, EM, was always a doctor.

The report of Gloucestershire's season emphasised how comparatively unsuccessful the county was in 1879, but:

Mr W. G. Grace again stands in the foremost position, both in the batting and bowling departments. In the latter he claims 75 wickets at a cost of a little over a dozen runs each. Midwinter comes second with 41 wickets for 671 runs, and Mr G. F. Grace third with 15 for 258. In batting he more than doubles the average of any of his companions. He took part in all the matches and completed 15 innings for an average of 54.7.

CHAPTER 3
PLAYING DAYS – 1880 ONWARDS

"Mr Grace's absolute supremacy over all the cricketers who have ever lived"

In 1880, WG celebrated his 32nd birthday. He had qualified as a doctor the previous year, and it was assumed that he would therefore play less cricket in future. During the first three years of the decade, his doctoring duties did indeed keep him away from the cricket field more often than had been the case in the past, but if it was ever his intention to retire from cricket and become a fulltime country GP, his love of cricket soon took precedence over his love of medicine, and, with a locum in place, he returned to regular first-class cricket from 1884 onwards. He played a total of 94 first-class matches in the five seasons 1879 to 1883, but as many as 195 in the next six years to 1890. He scored 1,000 runs in each season from 1883, and performed the double of 1,000 runs and 100 wickets twice more, in 1885 and 1886. Even when he was not playing regularly, he was still the giant of English cricket.

His brother EM, who was almost 40 when the decade began, was still playing regularly and still among the very best cricketers in England, but was inevitably in the shadow of his younger brother. Even so Wisden was able in 1889 to write of "the veteran, Mr E. M. Grace, who worthily maintained his reputation of being one of the best of batsmen at the pinch of a game."

WG played on. And on. As Wisden wrote in 1890, "Mr W. G. Grace, as he has done for so many years, came out a long way ahead of his colleagues." He was still the benchmark against whom to judge all other players, even in his early forties.

WISDEN 1881

Apart from his century in the England v Australia Test at The Oval, WG had a comparatively quiet year in 1880.

Gloucestershire v Yorkshire
At Clifton, August 23, 24 and 25, 1880

Gloucestershire 302 (W. G. Grace 89; Peate 4–85) and **84 for 4** (W. G. Grace 57*; Peate 4–29);
Yorkshire 195 (Emmett 45; Gilbert 4–36) and **190** (Pinder 57; W. G. Grace 4–78).
Gloucestershire won by six wickets.

In this match Mr [*sic*] W. G. Grace had another opportunity of showing the wonderful power he possesses of scoring against time. Owing to the interruption by rain on the first day, the very large scoring of the Gloucestershire men in their first innings, and the good totals obtained by the Yorkshire team in both innings, there was only an hour and a half left to the West Countrymen to score the required 84 runs to secure them a victory; but with such astonishing rapidity did Mr Grace add to the score, that, despite the time lost through four wickets falling, the necessary runs were obtained in an hour and a quarter, Mr Grace making 57 out of 77 from the bat. It would be impossible to speak too highly of Mr Grace's batting in this match; it was equal to anything he had previously done.

The very first Test match on English soil was not given as much space as Wisden's *editor, nor modern cricket historians, would have liked.*

All three Grace brothers played – all were making their Test debuts, but neither EM nor GF ever represented their country again. Fred caught pneumonia, and was dead two weeks later. He bagged a pair and did not bowl, but his catch to dismiss George Bonnor in the first innings has gone down in cricket history. Bonnor hit the ball high towards the gasholder and the batsmen had completed two runs as the ball "hung, hawk-like, high in the sky" as Simon Rae puts it in his 1998 biography of WG. Fred made the catch look simple but it was a "truly magnificent catch", the cheering for which could be heard all the way to Vauxhall Station.

WG's century was the first ever by an Englishman in Tests.

England v Australia
At Kennington Oval, September 6, 7 and 8, 1880

The compiler much regrets that the limited space allotted to the Australians' matches in this book precludes the possibility of giving a lengthened account of this famous contest.

He must therefore rest content to put on record the following facts anent the match: That in the history of the game no contest has created such worldwide interest; that the attendances on the first and second days were the largest ever seen at a cricket match; that 20,814 persons passed through the turnstiles on Monday, 19,863 on the Tuesday, and 3,751 on the Wednesday; that fine weather favoured the match from start to finish; that the wickets were faultless; that Mr Murdoch's magnificent innings of 153 not out was made without a chance.... ; that superb batting was also shown by Mr Lucas, Lord Harris, Mr McDonnell, and Mr Steel; that the fielding and wicketkeeping on both sides was splendid; that a marvellous change in the aspect of the game was effected on the last day; that universal regret was felt at the unavoidable absence of Mr Spofforth; and that England won the match by five wickets.

England v Australia
At The Oval, September 6, 7 and 8, 1880

England

Dr. E. M. Grace c Alexander b Bannerman	36	b Boyle	0
Dr. W. G. Grace b Palmer	152	not out	9
A. P. Lucas b Bannerman	55	c Blackham b Palmer	2
W. Barnes b Alexander	28	c Moule b Boyle	5
Lord Harris c Bonnor b Alexander	52		
F. Penn b Bannerman	23	not out	27
A. G. Steel c Boyle b Moule	42		
Hon. A. Lyttelton not out	11	b Palmer	13
G. F. Grace c Bannerman b Moule	0	b Palmer	0
A. Shaw b Moule	0		
F. Morley run out	2		
B 8, l-b 11	19	N-b 1	1
	420	**(5 wkts)**	**57**

Boyle 44–17–71–0; Palmer 70–27–116–1; Alexander 32–10–69–2; Bannerman 50–12–111–3; McDonnell 2–0–11–0; Moule 12.3–4–23–3.
Second innings—Boyle 17–7–21–2; Palmer 16.3–5–35–3.

Australia

A. C. Bannerman b Morley	32	c Lucas b Shaw	8
W. L. Murdoch c Barnes b Steel	0	not out	153
T. U. Groube b Steel	11	c Shaw b Morley	0
P. S. McDonnell c Barnes b Morley	27	lbw b W. G. Grace	43
J. Slight c G. F. Grace b Morley	11	c Harris b W. G. Grace	0
J. McC. Blackham c and b Morley	0	c E. M. Grace b Morley	19
G. J. Bonnor c G. F. Grace b Shaw	2	b Steel	16
H. F. Boyle not out	36	run out	3
G. E. Palmer b Morley	6	c and b Steel	4
G. Alexander c W. G. Grace b Steel	6	c Shaw b Morley	33
W. H. Moule c Morley b W. G. Grace	6	b Barnes	34
B 9, l-b 3	12	B 7, l-b 7	14
	149		**327**

Morley 32–9–56–5; Steel 29–9–58–3; Shaw 13–5–21–1; Dr. W. G. Grace 1.1–0–2–1.
Second innings—Morley 61–30–90–3; Steel 31–6–73–2; Shaw 33–18–42–1;
Dr. W. G. Grace 28–10–66–2; Barnes 8.3–3–17–1; Lucas 12–7–23–0; Penn 3–1–2–0.

Umpires: H. H. Stephenson and R. A. Thoms.
England won by five wickets

GLOUCESTERSHIRE IN 1880

This notice would indeed be incomplete were mention omitted of the very sad loss the county, and indeed the whole cricketing world, sustained by the death of Mr G. F. Grace. A brilliant field, a splendid batsman, at times a very successful bowler, and one of the most genial and popular men that ever appeared on a cricket field, his early decease will long be deplored, and his memory cherished by all who were acquainted with him, and it will be very difficult to fill the void his death has created.

Obituaries in 1880

BOWYER, JOHN (Surrey)	Feb. 12
ELLIS, CHARLES HOWARD (Sussex)	Jun. 17
GRACE, MR GEORGE FREDERICK (Gloucestershire)	Sept. 22
HINKLY, EDMUND (Kent)	Dec. 8
SOUTHERTON, JAMES (Surrey, Sussex, and Hampshire)	June 16
WENMAN, EDWARD GOWER (Kent)	Aug. 18

WISDEN 1882

GLOUCESTERSHIRE IN 1881

In all three important batting columns, Dr W. G. Grace again heads the list, and in each instance with better results than in the previous year... And the return to something like his old form was very conspicuous in Dr E. M. Grace, with second-highest aggregate of 469 and an average about eight points better than in 1880.

The bowling of Midwinter, Mr Grace, Woof and Mr Townsend was not so successful as in the previous year.

WG played 12 matches for the county, batted 19 times (once not out), and scored 720 runs at an average of exactly 40. His highest score was 182.

He bowled 486 overs, 196 of which were maidens. He was hit for 853 runs and took 47 wickets, at an average of 18.15.

Midwinter took 51 wickets for 827 runs, at an average of 16.22.

Wisden's list of first-class centuries in 1881 includes WG's name twice:

Dr W. G. Grace	100	bowled	Gentlemen v Players	The Oval
Dr W. G. Grace	182	lbw	Gloucestershire v Notts	Nottingham

But immediately below him in alphabetical order, Mr A. N. Hornby appears three times:

Mr A. N. Hornby	188	caught	Lancashire v Derbyshire	Old Trafford
Mr A. N. Hornby	102	caught	Lancashire v Kent	Old Trafford
Mr A. N. Hornby	145	caught	Lancashire v Derbyshire	Derby

For the first time in many years, WG also missed Canterbury Week, although no first-class matches were played, the three fixtures being Thirteen of Kent v Eleven of England, Twelve of Kent v Twelve Gentlemen of England, and I Zingari v Gentlemen of England.

Middlesex v Gloucestershire
At Lord's, June 13 and 14, 1881

Gloucestershire 160 (W. G. Grace 64, E. M. Grace 47; Burton 6–45) and **114–4** (Cranston 35*); **Middlesex 77** (W. G. Grace 7–30) and **195** (Vernon 88; Midwinter 6–53). Gloucestershire won by six wickets.

This match produced some very remarkable cricket. Gloucestershire, winning the toss, elected to bat, and on the brothers Grace going to the wickets, some surprising hitting, by Dr E. M., was soon witnessed. He early had a life at the hands of Mr Law, and encouraged by this, batted with astounding vigour. Off Clarke's bowling he scored five fours, and before he was caught at cover point, had made 47 runs while Dr W. G. put on 12. Mr L. M. Day filled the vacancy, and the Gloucestershire captain then batted with greater freedom, and the score was raised to 117 before a separation was effected by Mr Day being lbw to Burton. During the partnership, Dr W. G. compiled 39 while Mr Day made 19. At this stage of the game, Burton's bowling became so exceedingly destructive, that the remaining eight wickets were disposed of for an addition of only 43 runs. Dr W. G. Grace's excellent innings of 64 consisted of one five, three fours, two threes, 11 twos, and 19 singles.

Nottinghamshire v Gloucestershire
At Trent Bridge, July 28, 29 and 30, 1881

Gloucestershire 155 (W. G. Grace 51; Shore 5–40) and **483** (W. G. Grace 182; Tye 4–86); **Nottinghamshire 240** (Attewell 46*; W. G. Grace 3–60). Match drawn.

This match was productive of some large scoring, 878 runs being made for the loss of 30 wickets, giving an average of 29 runs per wicket… Gloucestershire, on going in, scored 155, of which number Dr W. G. Grace made 51, but should have been caught when he had made 11. The southern county had to follow on, and the Nottingham bowling was sorely punished. Dr W. G. Grace went in with the score at 82 and stayed until it reached 440. He was then out lbw for a splendid innings of

182, for which he was deservedly applauded on retiring. This is the highest score ever made in a county match on the Trent Bridge ground. His chief hits were 17 fours, 11 threes and 18 twos.

WISDEN 1883

WG did not score a first-class century in 1882.

GLOUCESTERSHIRE IN 1882

1882 will be remembered as the most disastrous season the West Countrymen experienced from the time the G. C. C. C. was formed in 1871. In only one year previously (1879) had the defeats exceeded the victories in point of number, that season's results being: 11 matches played; two won; three lost; six drawn. In 1882 the wins were three, the drawn matches three and the defeats seven.

A comparison of the batting averages of '81 and '82 will account for this very unsatisfactory result. In '82 the principal batsmen in the Eleven, except Midwinter, played with less success than in the previous year, and in most cases the falling-off was very great. The champion dropped from 40 to 30.6… Mr Gilbert from 27.10 to 12.5… and Dr E. M. Grace from 27.10 to 25.21. Midwinter's average rose from 17.16 to 27.1, and taking all things into consideration he was, too, the most successful bowler for the County. Midwinter, Dr W. G. Grace and Woof did about nine-tenths of the bowling, but their averages of 15.40, 16.70 and 17.4 runs per wicket respectively were much too high for the County's success when the batting of the team had shewn so marked a depreciation…

Perhaps the most remarkable circumstance connected with Gloucestershire cricket in 1882 was the failure of the champion to score a three-figure innings for his county; a thing that had not once occurred since the County club was formed. There were three scores of over 100 made – two by Dr E. M. Grace and one by Midwinter.

WG scored 666 runs in 22 innings, with a highest score of 88. He was still top of the averages and the most prolific run-scorer for the county. He also took the most wickets, 74, but at a higher average than Midwinter, who took 52.

Gloucestershire v Somersetshire
On The Spa Ground, Gloucester, Thursday, Friday, July 13 and 14, 1882

Somersetshire 62 (Fowler 39; W. G. Grace 8–31) and 109 (Welman 36; Woof 7–39); Gloucestershire 348 (E. M. Grace 108, Midwinter 107*; Fothergill 4–96). Gloucestershire won by an innings and 177 runs.

Considering the strength of the Gloucestershire team as compared with that of Somersetshire, the severe defeat the latter county sustained can hardly be wondered at. No one but Mr Fowler could make any stand against the bowling of the champion, who took eight wickets for 31 runs... Gloucestershire then went in and made an unfortunate start, Dr W. G. Grace being caught for a single. Mr Cranston now joined Dr E. M. Grace, and some splendid hitting was then shown, as when Mr [*sic*] E. M. Grace was bowled the score had reached 179. Of these Dr E. M. had made no less than 108, a grandly hit innings, played in quite his old form.

E. M. Grace was 41 years old by now.

Gloucestershire v Lancashire
At Clifton, Thursday, Friday, Saturday, August 10, 11 and 12, 1882

Lancashire 240 (Haigh 80; Woof 5–70) and **217** (Hornby 63; Midwinter 6–66);
Gloucestershire 196 (W. G. Grace 86; Barlow 5–32) and **248** (E. M. Grace 122; Nash 6–85).
Lancashire won by 13 runs.

A perfect wicket had been prepared for this match. Mr Hornby, with his usual luck, won the toss, and at 12.15, accompanied by Barlow, commenced the Lancashire innings, but the captain made an unfortunate start, being bowled by the first ball of the second over... The last four wickets gave little trouble, and the total reached 240, Barlow carrying out his bat for a well-played innings of 58. This was the fourth time this season, in county matches, that Barlow had gone in first and seen all the rest of the eleven out. Gloucestershire now commenced their innings, and by the time play ceased for the day had lost five wickets for 119 runs...

On resuming the next morning, the champion increased his score to 86, having been at the wickets three hours, for one of the best innings he had played in 1882... The [Lancashire second innings] total was 217, which left Gloucestershire 262 to get to win. They commenced the task with Dr E. M. Grace and Peake, who started by putting on 30 in a quarter of an hour. Mr Peake was caught, and soon after play ceased for the day, with the score at 56 for one wicket.

Messrs E. M. Grace and Gilbert resumed the next morning, taking the score to 85 when the latter's wicket fell. Dr W. G. Grace joined his brother, and brought the score to 144, when he was caught at the wicket. At luncheon time, the game looked almost a certainty for Gloucestershire, the total being 179, or 83 to win, with seven wickets to fall. After the interval, however, a change came over the game. Two wickets quickly fell, and soon after Dr E. M. Grace was stumped for a brilliantly played innings of 122, the highest he made for Gloucestershire in 1882. This was indeed a splendid performance, made without the semblance of a chance, and including 18 fours and 12 twos. With the last wicket to fall, 20 runs only were wanted to win, and the excitement was intense; but Mr Bush got his leg in front of the wicket when the score was 248, Lancashire thus winning by 13 runs.

W. G. Grace did not go out to Australia in the winter of 1881–82: a team of professionals led by Alfred Shaw, James Lillywhite and Arthur Shrewsbury lost 2–0 to Australia, but Grace was available to play for England in 1882, when the Australians came over to England.

Australia v England
At Kennington Oval, Monday, Tuesday, August 28 and 29, 1882

Australia 63 (Blackham 17; Peate 4–31) and **122** (Massie 55; Peate 4–40);
England 101 (Ulyett 26; Spofforth 7–46) and **77** (W. G. Grace 32; Spofforth 7–44).
Australia won by seven runs.

With these few remarks the compiler proceeds to give a short account of the contest, leaving the reader to attribute the Australian victory to the fact that the Colonists won the toss and thereby had the best of the cricket; to the fact that the English had to play the last innings; to the brilliant batting of Massie; to the superb bowling of Spofforth; to the nervousness of some of the England side; to the glorious uncertainty of the noble game; or to whatever he or she thinks the true reason.

Monday. Murdoch beat Hornby in the toss and deputed Bannerman and Massie to commence the innings. Massie was clean bowled by a yorker on the leg stump at six. At 21 Murdoch played a ball from Peate on to his wicket, and, after adding a single, Bonnor was clean bowled middle stump. Horan came in, and then, at 26, Bannerman was splendidly caught by Grace at point, left hand, low down, having been in an hour and five minutes for nine runs… At 59 Blackham skied a ball and was caught, and Spofforth, the last man, joined Jones. The Demon hit a four, and then Jones was caught at third man, the innings closing for 63.

At 3.30 Grace and Barlow started the first innings of England. Spofforth bowled Grace at 13, and Barlow was caught at forward point for 18. Eight wickets were down for 96 when Hornby came in. Read made a cut for three and Hornby scored a single, bringing up the 100. With only one run added, however, Hornby's leg stump fell, and the innings closed about five minutes before the call of time.

Tuesday. Massie and Bannerman commenced the Australians' second innings at 12.10, the Colonists being 38 to the bad. 30 went up after about 28 minutes' play, two bowling changes having been tried… When the score had been hit up to 99 rain fell, and luncheon was taken.

Resuming at 2.45, after another shower, Blackham was well caught at the wicket without any addition to the score. Jones filled the vacancy and a single by Murdoch sent up the 100. At 114 Jones was run out in a way which gave great dissatisfaction to Murdoch and other Australians. Murdoch played a ball to leg, for which Lyttelton ran. The ball was returned, and Jones having completed the first run, and thinking wrongly, but very naturally, that the ball was dead, went out of his ground. Grace put his wicket down, and the umpire gave him out. Several of the team spoke angrily of Grace's action, but the compiler was informed that after the excitement had cooled down a prominent member of Australian eleven admitted that he should have done the same thing had he been in Grace's place. There was a good deal of truth in what a gentleman in the pavilion remarked, amidst some laughter, that Jones ought to thank the champion for teaching him something…

England, wanting 85 runs to win, commenced their second innings at 3.45 with Grace and Hornby. Spofforth bowled Hornby's off stump at 15, made in about as many minutes. Barlow joined Grace, but was bowled first ball at the same total. Ulyett came in, and some brilliant hitting by both batsmen brought the score to 51, when a very fine catch at the wicket dismissed Ulyett. 34 runs were then wanted, with seven wickets to fall. Lucas joined Grace, but when the latter had scored a two he was easily taken at mid-off. Lyttelton became Lucas's partner, and the former did all the hitting. Then the game was slow for a time, and 12 successive maiden overs were bowled, both batsmen playing carefully and coolly. Lyttelton scored a single, and then four maiden overs were followed by the dismissal of that batsman – bowled, the score being 66. Only 19 runs were then wanted to win, and there were five wickets to fall. Steel came in, and when Lucas had scored a four, Steel was easily caught and bowled. Read joined Lucas, but amid intense excitement he was clean bowled without a run being added. Barnes took Read's place and scored a two, and three byes made the total 75, or ten to win. After being in a long time for five Lucas played the next ball into his wicket, and directly Studd joined Barnes the latter was easily caught off his glove without the total being altered. Peate, the last man, came in, but after hitting Boyle to square leg for two he was bowled, and Australia had defeated England by seven runs.

This was the Test that gave rise to the legend of The Ashes.

WISDEN 1884

In 1883, WG had more success than in the previous season, but there was a feeling that his cricket was nearer in standard to that of his fellow players than it had ever been. After all, he did celebrate his 35th birthday during the summer.

GLOUCESTERSHIRE IN 1883

With two bowlers to start with and not a single effective one to back them up, the good averages of five or six of the batsmen were powerless to save the county from another disastrous season…

Dr W. G. Grace was considerably the highest aggregate scorer; was credited with an innings of three figures – the only one he made in first-class matches in the past two seasons; and has the splendid average of 39.13, the merit of which is enhanced by the fact that it was obtained without the aid of a single not-out innings…

Mr Gilbert's batting proved of great service, and he occupies fourth position with an average of 24.16. The veteran Dr E. M. Grace commenced the season in fine form, and when half the Gloucestershire programme had been gone through his average was a trifle higher than his brother's. He was not so successful in the later matches. However, but nevertheless has the good average of 23.13.

No county was so deplorably weak in bowling as Gloucestershire, the 167 wickets credited to the bowlers costing no less than 26 runs each. With such a result it is a matter for wonder that the Western County could win a single match.

WG scored 871 runs in 22 innings, and took 50 wickets at 20.31. The slow left-arm bowler William Woof took fewer wickets – 50 – but at a better average (20.31).

Only two men scored more runs in county cricket that season than WG – Walter Read of Surrey who made 1,637 runs at 46.27, and George Ulyett of Yorkshire who scored 956 at 41.1. Apart from these two men, only three other batsmen, the Hon. A. Lyttelton, A. W. Ridley and C. T. Studd, all of Middlesex, had a higher average for their county. So even in a bad year, WG was among the top six batsmen. He also scored another 169 runs in MCC matches, bringing his aggregate over the 1,000-run mark.

North v South

At Lord's, Whit Monday, Tuesday, Wednesday May 14, 15 and 16, 1883

North 115 (Lockwood 30; Woof 5–35) and **247** (Lockwood 60; W. G. Grace 4–56);
South 128 (W. G. Grace 64; Peate 7–45) and **64** (Lucas 22; Peate 5–17).
North won by 170 runs.

Monday… The most noteworthy bit of cricket was the magnificent catch by Dr Grace which disposed of Wyld. Of that catch a critic remarks, "The ball was driven back hard, but he sprang up and took it most brilliantly with his left hand. Nothing in the day's cricket provoked louder cheering."

The first innings of the North was over at 4.05, and at 4.25 the Southern team commenced batting with Dr Grace and Mr Lucas. With the score at only 15, three wickets had fallen. Mr Cave then joined his captain, and was directly missed at the wicket by Wyld. Profiting by this mistake, Mr Cave, by careful defensive play, stayed at the wickets while 38 runs were put on. Dr Grace was sixth out, the score at 96, having been at the wickets an hour and 50 minutes. He gave one chance to Peate at slip when the total stood at 67, but his innings was nevertheless a splendid one, and comprised seven fours – one a drive off Bates on to the top of the reserved enclosure – two threes, six twos and 18 singles...

Tuesday... The South's innings was finished off without the addition of a single run. Mr Tylecote unfortunately arrived too late to go in... The North were 13 runs to the bad when they commenced their second innings... Towards the close of the innings Dr Grace unfortunately received a severe blow on the finger in stopping a hard return by Wyld, an accident which prevented his taking any further part in the match.

WG was playing again five days later, for MCC against Yorkshire.

Wisden was still sometimes critical of WG's play, as when Middlesex played Gloucestershire at Lord's at the end of May.

Dr W. G. Grace batted splendidly until he had scored 80, but after that he made several bad hits and was thrice missed. His 89 included ten fours, one three and ten twos.

WG also took 12 wickets for 156 runs during the match, but Wisden *made no mention of his bowling.*

Surrey v Gloucestershire
At Kennington Oval, Thursday, Friday, May 31 and June 1, 1883

Gloucestershire 174 (E. M. Grace 71; Barratt 5–69) and 198 (Cave 42; Henderson 6–17);
Surrey 167 (Abel 46; Woof 5–53) and 208-3 (J. M. Read 113*, W. W. Read 79*;
W. G. Grace 2–55).
Surrey won by seven wickets.

When play ceased on the opening day each side had played an innings and were on very even terms. Gloucestershire had first turn at the wickets, and their brilliant start was but weakly followed up. The brothers Grace scored 75 for the first wicket. Surrey, on the other hand, commenced very badly and finished up well... A feature of the first innings of Gloucestershire was the success of the Grace family, and the utter failure of the other batsmen. The brothers Grace and Mr Gilbert scored 155; the other eight members of the team only 16 between them. Dr W. G. Grace scored at a lower rate than usual, but his brother and Mr Gilbert hit freely and well, the former being seen to special advantage. His 71 included nine fours, two three, and four twos, and Mr Gilbert's 51 six fours, two threes and four twos.

Somersetshire v Gloucestershire
At Taunton, Monday, Tuesday, Wednesday, August 13, 14 and 15, 1883

No fewer than 1,047 runs were scored in this match for the loss of 32 wickets at an average of more than 32 per wicket. Of the number Mr Sainsbury made 175, Mr Moberly 163 and Dr W. G. Grace 133. The Gloucestershire captain was also far and away the most successful bowler in the match, as he was credited with 11 wickets at a cost of 154 runs – a fine performance, considering the heavy scoring… Gloucestershire won the match by eight wickets.

Gloucestershire v Lancashire
At Clifton, Monday, Tuesday, Wednesday, August 27, 28 and 29, 1883

Gloucestershire 324 (Cranston 127, W. G. Grace 112; Crossland 4–80) and **81–4** (Pullen 35); **Lancashire 190** (Pilling 46*; Gilbert 3–17) and **213** (Robinson 90; Woof 4–56). Gloucestershire won by six wickets.

The splendid batting of Dr W. G. Grace and Mr Cranston on the opening day enabled Gloucestershire to score a most creditable victory in the last match of the most disastrous season the West countrymen have ever experienced. Mr Grace's 112 was the first three-figure innings scored by him in a first-class contest during two seasons, and Mr Cranston's 127 the highest score he had made in a county match. The two batsmen became partners when three wickets had fallen for 75 and were not separated until they had added 126. Their batting was of the finest description, and Mr Cranston did not give the slightest chance during his two hours and three-quarters stay at the wickets. Mr Grace was missed at slip when he had made 108, but his batting was otherwise absolutely free from fault.

In Wisden*'s list of "The 200s Hit in 1883", Dr E. M. Grace's is the only name to appear twice: 243 for Thornbury v Chepstow; and 207 for Thornbury v Newport, Mon.*

WISDEN 1885

GLOUCESTERSHIRE IN 1884

… A disastrous season was not the result of a total failure in the batting department, which as usual was headed by Dr W. G. Grace, with highest aggregate, and best average – 37–6. The Gloucestershire captain was not quite so successful as in the previous year, for notwithstanding his average was assisted with four not-out innings, it was a couple of points lower than in 1883... Of the other leading batsmen, Dr E. M. Grace, and Messrs Gilbert, Page, and Townsend did not gain quite such good averages as in the previous year.

Woof took 81 wickets, against 50 in 1883, and they were secured at almost exactly the same cost. Mr Gilbert obtained 18, at an average of 19–16, but Dr W. G. Grace, who was credited with 64 in 1883, at an average of 22–7, only secured 40 in 1884, and at the increased cost of 27–27.

In 1884, the Australians toured again, playing three Tests against England. WG played in all three games, without much distinction, but in other games against the tourists, he scored prolifically.

WG played against the Australians for Lord Sheffield's XI (one and 30; and six for 72); for MCC and Ground (see below); twice for Gentlemen of England (21 and 20; and none for 21; and then 107 and 30; and three for 74); for Gloucestershire (see below); and for South of England (24 and 26; and none for 13).

MCC and Ground v The Australians
At Lord's, Thursday, Friday, May 22 and 23, 1884

MCC and Ground 481 (Steel 134, Barnes 105*, W. G. Grace 101; Spofforth 4–98);
Australians 184 (McDonnell 64; C. T. Studd 6–96) and **182** (Murdoch 58*;
W. G. Grace 4–61).
MCC and Ground won by an innings and 115 runs.

Grace's splendid innings of 101 consisted of four fours, four three, eleven twos and 51 singles, and was made while 199 runs were put on... It will be seen that Grace was the most successful bowler in the match, taking seven wickets for 79 runs.

England v Australia
First Test Match, at Old Trafford, Friday, Saturday, July 11 and 12, 1884

England 95 (Shrewsbury 43; Boyle 6–42) and **180–9** (W. G. Grace 31;
Palmer 4–47); **Australia 182** (Midwinter 37; Ulyett 3–41).
Match drawn.

This was the first of three matches arranged to be played between the Australians and the full strength of England. Owing to unfavourable weather the wicket was unfit for cricket on the Thursday, and play was consequently confined to the Friday and Saturday. The result was a draw in favour of the Australians, England being 93 runs on with a wicket to fall in their second innings.

Shrewsbury and Lucas played admirable cricket in both innings. Grace exhibited great skill and judgment in scoring his 31, and O'Brien made runs at a time they were badly wanted. Grace was one hour and a quarter scoring his 31, and Lucas was at the wickets two hours for his 24. The Australians hit with more vigour and confidence than their opponents, and McDonnell, Murdoch and Midwinter contributed capital innings.

Thanks to Steel's 148, England were able to win the second Test at Lord's by an innings and five runs, but WG's contribution of 14 runs, one wicket and one catch went unremarked by Wisden.

Gloucestershire v Australians
At Clifton, Thursday, Friday, Saturday, August 7, 8 and 9, 1884

Gloucestershire 301 (W. G. Grace 116*; Midwinter 4–41) and **230–2** (Brain 108); **Australians 314** (Scott 79; Woof 6–82).
Match drawn.

The heavy scoring in this match caused it to result in a drawn game… Gloucestershire were batting almost the whole of the first day. E. M. Grace and Gilbert scored 78 for the first wicket, both playing admirable cricket, and when the total was 84 for two wickets, W. G. Grace went in, and for the third time in the season scored an innings of over 100 against the Australians. His 116 not out was an innings worthy of his best days. [In the second innings] Grace carried out his bat for 27, and it will be seen that altogether he scored 143 runs in this match without being once dismissed.

The reference to his innings being 'worthy of his best days' perhaps implies that Wisden's *contributors felt that WG's best days were already behind him at 36 years of age.*

England v Australia
Third Test Match, at Kennington Oval, Monday, Tuesday, Wednesday, August 11, 12 and 13, 1884

Australia 551 (Murdoch 211; Lyttelton 4–19); **England 346** (W. W. Read 117; Bonnor 5–33) and **85–2** (Shrewsbury 37).
Match drawn.

The third and last of the three great matches arranged to be played against the full strength of England resulted in a draw, England wanting 120 runs to avert a single-innings defeat, with eight wickets to go down. The fact that three individual scores of over 100 runs each were scored on the first day rendered the match unique in the annals of the game. When stumps were drawn on the first day, the score stood at 363 for two wickets, Murdoch having scored 145, and Scott 101 undefeated, the pair having added 205.

Bannerman was out with the score at 15, and McDonnell at 158, but 205 more runs were added that day without further loss. On the Tuesday Scott was caught at the wicket after adding a single to his overnight score, but Murdoch was not dismissed until he had compiled 211, being the sixth batsman out with the total at 494. The remainder of the innings was alone remarkable for the success which attended Lyttelton's lobs. He went on for the second time when six wickets were down for 532, and took the last four wickets in eight overs for only eight runs.

All 11 England players bowled during Australia's innings (declarations were not allowed at this time), and when Lyttelton, the wicketkeeper, went on to bowl, WG took his place behind the stumps. His old Gloucestershire friend and sometime England team-mate Billy Midwinter, was out "c Grace b Lyttelton 30", caught off the first ball of WG's wicketkeeping stint. This is yet another record for the Champion – nobody else has ever taken a catch or made a stumping or run-out from his very first ball as a Test wicketkeeper.

WISDEN 1886

GLOUCESTERSHIRE IN 1885

Gloucestershire had a far more successful season than in either of the three preceding years, notwithstanding the fact that Dr E. M. Grace was an absentee from the county ranks during the entire season...

Dr W. G. Grace was in splendid form in 1885, and his batting was the feature of the Gloucestershire season. He scored 1034 runs for Gloucestershire, and with innings of 221 not out, 69 and 54 against Middlesex, 132, 54 and 34 against Yorkshire, 104, 55, and 19 not out against Surrey, and 50, 49 and 39 against Lancashire, gained the very fine average of 43–2 – a better record than for several years previously. Mr Townsend, too, had not been seen to such advantage for several seasons, and secured second place in the batting list with an average of 25–2, being closely followed by Mr W. R. Gilbert, with an average of 24–9 and second highest aggregate. Mr Gilbert's best innings were his 102 against Yorkshire and 95 and 51 against Sussex...

Dr W. G. Grace took 63 wickets at an average of 21–5, and therefore was more successful than in 1884.

But it was not only for Gloucestershire that WG excelled in 1885:

MCC and Ground v Nottinghamshire
At Lord's, Thursday, Friday, May 28 and 29, 1885

Nottinghamshire 96 (Daft 23; W. G. Grace 7–40) and 44 (Scotton 12;
W. G. Grace 9–20); **MCC and Ground 199** (W. G. Grace 63; Flowers 4–35).
MCC and Ground won by an innings and 59 runs.

To the brilliant all-round cricket played by Dr W. G. Grace in this match the crushing defeat of the powerful Notts Eleven by an innings and 59 runs was mainly due...

Notts had first innings, and going in at five minutes after noon, were all out half an hour after luncheon for 96... On the whole the batting was feeble... When the MCC went in to bat Selby took Shrewsbury's place at point, but being unused to the position made several mistakes, for which Notts had to pay dearly. Messrs Grace and Russell put on 54 runs for the first wicket, but at starting the Gloucestershire captain did not seem quite at home and gave three difficult chances. Afterwards, however, he played in his old form, although he scored rather more slowly than usual. The Notts total was passed for the loss of two wickets. Dr Grace, after being in for two hours and a quarter for 61 [*sic*] out of 109, was bowled ...

There was a good deal of rain overnight, and the hot sun on Friday morning rendered the wicket slow and treacherous. The bowlers therefore had matters all their own way... Notts began their second innings at ten minutes to one, Dr Grace bowling from the Pavilion wicket, where Flowers had met with so much success. Scotton was in an hour and 20 minutes for 12, and Mr Daft played very steadily and well for ten, not out, but the other batsmen only offered the feeblest resistance to the bowling of Dr Grace, and in two hours the innings closed for 44, and the MCC gained an easy victory. In scoring 63 and taking 16 wickets at a cost of only 60 runs in such a match, Dr Grace achieved one of the greatest successes attached to his name.

By this time, WG was of course a huge boost to the gate of any game he played in, as Wisden *acknowledged in a note on the North v South match at Manchester in July:*

Dr W. G. Grace's presence gave the fixture an importance and attraction unfortunately lacking in the North and South contest for Richard Humphrey's benefit a fortnight previously at The Oval.

Gentlemen v Players
At Scarborough, Thursday, Friday, Saturday, September 3, 4 and 5, 1885

Gentlemen 263 (W. G. Grace 174; Attewell 5–42); **Players 59** (Ulyett 14;
Christopherson 7–24) and **179** (Gunn 82; Evans 5–20).
Gentlemen won by an innings and 25 runs.

The third and last of the three Gentlemen v Players matches of 1885 resulted in a crushing defeat for the Players…. the merit of the splendid victory resting almost exclusively with three men – with Dr W. G. Grace, for his magnificent batting, and with Messrs Christopherson and Evans for their fine bowling… The Gentlemen, in batting first, had undoubtedly the best of a wicket which was slow and treacherous throughout, but which played more falsely on the second day owing to the action of a hot sun. On the Thursday, owing mainly to the remarkable batting of Dr Grace, 234 runs were scored for the loss of eight wickets; on the Friday 16 wickets fell for 192 runs; and on the Saturday six batsmen were dismissed for 75 runs. Dr Grace's brilliant batting was, of course, the feature of the first day's play. Out of 230 runs scored from the bat, he made the large proportion of 163, and it is worthy of note that at the conclusion of this match, Dr Grace had played consecutive innings of 104, 19 not out, 221 not out, 68, and 174, or an aggregate of 586, and wonderful average of 195–1.

… On the Friday… Ulyett and Peate took up the bowling, but the former soon gave way to Attewell, from whose seventh ball Mr Grace was caught at slip, the total being 247. Mr Grace had been batting only three hours and 55 minutes, and considering the treacherous state of the wicket the whole time he was in, the performance was one of the finest ever credited to a batsman, and the enthusiastic reception accorded to him on his retirement was therefore thoroughly merited.

WISDEN 1887

The season of 1886 was not one of Grace's best.

Mr W. G. Grace, although he batted grandly in some of the big matches against the Australians, fell far below his usual form in purely county matches, his last eight innings for Gloucestershire producing an aggregate of only 105 runs…

The first thing that stands out prominently is the falling-off in Mr W. G. Grace, who scored only 560 runs, with an average of 28, as against an aggregate of 960 in 1885, at an average of 45.15… Mr W. G. Grace took exactly the same number of wickets in county matches as in the season of 1885, but at a cost of one run more each… Good fielding made up to some extent for indifferent bowling, the brothers Grace at point, or close in elsewhere... being especially brilliant.

All the same, overall WG ended up fifth in the season's batting averages, with 1,846 runs – the highest aggregate of the season at an average of 35.26. He was also one of only five bowlers to take 100 wickets, Wisden *crediting him with 122 at an average of 19.12.*

Ten of those wickets were taken in one innings.

Oxford University v MCC and Ground
In the Parks at Oxford, Monday, Tuesday, June 21 and 22, 1886

Oxford University 142 (Page 49; Wright 4–31) and **90** (Page 26; W. G. Grace 10–49);
MCC and Ground 260 (W. G. Grace 104; Wreford-Brown 4–42).
MCC and Ground won by an innings and 28 runs.

This, the last home match of the Oxford season, was rendered remarkable by the extraordinary performance of Mr W. G. Grace, who scored an innings of 104, and took the whole of the ten Oxford wickets, this being the only instance in first-class cricket in 1886 of all ten wickets being taken by the same bowler. The match was robbed of a great deal of importance from the fact that a large number of the Oxford eleven were engaged in the schools and unable to appear for the team, and the weakness of the home team will readily be seen when it is noted that there were only five men taking part in the match who subsequently appeared against Cambridge... In their second innings the Oxonians failed completely before the bowling of Mr Grace.

Oxford University

Mr. J. H. Brain c Nepean b Wright	19	c Hine-Haycock b Grace	15
Mr. P. Coles b Wright	14	c Attewell b Grace	1
Mr. A. K. Watson c Grace b Attewell	9	b Grace	0
Mr. H. V. Page b Attewell	49	st Kemp b Grace	26
Mr. W. Rashleigh b Wright	2	b Grace	19
Mr. C. Wreford-Brown c Kemp b Grace	4	c Attewell b Grace	13
Mr. E. H. F. Bradby c Hine-Haycock b Grace	4	b Grace	0
Mr. E. H. Buckland b Titchmarsh	20	b Grace	4
Mr. A. R. Cobb b Wright	6	c de Paravicini b Grace	0
Mr. H. W. Forster c Grace b Attewell	8	not out	0
Mr. J. H. Ware not out	4	lbw b Grace	10
B 2, l-b 1	3	L-b 2	2
	142		**90**

Mr. Grace 32–11–60–2; Wright 59–42–31–4; Attewell 38.1–22–39–3; Titchmarsh 11–7–9–1.
Second innings—Mr. Grace 36.2–17–49–10; Wright 25–12–28–0; Attewell 11–7–11–0.

MCC and Ground

Mr. W. G. Grace lbw b Page 104	W. Wright c Wreford-Brown b Buckland ... 9
Mr. E. J. C. Studd c Wreford-Brown b Forster ... 36	W. Attewell c Buckland b Wreford-Brown .. 22
Mr. C. Booth c Buckland b Wreford-Brown .. 14	Lord George Scott not out 25
Mr. T. R. Hine-Haycock c Forster	Mr. E. A. Nepean c and b Buckland 6
b Wreford-Brown 0	V. A. Titchmarsh st Cobb b Forster 10
Mr. P. J. de Paravicini c Coles	
b Wreford-Brown 9	B 8, l-b 2 10
Mr. M. C. Kemp c and b Forster 15	260

Mr. Buckland 44–23–55–2; Mr. Forster 32.3–12–65–3; Mr. Ware 14–2–43–0;
Mr. Page 15–1–45–1; Mr. Wreford-Brown 23–8–42–4.

MCC and Ground won by an innings and 28 runs.

WG remains a century after his death one of only two men ever to take all ten wickets in an innings and score a century in the same match, the other being his near-contemporary V. E. Walker, who achieved the feat for England against Surrey in 1859. E. M. Grace, for MCC v Gentlemen of Kent in a 12-a-side match at Canterbury in 1862, scored 192 not out and took five for 77 and ten for 69.

In May that year, WG played against a new opponent:

MCC and Ground v Parsees
At Lord's, Thursday, Friday, May 27 and 28, 1886

MCC and Ground 313 (Lindsay 74; Major 5–91); **Parsees 23** (Grace 7–18) and **66**
(Morinas 28*; Walker 5–28).
MCC and Ground won by an innings and 224 runs.

For this match the Marylebone Club put an altogether unnecessarily strong team into the field to oppose the Parsees, and there was really no serious interest in the game. From the first it was seen that the Parsees were utterly overmatched, and had not the smallest chance of success. Their notions of bowling and fielding were at that time of the most elementary description. It should be stated, however, that Mr W. G. Grace played at the request of the Parsees, who were anxious to have the champion on the opposing side once during their tour... Mr W. G. Grace's 65 included two fours, ten threes, one two and 25 singles...

Although the Parsees had done so badly in bowling and fielding, the spectators were hardly prepared for the poor batting display that was given. Between 20 minutes to three and ten minutes to six the Parsees were twice got rid of for a gross total of 89 runs. In the first innings they could do nothing at all with the bowling of Messrs Grace and Robertson and in the second innings they did little better against Mr Walker's lobs and Mr Grace.

In 1886, another Australian team toured England, but, as Wisden *made clear,*

The fifth tour of Australian cricketers in England was emphatically a failure, whether we regard it as an event of itself, or compare it with the previous visits to this country of the picked teams of the Australian colonies.

Rumours of bloodstains in railway carriages used by the tourists, and other clear signs of an unhappy touring party, were largely overlooked by Wisden, *who did nevertheless comment:*

It would not be possible to deal exhaustively with the various arguments that have been put forward to account for the non-success of the recent trip. The leading points have been briefly described above, and before commencing to describe the matches in their chronological order, we should say that it is emphatically a satisfactory and pleasant thing for English cricketers and lovers of the game in England, that our strength should have been so happily proved, and our superiority so clearly demonstrated.

Wisden *also noted in passing the fact that WG was no longer necessarily the Champion, even though*

… we still had in Mr Grace and Mr Read batsmen who were equal to the greatest emergencies.

Giffen was emphatically the success of the tour, and the fact that he came out first in both batting and bowling speaks volumes for his excellence. Indeed it would be impossible at the present day to name his superior as an all-round cricketer.

WG did little in the first two Tests, both of which England won, but came into his own in the Third. Just a week after hitting a century for Gloucestershire against the tourists, he repeated the dose at The Oval.

England v Australia
Third Test Match, at The Oval, Thursday, Friday, Saturday,
August 12, 13 and 14, 1886

England 434 (W. G. Grace 170; Spofforth 4–65); **Australia 68** (Lohmann 7–36)
and **149** (Giffen 47; Lohmann 5–68).
England won by an innings and 217 runs.

For the second time the Englishmen won the toss, and once more they took full advantage of their opportunity. Curiously enough the Australians were engaged for the whole day in getting down two wickets, just as they had been a fortnight before in the return match against Surrey. On the present occasion, however, the batting was not of such a high quality. Although Mr W. G. Grace made the highest innings he had ever scored against Australian bowling, it was pretty generally admitted that his cricket was more faulty than usual. He gave an easy chance to Scott at short slip when he had made six, when his score was 23 he hit a ball very hard back to Giffen, which was a possible chance to that bowler's left hand; when he had scored 60 he might perhaps have been caught in the long field, had Bruce started earlier for the ball, and when his total was 93 McIlwraith had a difficult one-handed chance of catching him at slip. Moreover, just before getting out, when his total was 169 he hit a ball straight back to Garrett, who failed to hold it. Still, these blemishes notwithstanding, the innings was a very fine one. He made the enormous proportion of 170 out of 216 during his stay, which lasted altogether four hours and a half, and his figures were 22 fours, four threes, 17 twos and 36 singles. In an hour and 52 minutes before luncheon Mr Grace made 40 runs, and consequently in two hours and 38 minutes afterwards he made 130.

This marked difference in the rate of scoring was certainly accounted for to a large extent by the state of the wicket, which was by no means perfect up to the interval, but which improved steadily as the afternoon wore on. Scotton batted with extraordinary patience even for him, and contented himself by keeping up his wicket while Mr Grace hit. The two batsmen put on 170 runs before they were parted, this being the largest number ever scored for the first wicket against an Australian team in England. Scotton's 34 – an innings of immense value to his side – occupied no less a time than three hours and three quarters, and at one period the famous Notts left-hander was in an hour and seven minutes without making a single run.

WISDEN 1888

GLOUCESTERSHIRE IN 1887

Gloucestershire cricket in 1887 may be summed up in a phrase – Mr W. G. Grace had a great personal triumph, but the county failed… Mr W. G. Grace, as we have said, enjoyed a personal triumph, and the records of first-class cricket might be searched in vain for another instance of a batsman doing such big things and yet finding his county rewarded by only one win in 14 matches. Mr Grace scored 113 against Middlesex at Lord's, 92 and not out 183 against Yorkshire at Gloucester, 97 against Yorkshire at Dewsbury, 113 not out against Notts at Clifton, and 101 and not out 103 against Kent at Clifton – a splendid series of scores indeed. The Kent match formed a worthy climax to the best season Mr Grace had had since 1876, for after an interval of 19 years he repeated his Canterbury feat of scoring two hundreds in one game. No one else in modern days has done this in a first-class match, and the fact of his having twice accomplished a performance so remarkable will stand out among the leading incidents of Mr Grace's career... It was not alone as a batsman that our great cricketer did good work in 1887 for his county. As will be seen from the average tables, he took 64 wickets at a cost of just under 22 runs each, and badly as this record may compare with what he has done as a bowler in some previous years, it was very good for a man who scored 1,405 runs with an average of 63.19 per innings.

... Mr E. M. Grace, who has now been playing longer in first-class matches than any other cricketer now before the public – he was the greatest run-getter in England before Alfred Shaw and Emmett were heard of – worked very hard for the side, and made several good scores. Advancing years do not make him more orthodox than he was in his youth, and he still plays his own game – a remarkable game it is true, but not one that can be pointed to as a model for the beginner.

WG scored almost three times as many runs as the next man (1,405 to his brother's 552) at an average almost three times as good as any of his team-mates (63.19 to Newnham's 22.4). He took twice as many wickets as anybody else (64 to 29 by Roberts).

In all matches in 1887, Grace scored 2,062 runs at an average of 54.10, putting him first in the country in aggregate but second to Arthur Shrewsbury's average of 78.15. He took 97 wickets at an average of 21.41, the fifth-highest total of wickets by any bowler that year.

Typical of WG's season was the match against Yorkshire, for many seasons a side against whom WG tended to excel, even by his own standards:

Gloucestershire v Yorkshire
At Gloucester, Thursday, Friday, Saturday, June 30, July 1 and 2, 1887

Gloucestershire 369 (W. G. Grace 92; Emmett 3–55) and **338** (W. G. Grace 183*; Emmett 3–61); **Yorkshire 300** (Ulyett 104; E. M. Grace 7–120).
Match drawn.

The weather was delightfully fine on the Thursday, when the brothers went in for Gloucestershire, Mr W. G. Grace having fortunately won the toss on the splendid wicket. The pair put on 48 runs for the first wicket, and then Mr Troup joined Mr W. G. Grace, the total being carried to 149 before they were parted. Mr Grace, who had been in for two hours and 40 minutes, had put together a faultless innings of 92, in which were 12 fours, two threes and five twos...

[When Yorkshire had made 173 for one] the innings promised to be a very long one, but a complete change came over it, and wickets fell so rapidly that nine were down for 286, when four runs were still wanted to avert the "follow-on". This, however, was saved by the last two men, and the total reached 300... Mr E. M. Grace took seven wickets with his lobs...

On Saturday the play before luncheon did not give promise of anything sensational, for at the interval seven wickets had fallen for 138 runs, Mr W. G. Grace being not out for an admirable 64. Soon after resuming another wicket fell, and, eight being down for 146, it seemed just possible that Gloucestershire might lose, but then Mr Newnham joined his captain, and the pair completely mastered the bowling. Both hit with great brilliancy, Mr Grace, after completing his hundred, showing astonishing power. Before the separation came, no fewer than 143 runs were added, the score having been nearly doubled in an hour and 50 minutes. Mr Newnham was out for a capital 56, in which were six fours, three threes and three twos. Mr Griffiths, the last batsman, stayed some time while Mr Grace continued his grand hitting, but he was at length got rid of, and the innings closed at 5.35 for 338... Mr Grace's not-out innings of 183 was a magnificent display without a blemish. He was batting five hours and 25 minutes, his hits being 21 fours, four three, 19 twos and 49 singles.

Against Nottinghamshire a month later, Gloucestershire lost by an innings, but WG again carried his bat through the second innings:

Gloucestershire v Nottinghamshire
At Clifton, Monday, Tuesday, Wednesday August 8, 9 and 10, 1887

Nottinghamshire 423 (Shrewsbury 119*; Woof 2–45); **Gloucestershire 172**
(E. M. Grace 42; Richardson 5–43) and **186** (W. G. Grace 113*; Barnes 5–31).
Nottinghamshire won by an innings and 65 runs.

The batting in the first innings of Gloucestershire presented few features of interest, and though the brothers Grace put on 52 runs for the first wicket, the whole side were out for 172... Going in a second time against a majority of 251, Gloucestershire before the close of play scored 43 for the loss of two wickets. Mr W. G. Grace was not out 32.

Not very much interest remained in Wednesday's play, as scarcely a doubt could be felt as to the ultimate success of Notts. Mr W. G. Grace certainly played a fine, though not a faultless, innings of 113 not out, but even his batting could not save his side from a crushing defeat. Except Mr Grace, no man on the Gloucestershire side scored more than 30.

The last match of the season proved to be a personal, if not a team, triumph:

Gloucestershire v Kent
At Clifton, Thursday, Friday, Saturday, August 25, 26 and 27, 1887

Gloucestershire 277 (W. G. Grace 101; Wootton 4–80) and **182–2** (W. G. Grace 103*);
Kent 317 (Rashleigh 108; Peake 5–120).
Match drawn.

This was the first time a Kent team had ever played on the Clifton College ground. Mr W. G. Grace, after winning the toss, went in first with his brother, and the pair made so good a start that 127 runs were scored before the elder batsman was got rid of. Mr E. M. Grace, who had given a ridiculously easy chance when 32, made 70 in his usual unorthodox fashion… After he left, Mr W. G. Grace could find no one to stop with him, and he himself was run out, after a superb display, from the next ball after completing his hundred. His innings was nearly faultless, and lasted two hours and 55 minutes…

Saturday's cricket was hardly expected to prove interesting as there was little probability of the game reaching a definite conclusion, but the weather was fortunately fine again and the large company present witnessed another grand batting performance by the champion… When Gloucestershire went in a second time, two hours and 20 minutes remained for cricket and the Graces once more made a good start. After Mr E. M. Grace left, Mr Pullen came in and during his partnership with Mr W. G. Grace, it began to look as though the latter had a chance of making his second hundred in the match. When Mr Pullen got out, about a quarter of an hour before time, Mr Grace still wanted 18 runs, but, hitting whenever the opportunity served, he managed to complete the hundred with a three to square leg from the last ball but one of the day. He was most enthusiastically cheered at the close for a performance that, as we have said, has not been equalled in modern days in first-class matches, except by himself. His second innings was absolutely faultless, and his figures included eleven fours, six threes and 11 twos. It was a performance in every way worthy of the great cricketer's reputation, and worthily wound up what proved to be his best season since 1876.

WISDEN 1889

The 1889 Wisden featured the first appearance of what was to become the famous Five Cricketers of the Year, and it also featured articles about cricket in general, rather than mere match reports, for the first time.

"A Few Jottings," by Robert Thoms, perhaps the most famous umpire of his day, looked at the bowling of the time:

But this dissertation leads me on to recount that it is improvement in the grounds that has to a great extent made the fast bowler more harmless; and batsmen in due course came along, of whom the marvellous little Doctor (E. M. Grace) was the pioneer, who upset all the stereotyped fast-footed play by going to the ball, when the pitch suited, and cracking it all over the shop. Not that I for a moment put less value on the fast bowler in these days of good wickets; for I well know he is still the most effective; but length and pace, without spin, break-back, or rearing-up qualities, don't count for much on modern wickets.

In 1888, WG reached the age of 40. He saved his best performance of the summer, as usual, for Yorkshire.

GLOUCESTERSHIRE IN 1888

Whereas in 1887 Mr W. G. Grace's great batting triumph was almost the only creditable feature of Gloucestershire cricket, the Western county in 1888 made a distinct advance at all points, despite the fact that Mr Grace's record fell far below that which he achieved in the previous season. The Gloucestershire captain played three big innings, but otherwise his batting was in no way sensational, yet from eighth place in 1887 the county rose to the fourth position last summer, passing Lancashire, Notts, Middlesex and Sussex...

As was only to be expected in so terribly wet a season, Mr W. G. Grace failed to maintain his wonderful figures of 1887, his aggregate falling from 1,405 to 902, and his average from 63 to 39, but these figures, both in aggregate and average, were really superior to those of any other batsmen. Three times he played an innings of three figures, scoring 215 against Sussex at Brighton, and 148 and 153 in the return match with Yorkshire at Clifton. This latter feat – two hundreds in the one match – Mr Grace alone of contemporary batsmen can claim to have achieved in a first-class fixture, and he accomplished it in the last county match he took part in in 1887, making 101 and 103 not out against Kent at Clifton. Moreover, Mr Grace attained a similar honour just 20 years ago at Canterbury, where he made 130 and 102 not out. The fact of the great batsman having thrice done what no one else has accomplished since W. Lambert's famous scores for Surrey against Epsom in 1817, will be some proof, were any needed, of Mr Grace's absolute supremacy over all the cricketers who have ever lived...

The veteran of the team, Mr E. M. Grace, who has now been before the public for more than a quarter of a century, played one or two of his characteristic innings, and, as the table of averages will tell, was of more use as a batsman than some of the younger members of the county team. His fielding, too, at point, if not showing the marvellous dexterity which used to characterise his efforts in that position, was still very smart and accurate...

Mr W. G. Grace was not so hard worked as a bowler as usual, but he took 47 wickets at a cost of less than 21 runs each.

Sussex v Gloucestershire
At Brighton, Monday, Tuesday, Wednesday, May 21, 22 and 23, 1888

Gloucestershire 428 (W. G. Grace 215; Humphreys 3–71) and 174 (Radcliffe 68; C. A. Smith 5–49); **Sussex** 354 (Hide 130; Newnham 5–77) and 161–4 (Newham 81*; Radcliffe 3–52).
Match drawn.

Big scoring was certainly pretty frequent about this time in May, but among the seventies, eighties and nineties recorded contemporaneously with the contest we are about to describe, the innings of Mr Grace stood out prominently as a thing of itself… Gloucestershire won the toss, and at the end of the first day Mr Grace was 188 not out… and except for one chance to Tester at mid-off when he had made 26, his batting was altogether free from fault. The Gloucestershire score was 361 for six wickets, and nine of the Sussex bowlers had been tried… On the second day, Gloucestershire continued their hitting until the score was 428. Mr Grace was ninth out for 215, hitting his wicket in playing at a lob. The champion was in for very nearly seven hours, and only gave the one chance we have mentioned. He hit 20 fours, three threes, 26 twos and 74 singles, and his innings of 215 was the largest score in first-class county matches in 1888.

Gloucestershire v Yorkshire
At Clifton, Thursday, Friday, Saturday, August 16, 17 and 18, 1888

Gloucestershire **248** (W. G. Grace 148; Preston 7–82) and **316** (W. G. Grace 153; Preston 4–99); **Yorkshire 461** (Hall 129*; Woof 5–87) and **28–0**.
Match drawn.

This was one of the heaviest scoring matches of the season, 1,053 runs being obtained in the course of three days for the loss of only 29 wickets. Apart from the heavy scoring, it was rendered remarkable by the wonderful achievement on the part of Mr W. G. Grace, who, for the third time in his career, succeeded in making over 100 runs in each innings. The ground was in exceptionally good order, but that the feat also was exceptional is fully proved by the fact that no other cricketer within the last 50 years has ever succeeded in accomplishing it in a first-class match… While no one but Mr Grace has ever scored so well in a big match, the feat has been accomplished in minor engagements by Mr W. Townshend, Mr D. G. Spiro and Mr F. W. Maude. To return to the match, we may say that Gloucestershire, after winning the toss made a wretched start, losing Mr E. M. Grace, Mr Pullen, Mr Champain (the Cheltenham captain) and Painter for 26 runs, Peel and Preston taking two wickets each. At this point Mr Radcliffe came in and rendered his captain such great assistance that 107 runs were put on for the fifth wicket; while after Mr Radcliffe's departure Mr W. G. Grace and Mr Brain took the score from 133 to 221… It may be of interest to state that Mr Grace scored 50 out of 75, and reached his hundred when the total was 147. He was sixth out with the total at 221, having played an absolutely faultless innings of 148, which lasted three hours and a half, and was made up by 16 fours, 11 threes, eight twos and 35 singles. After Mr Grace's dismissal, the innings was quickly finished off…

With arrears of 213 to clear off, Gloucestershire commenced their second innings, and before Mr Grace left the score stood at 253. The Gloucestershire captain gave a chance at the wicket when he had only made 12, but in other respects his batting was masterly, and included in his splendid innings of 153, which lasted three hours and ten minutes, were 22 fours, five threes, 12 twos and 26 singles. Mr Pullen and Mr Radcliffe were fairly successful, but of course Mr Grace's batting dwarfed everything else. But for his wonderful performance Gloucestershire would undoubtedly have been beaten.

WG did not achieve much against the visiting Australians in the Tests, but for the Gentlemen of England during the sunny month of May, he excelled:

Australians v Gentlemen of England
At Lord's, Monday, Tuesday, May 28 and 29, 1888

Australians 179 (Jones 61; C. A. Smith 4–45) and 213–1 (Bonnor 119);
Gentlemen of England 490 (W. G. Grace 165; Turner 6–161).
Match drawn.

The check received at Manchester [where Lancashire had won by 23 runs] was followed up by some superb hitting by the Gentlemen, and for the first time Turner and Ferris were very expensive. McDonnell and Jones put on 73 runs between them, but the whole side were out early in the afternoon, and then Grace and Shuter gave one of the grandest exhibitions of batting seen throughout the summer. The Surrey captain was out first at 158. After completing his hundred the champion hit with astonishing freedom, and made his last 50 in about half an hour. The Gentlemen had made 236 with only one man out when time was called. On the Tuesday Grace was soon out for 165 consisting of 18 fours, a five (two for an overthrow), three threes, 19 twos and 41 singles.

WG top-scored in the Lord's Test – just – but it did England no good:

England v Australia
First Test Match, at Lord's, Monday, Tuesday July 16 and 17, 1888

Australia 116 (McDonnell 22, Blackham 22; Peel 4–36) and 60 (Ferris 20*; Peel 4–14);
England 53 (Briggs 17; Turner 5–27) and 62 (W. G. Grace 24; Ferris 5–26).
Australia won by 61 runs.

The Australians left out Lyons and Boyle, and McDonnell, having won the toss, went in with Bannerman to commence a match about which everyone's nerves were in a high state of tension, and at a time when it is not too much to say that all concerned, from batsmen, bowlers, and umpires down to the merest spectators, felt the importance of the issue, and how much was at stake. We ought, however, to say that to the best of our knowledge there was little or no betting of any consequence, and certainly, with all the eagerness and keenness of feeling, there was no bitterness or acrimony on either side.

The game has been often described, and it is not our intention to follow the play in detail. It was one in which the Australians, starting with a distinctly inferior team, played with great courage and spirit, and achieved a performance for which they were fully entitled and for which they received a large amount of credit. The Australians played quite the right game, hitting out pluckily, and never attempting to show correct cricket. The Englishmen started well enough, getting rid of Bannerman and Trott for three runs, but then Bonnor and McDonnell were both missed. The total was only 82 when the ninth wicket fell, and, though this score was not a bad one under the conditions, it was not good enough to look like winning. Ferris, the last man, joined Edwards, who should have been easily run out, and then this pair, by some invaluable and fearless hitting, put on 30 runs before they were separated. The Englishmen went in in a bad light, and lost Abel, Barnes and Lohmann for 18 before stumps were drawn for the day.

On Tuesday morning play began at half-past 11, and W. G. Grace did not add to the ten he had made overnight. Wicket after wicket fell until eight men were out for 37, and it looked quite possible that England would have to follow on. Briggs and Peel averted this disaster, but the whole side were out before half-past 12 for 53, or 63 to the bad. The English bowling and fielding during the second innings of Australia were superb, and the ground was altogether against batsmen, so that it was no wonder the Australians were out for 60. Indeed, but for Ferris's capital hitting the total would not nearly have reached that number. But it was clear England was at a great disadvantage, and that the 124 wanted to win would be more than could be made. Mr Grace began really well, and 29 runs were made before the first wicket fell. At 34, however, the champion was out, and from that time Turner and Ferris carried everything before them. The Australians played a winning game with tremendous energy and unfailing skill, and at 25 minutes past four in the afternoon they were successful with 61 runs to spare… So ended a game that will never be forgotten in cricket history, and one which practically ensured the fame of the Australian team.

WG also top-scored in the Third Test, and this time England won. What's more, his performance as captain was favourably commented upon, a rare occurrence in Wisden:

England v Australia
Third Test Match, at Manchester, Thursday, Friday, August 30 and 31, 1888

England 172 (W. G. Grace 38; Turner 5–86); **Australia 81** (Lyons 22; Peel 7–31) and **70** (Lyons 32; Peel 4–37).
England won by an innings and 21 runs.

There had been a great deal of rain just before the contest, and the ground was very soft when play commenced, so that when the Englishmen for the first time in the three matches, won the toss, they obtained a great advantage. It would perhaps be going a little beyond the truth to say that the advantage was so great as it had been at Lord's, but nevertheless there can be no doubt that the first innings gave the side that took it, an immense chance of victory.

The ground could scarcely get better, while it was almost sure to be exceedingly difficult as it dried. This is what really happened, and, after the Englishmen had made a good score under the existing conditions, the Australians were helpless against Peel, with Lohmann and Briggs to help him. Turner at once began to do wonders, as he bowled Abel before a run had been scored, and clean bowled Ulyett with the first ball he had at him. Walter Read and W. G. Grace then hit freely until at 58 the Surrey man was out to a good ball. After this nearly everybody made runs, the champion's 38 being the highest, and the best innings in the match.

Mr Grace was out to a wonderful catch at long-on; Bonnor with the sun in his eyes could not judge the ball properly, but got to it just on the boundary, and made the catch with his right hand high up in the air. Briggs and Pilling, getting together when nine wickets were down at 136, put on 36 runs for the last wicket, and took the total to 172. The finish of the first day's play saw the Australian score at 32 for two wickets, McDonnell and Bannerman being out.

On the Friday play started at a quarter past 11, and at five minutes to two the game was over... It will be seen that Peel's bowling was again very successful, but this time Lohmann and Briggs had a considerable share in taking the wickets. However, Peel's performance in the match – 11 for 68 – was altogether admirable. The Australians undoubtedly had the worst of the luck, but England, brilliantly led by W. G. Grace, played a grand game. Not only was their batting strong and good throughout, but their bowling, wicketkeeping, and fielding would have done immense credit to any team. Notwithstanding the threatening weather on the opening day, 8,080 spectators paid admission at the gates, while on Friday there was a good crowd present in the morning, and it is not too much to say that several thousands more were prepared to go up to the ground in the afternoon from Manchester and the surrounding towns, where the news of the collapse of the Colonial batting created a great deal of excitement. This result gave England the "rubber", and was received with extreme satisfaction throughout the country.

Wisden's table of "English Batting In Representative Matches" against the Australians shows WG on top, thanks largely to his 165 for the Gentlemen of England. He hit the most runs (342) at the highest average (31.1) and made the highest score (165) against the tourists. He also hit the most runs (355) and made the highest score of the season (95) for MCC, but he had only the third-highest average (29.7). Over the season, he scored more runs (1,886) than any other player, *but had to take second place in the averages (36.1 to 32.3) to Walter Read, who hit 338 for Surrey against Oxford University that summer.*

WISDEN 1890

For the 1890 edition, Wisden chose to spotlight "Nine Great Batsmen Of The Year", a selection which, remarkably, left out WG. The comparisons with him were still made, though:

ARTHUR SHREWSBURY

Just before he went to the Colonies his health was so delicate as to cause considerable anxiety, but a winter in the warmer climate of Australia did wonders for him; and his batting during the last few years, as all cricket readers are well aware, has been some of the most remarkable in the history of the game. Indeed, on performances he can claim superiority over all English batsman save and except Mr W. G. Grace. In the season of 1887 his batting average in first-class matches was 78, which, curiously enough, just tied the highest average that Mr Grace had ever obtained. Certainly no batsman has ever equalled Shrewsbury in mastering the difficulties of slow wickets, and his supremacy in this direction is freely admitted by all cricketers.

The 1890 edition also gave more prominence to the section which would become the bedrock of Wisden's reputation for accuracy – the Records. W. G. Grace dominated. The first four paragraphs read as follows:

SOME CRICKET RECORDS

Mr W. G. Grace scored 344 for the MCC v Kent at Canterbury in August 1876, this being the highest individual score ever made in a first-class match.

The next-highest individual score in first-class matches is 338 by Mr W. W. Read, for Surrey against Oxford University at Kennington Oval in June 1888, and the only others of over 300 in first-class matches are 321, by Mr W. L. Murdoch, for New South Wales against Victoria at Sydney in February 1882, and 318 not out by Mr W. G. Grace, for Gloucestershire v Yorkshire at Cheltenham in August 1876. This last is the highest innings in a first-class county match.

Mr A. E. Stoddart made 485 for the Hampstead Club against the Stoics in August 1886, this being the highest score obtained in any match.

Mr W. G. Grace made 400 not out for the United South Of England Eleven v Twenty-Two of Grimsby at Grimsby in July 1876, this being the highest score ever obtained against odds.

Further down the page there is a reference to another of his records:

Mr W. G. Grace is the only batsman of modern days who has made two separate hundreds in a first-class match, but he has performed this most exceptional feat three times during his career.

And again:

Mr W. G. Grace and Mr B. B. Cooper, for the Gentlemen of the South v the Players of the South at Kennington Oval, in 1869, scored 283 for the first wicket, Mr Grace making 180 and Mr Cooper 101. This performance has never been quite equalled in a first-class match, but in June 1887, for England against the MCC at Lord's, Shrewsbury and Mr Stoddart scored 266 together for the first wicket, Shrewsbury making 152 and his partner 151. Mr K. J. Key and Mr Rashleigh scored 243 for the first wicket for Oxford v Cambridge at Lord's, in 1886; Mr W. G. Grace and Mr T. G. Matthews 238 for Gloucestershire v Yorkshire at Sheffield in 1872; and Mr W. G. Grace and Abel 226 for South v North at Scarborough in September 1889.

The only bowling record included is the feat of taking all ten wickets in an innings:

... some notable instances being the late John Wisden in a North v South match at Lord's in 1850;... Mr E. M. Grace for MCC v Gentlemen of Kent at Canterbury in 1862;... Mr W. G. Grace for the MCC against Oxford University at Oxford in 1886.

GLOUCESTERSHIRE IN 1889

[Of] Gloucestershire's three successes, it is not a little curious that one of the victories should have been scored over Lancashire, who divided the honours of the season with Notts and Surrey. This very welcome win was gained in a small-scoring match at Liverpool, when Gloucestershire won by three wickets – a result mainly due to the coolness and nerve of the veteran, Mr E. M. Grace, who worthily maintained his reputation of being one of the best of batsmen at the pinch of a game...

Though he did not have quite so good a season as in 1888, Mr W. G. Grace, as he has done for so many years, came out a long way ahead of his colleagues. He scored 884 runs – over 200 more than Mr Cranston – and he had the really splendid average of just under 37. Twice he made over a hundred – 127 not out and 101, both against Middlesex – but perhaps his best innings was played against Sussex at Bristol, when on a really bad wicket he scored 84 without giving a single chance.

Increasing years are telling upon Mr E. M. Grace, but the veteran fairly won – as we have said above – the return match with Lancashire... As has been the case for years, Gloucestershire's weakness was in bowling. Woof did extremely well, and under the circumstances his record of 65 wickets at a cost of about 16½ runs each does him great credit. Roberts got through a lot of hard work, but he, like Mr Townsend, Mr W. G. Grace and Mr Radcliffe, proved expensive.

E. M. Grace scored only 183 runs for Gloucestershire in 1889, at an average of 10.3, but headed the bowling averages with ten wickets at 15.8 with his lobs. W. G. Grace took 32 wickets at 25.24, although he also took eight for 29 for MCC against Sussex.

Over the whole season, Wisden credits WG with 1,396 runs at an average of 32.3, and 44 wickets at 23.2.

Playing for The South against The North at Scarborough in September, WG rolled back the years:

North v South
At Scarborough, Thursday, Friday, Saturday, September 5, 6 and 7, 1889

North 360 (Barnes 79; Woods 3–73); **South 197** (Stoddart 77; Shacklock 5–79) and **278–3** (W. G. Grace 154, Abel 105).
Match drawn.

A truly remarkable match brought the Scarborough Festival to a conclusion. On the last morning the South had to follow their innings against a majority of 163 runs, and so splendidly did Mr W. G. Grace and Abel play, that before they were separated the score had reached 226. This performance takes rank among the best stands ever made for the first wicket in a big match… The two batsmen were together for three hours and three-quarters and Abel, who left first, was out unluckily, playing a ball on to his wicket… Mr Grace was at the wickets for four hours and 35 minutes, scoring at much the same pace nearly all the time, and when a catch at short leg closed his innings, stumps were pulled up and the match was left drawn. He gave a difficult chance at cover slip when he had scored 22, and was missed at the wicket when his total was 139, while a ball that he put up between the wickets was just a possible chance to the bowler, but these were very small blemishes in a superb display.

CHAPTER 4
THE 1890s

"Mr Grace's confidence in himself was not misplaced."

1890 was the start of what many describe as the "Golden Age" of cricket. The final decade of the 19th century and the first years of the 20th, up to the outbreak of war in 1914, was an era during which cricket was at its most popular and its most fashionable. Great names bestrode the cricket field – men like Archie MacLaren and Stanley Jackson, who both made their first-class debuts in 1890, C. B. Fry and Ranjitsinhji, who first played in 1892 and 1893 respectively, and other legendary names like Tom Hayward, the second man to score 100 hundreds after WG, Victor Trumper, the first supreme Australian batsman, and bowlers like Jack Hearne, Tom Richardson, Wilfred Rhodes and Colin Blythe. But despite advancing years and ever-increasing girth, W. G. Grace still competed with the very best of them. In 1895, the year in which he turned 47, he broke many of his own records, playing with a freedom and ruthlessness which brought back memories of the agile youth who had forced people to rethink the boundaries of the game in the early 1870s, almost a quarter of a century earlier. Wisden was as enthusiastic as the rest of the country in praising the Champion.

Scoring 1,000 runs in the month of May, racking up a total of 100 first-class hundreds, and scoring a triple-century 20 years after he had first managed the feat were just three of WG's achievements in 1895 and 1896. He still had the power to astonish. He also had the power to disturb: before the decade was out, he had parted company somewhat acrimoniously with Gloucestershire County Cricket Club, and set up his own team, London County, which played its home games at the Crystal Palace ground, and he also played for several other teams during each season – England, MCC, the Gentlemen, and scratch sides such as The South. He played over 260 first-class games during the 1890s, a significantly larger number than in the 1880s, and such was his continued enthusiasm for the game, and his belief in his own play, that he no doubt hoped to play even more in the first decade of the new century.

Wisden now had more rivals to compare him with, players who were doing things that not even Grace in his prime might have thought possible, but even though MacLaren hit 424 not out, C. B. Fry scored six hundreds in six innings and Ranji scored more than 3,000 runs in a season – feats that WG never achieved – Wisden did not put these players on a pedestal with Grace. It was always understood that WG was a man apart as far as his cricketing talents were concerned.

WISDEN 1891

GLOUCESTERSHIRE IN 1890

Not the least noteworthy fact in connection with the season's work was the great amount of success achieved by Mr E. M. Grace – now the oldest cricketer taking part in first-class matches. His record in county contests – 512 runs at an average of 20.12 – is one of which many a younger batsman might feel proud, but when it is remembered that Mr Grace reached the zenith of his fame 27 years ago, his achievements are little short of marvellous. In the first five matches he did little or nothing, but subsequently he fairly astonished everyone by playing a splendid innings of 96 against Kent at Gloucester, and he followed this score by making a few days afterwards at Bristol 77 against the Surrey bowlers, while later in the season he hit up 78 against Sussex, and 69 against Lancashire. We should state that his innings of 96 was the highest the veteran had played since the summer of 1882, when against Lancashire at Clifton he made 122. As showing the great extent to which Mr Grace recovered his form, it is worthy of special mention that twice in one week he went in first with his brother Mr W. G. Grace, and the famous pair scored over 100 runs before being separated – 117 against Sussex and 139 against Lancashire. In the field Mr Grace displayed considerable activity, and though, as was only to be expected, he has lost some of his old brilliancy, he proved himself still to be one of the best points of the present day. Altogether Mr Grace has every reason to be thoroughly satisfied with the past season, and he has such abundant vitality that we may expect him to retain his place in the eleven for three or four years to come.

As has been the case for so many years, Mr W. G. Grace comes out at the head of the batting, having the really fine average of 36.4, and an aggregate of 832 runs – a record very similar to that of the preceding year. Only once – in a match against Kent at Maidstone, when he went in first, and took out his bat for 100 – did the champion succeed in scoring a three-figure innings, but on three other occasions he made 90 runs and upwards. During the middle part of the summer his batting fell off somewhat, but from the time he got back to form with his innings of 75 not out in the England and Australia match at Lord's, he played most brilliant cricket, and in a fortnight scored 94 and 90 in the two Lancashire matches, and 98 against Yorkshire at Dewsbury. Perhaps, however, his finest achievement was accomplished at Clifton, when on a difficult wicket, and against the famous Nottingham bowlers, he played a faultless innings of 70 not out.

Although WG finished the season with 1,476 runs at an average of 28.2, this placed him only eighth in the national averages. Arthur Shrewsbury (1,568 runs at 41.10) and Billy Gunn (1,621 at 34.23) beat both his aggregate and his average. Grace's 61 wickets at 19.24 was the second-highest tally by an amateur bowler, but pales into insignificance behind George Lohmann's 220 wickets at 13.14.

England v Australia

First Test Match, at Lord's, Monday, Tuesday, Wednesday, July 21, 22 and 23, 1890

Australia 132 (Lyons 55; Attewell 4–42) and **176** (Barrett 67*; Lohmann 3–28);
England 173 (Ulyett 74; Lyons 5 for 30) and **137–3** (W. G. Grace 75*; Ferris 2–42).
England won by seven wickets.

This was emphatically the great match of the Australian tour. No other game was looked forward to so eagerly and to the result of no other game was so much importance attached. Victory on this special occasion would to a very large extent have made up to the Australians for all their previous defeats and disappointments, and given, as it were, a fresh start to the trip. As everyone interested in cricket is well aware, the result of the match was a victory for England by seven wickets, but repeating in other words what we have said a few pages back, we may state emphatically that scarcely any one of their 38 engagements reflected so much credit on the Australians as this encounter with the representative England eleven... The England team was an immensely strong one, and yet not quite so powerful as that originally chosen by the MCC committee, the places intended for Mr Stoddart and Briggs being given to Maurice Read and Barnes. Mr Stoddart preferred playing for Middlesex against Kent at Tonbridge, and Briggs very properly resigned his place when he found that he had not sufficiently recovered from a strain to enable him to bowl...

The Australians, who won the toss, were batting on the Monday from just after 12 o'clock till a quarter to four, for a total of 132... When England went in the cricket was of the most sensational character, Grace, Shrewsbury, W. W. Read, and Gunn – unquestionably the four best bats on the side – being all got rid of for 20 runs. With things looking very black indeed for their side, Maurice Read and Ulyett then became partners, and in the course of an hour and a half, against superb bowling and fielding, put on 72 runs. The stand they made, coming when it did, was invaluable, and it would be difficult to praise them beyond their deserts. At the close of play the score was 108 for five wickets, and on the Tuesday the innings finished at 20 minutes past one for a total of 173, or 41 runs to the good...

Going in for the second time at 20 minutes to two, the Australians were batting all the rest of the afternoon, and at the drawing of stumps had made 168 for nine wickets. Lyons again hit brilliantly, scoring 33 runs in 25 minutes, but the feature of the day was the wonderful defence of Barrett. On the third morning the

Australian innings closed for 176, Barrett, who had gone in first, taking out his bat for 67. England had 136 to get to win, and with the wicket in capital order there was not much doubt about the task being accomplished. Shrewsbury was out at 27, but Grace and Gunn took the score to 101 and thus practically decided the match. Towards the finish Grace hit magnificently, and his not-out innings of 75 was entirely worthy of his reputation.

England v Australia

Second Test Match, at Kennington Oval, Monday, Tuesday, August 11 and 12, 1890

Australia 92 (Trott 39; Martin 6–50) and **102** (Trott 25; Martin 6–52);
England 100 (Gunn 32; Ferris 4–25) and **95–8** (M. Read 35; Ferris 5–49).
England won by two wickets.

The colonial players had sustained so many defeats that it was unreasonable to expect the same amount of interest that had been excited in previous years by the meeting with England at The Oval, but when the Surrey ground the day before the match was saturated by rain, good judges, remembering what Turner and Ferris are capable of on a damaged wicket, confidently predicted a capital game, and their anticipations were more than realised. The opening day's play was just what might have been expected after the great amount of rain that had fallen. The ball beat the bat all through the afternoon, and between 12 o'clock and the drawing of stumps 22 wickets went down for an aggregate score of only 197.

The Australians, who won the toss, and of course took first innings, were batting nearly two hours and a half for a total of 92... England on going in to bat started very badly, Grace being easily caught at slip from the first ball he received; Shrewsbury at the end of half an hour's cricket being finely taken at point with the score at ten; and Mr W. W. Read being bowled at 16... the innings being finished off for a total of 100, or only eight runs to the good. With the ground in a very difficult state, the Australians lost Barrett and Ferris in their second innings for five runs, and the second day they stayed in till 25 minutes to two, the last wicket falling for 102, which left England 95 to get to win. Under ordinary circumstances the task of getting 95 runs would have been an easy matter for the England team, but with the wicket as it was it was impossible to feel over-confident. Mr Grace ought for the second time in the match to have been caught from the first ball that he received, but Trott at point dropped a ball that was cut straight into his hands. Despite this lucky let-off, however, the four best England wickets fell for 32 runs, the interest then reaching a very acute point.

... As it was, the score had been taken to 83 – only 12 to win with six wickets to fall – when Maurice Read was caught at long-on for an invaluable 35. On his dismissal there came a collapse that recalled the great match in 1882, Mr Cranston, Lohmann and Barnes being dismissed in such quick succession that with eight men out two runs were still wanted to win. Amid indescribable excitement Sharpe became Mr MacGregor's partner, and five maiden overs were bowled in succession, Sharpe being beaten time after time by balls from Ferris that broke back and missed the wicket. Then at last the Surrey player hit a ball to cover point, but Barrett, who had a chance of running out either batsman, overthrew the ball in his anxiety, and a wonderful match ended in a victory for England by two wickets.

The Third Test match was abandoned without a ball being bowled.

WISDEN 1892

For the first time ever, W. G. Grace's form deserted him for an entire season. Wisden *was phlegmatic about his cricket, putting the decline down to injury.*

GLOUCESTERSHIRE

There is no inducement to dwell at great length upon the doings of the Gloucestershire eleven in 1891, as the season was one of the most disastrous experienced by the club. Now and then the team showed some approach to their old ability, but their good displays were few and far between and were scarcely sufficient to brighten the summer's work...

It is perhaps a little ungenerous to include Mr E. M. Grace among those who were not so successful as in the preceding season, for it was hardly reasonable to expect that the veteran cricketer would be able to repeat his achievements of 1890. That was a veritable Indian summer for Mr E. M. Grace, and it is only for the purpose of showing one of the causes of Gloucestershire's misfortunes that we draw attention to the fact that his average declined from 20.12 to 15.10...

Though... Mr W. G. Grace had an unsuccessful season – indeed, the worst he has ever experienced – there is no cause for apprehension. The champion commenced the summer fairly well, but early in July, while playing at Edinburgh, he had the misfortune to sprain his knee. Instead of taking a complete rest Mr Grace, though very lame, continued to take his place in the eleven, until he was absolutely compelled to give way. Following the recovery from this injury Mr Grace wrenched his back while practising at Trent Bridge, and was again forced to stand down. These unfortunate mishaps naturally affected his cricket, and in a great measure accounted for his comparative failure. In 1890 Mr Grace had an aggregate of 832 and the splendid average of 36.4, but this season he only scored 440 runs, and his average fell just short of 21. In the case of many other batsmen on the side such a measure of success would be deemed creditable, but the great cricketer has so accustomed us to large scores that the figures cannot be considered at all satisfactory. His inability to do justice to himself had a serious effect on the other members of the side... For Mr Radcliffe, who had the rare distinction of beating Mr Grace in the averages, we have only words of praise.

The bowling tables clearly show that... Mr W. G. Grace was also more effective than he had been for some years, and had he not broken down it is probable that he would have been able to show an even better record than 37 wickets for less than 17 runs each.

A. H. Grace, nephew of WG and EM, played in the first match of the season, against Kent, but scored a duck and did not bowl. He did not appear for the county again that year, and Wisden *failed to pass comment on him.*

WISDEN 1893

Among the Five Great Batsmen chosen for profile by Sydney Pardon was Walter Read. No comparisons with WG were made, but E. M. Grace's name was used as a gold standard.

The Surrey cricketer often bowls lobs with success; can keep wicket on occasions; and is a capital field at point – not an E. M. Grace, but still very safe and dependable.

THE ENGLAND TEAM IN AUSTRALIA, 1891–92

The tour undertaken by Lord Sheffield's team in the Australian season 1891–92 was in one respect unique. Never before in the history of visits paid by English cricketers to Australia or by Australian cricketers to the mother country had the enterprise been undertaken and carried out by a single individual. In as much as two of the three Test matches against Combined Australia ended in the defeat of the English players, the tour was in one sense a disappointment to all lovers of the game in Great Britain, but this was only the fortune of war. Moreover, our defeats had one very beneficial effect, the double triumph of the Australians restoring the game to its old place in the affections of the Colonial public.

Apart from the fact of two of the big matches having been lost, the tour was a great success, Lord Sheffield's action in arranging the trip, and the manner in which he carried it out, earning unstinted praise from every organ of public opinion in Australia. It was understood that the expenses of the tour considerably exceeded the receipts, but this was largely due to the liberal scale on which everything was done. That Lord Sheffield was well satisfied with his own reception in Australia was best proved by the fact that he presented a handsome trophy to be competed for by the different Colonies. Except for the very important fact that Arthur Shrewsbury and William Gunn declined to accept the terms offered them, the team was, on the form shown during the English season of 1891, fully representative. It consisted of

Mr W. G. Grace, Gloucestershire (captain).
Mr A. E. Stoddart, Middlesex.
Mr G. MacGregor, Cambridge University.
Mr O. G. Radcliffe, Gloucestershire.
Mr H. Philipson, Northumberland.
G. A. Lohmann, Surrey.
R. Abel, Surrey.
Maurice Read, Surrey.
J. W. Sharpe, Surrey.
W. Attewell, Notts.
R. Peel, Yorkshire.
J. Briggs, Lancashire.
G. Bean, Sussex.

Alfred Shaw acted as general manager of the team on Lord Sheffield's behalf, and earned praise on all hands for the tact and good judgment with which he discharged a by no means easy task. Beyond everything else the tour was remarkable for the reappearance in Australia, after an interval of 18 years, of Mr W. G. Grace. When the most famous of all cricketers visited the Colonies in 1873 he was at the very height of his powers, and not a few of his warmest admirers regarded it as rather a hazardous venture on his part to go out again at so late a period of his career. Events proved, however, that Mr Grace's confidence in himself was not misplaced. Alike in the 11-a-side matches and in all engagements he came out at the head of the batting averages. When we remember that he was in his 44th year, and that his position as the finest batsman in the world had been established at a time when all the other members of the team were children, this feat must be pronounced nothing less than astonishing.

It is true that in the matches against odds he was favoured with more than his fair share of luck, but, so far as we could gather from the detailed reports that appeared in the Australian papers, he was not more fortunate in the first-class fixtures than his colleagues. His only big score was 159 not out in the first match against Victoria, but he played most consistently all through the tour, and rarely failed to make runs.

Lord Sheffield's Team v Victoria
At Melbourne, Friday, Saturday, November 27 and 28, 1891

Victoria 73 (Carlton 17*; Sharpe 6–40) and **104** (Bruce 25; Attewell 5–41, Lohmann 5–41);
Lord Sheffield's Team 284 (W. G. Grace 159*; Barrett 4–51).
Lord Sheffield's Team won by an innings and 107 runs.

Though in other respects uneventful, the match will be remembered for W. G. Grace's not out innings of 159. The wicket did not play perfectly, and the excellence of his performance may be judged from the fact that the other ten batsmen on the side only scored 119 between them. The only chance he gave was one in the slips when he had made 14, and from first to last he timed and placed the ball in his best style. His innings included ten boundary hits and a big square-leg hit over the chains.

This was WG's only century between 1890 and 1893.

England v Australia
First Test Match, at Melbourne, Friday, Saturday, Monday, Tuesday, Wednesday, January 1, 2, 4, 5 and 6, 1892

Australia 240 (Bruce 57; Sharpe 6–84) and **236** (Lyons 51; Peel 2–25);
England 264 (W. G. Grace 50; McLeod 5–53) and **158** (Stoddart 35; Turner 5–51).
Australia won by 54 runs.

This, the first of the three matches against Combined Australia, excited an extraordinary amount of interest. It lasted into the fifth day, and, after a struggle which by general consent had rarely or never been surpassed in the colonies, was won by the Australians by 54 runs. The Englishmen lost the game on the Tuesday afternoon, when they went in for the last innings with 213 runs wanted to win. With the wicket still in good order they entertained little doubt of accomplishing their task, and when Grace and Stoddart, on starting the innings, had hit up 60 runs without being separated, Australia's chance seemed very remote. However, at 60 Grace was caught at mid-off and Stoddart bowled in trying to pull a long-hop. Then came such a collapse on the part of the English batsmen that before the drawing of stumps there were seven wickets down. On the Wednesday morning the remaining players did their best, but the innings was all over for 158. In the early stages of the match some fine cricket was shown on both sides… W. G. Grace's 50 was a capital display…Turner and Trott bowled admirably in the last innings, but the most sensational piece of bowling in the match was that of McLeod, who, in the Englishmen's first innings, got rid of Abel, Grace, and Stoddart in two overs.

Australia v England
Third Test Match, at Adelaide, Thursday, Friday, Saturday, Monday, March 24, 25, 26 and 28, 1892

England 499 (Stoddart 134; Turner 3–111);
Australia 100 (Lyons 23; Briggs 6–49) and **169** (Bruce 37; Briggs 6–87).
England won by an innings and 230 runs.

The third meeting with Combined Australia was the last match of the tour. As some compensation for their defeats at Melbourne and Sydney, the Englishmen won in a single innings with 230 runs to spare. It was a brilliant victory, but inasmuch as the Englishmen batted on a perfect wicket, and the Australians had to go in when the pitch had been ruined by rain, it cannot be pretended that the result represented with any accuracy the merits of the two elevens. In justice to the English team, however, it should be mentioned that before the rain came on they had scored 490 for nine wickets. This being the case, it is not unreasonable to suppose that even had the weather remained fine, the game would still have ended in their favour. Stoddart's batting and Briggs's bowling were the features of the game. In scoring 134 Stoddart was at the wickets three hours and 50 minutes, his hits including two fives and 15 fours. He gave three chances, but not one of them was easy, and from first to last he played in his best form. Grace's 58 was quite faultless, and the only mistake in Peel's admirable 83 – an innings which lasted three hours – was a hard return to Giffen when he had scored 60.

GLOUCESTERSHIRE

Though Gloucestershire escaped the unenviable distinction of being last on the list among leading counties – a position held by the western eleven in 1891 – the season was every whit as disastrous…

The batting, however, affords agreeable subject for contemplation, and it is gratifying to be able to record a brilliant season for Mr W. G. Grace. In 1891, the champion had for him an unsuccessful year, but though fears were expressed in some quarters that his powers were declining we took occasion to point out that there was no cause for apprehension. The correctness of our view was quickly borne out by his series of achievements in Australia during the winter, and further exemplified by his consistently good batting during the season under notice. In 25 innings for his county the great batsman scored 802 runs, with the splendid average of 36–10, this record being curiously similar to that of two years ago, when he went to the wickets the same number of times, scored 832 runs and had an average of 36–4. Mr Grace's figures are the more noteworthy as he did not have any exceptionally big innings to help him. His highest and best innings was 99 against the Sussex bowlers at Gloucester, and on that occasion he batted with the freshness, vigour and rapidity of his earlier days. As a rule, however, the famous cricketer played a slower game than that to which he has so long accustomed us, but this was perhaps only to be expected. Among his other achievements we may mention that he scored 47 and 72 not out against Middlesex at Lord's, and 89 in the return match with the same county. He also showed his old partiality for the Yorkshire bowling, obtaining 53 and 32 at Bradford, and 61 in the return.

… On occasions Mr E. M. Grace played extremely well, the veteran being seen to the best advantage in the first match with Somerset, when he scored 70 and 31.

In all matches, Wisden records that WG finished the year with 1,055 runs at an average of 31.1. He was one of nine players to score 1,000 runs that year. E. M. Grace finished with 440 runs at 15.5. WG only took 31 wickets that summer, at an average of 30.28, while his brother's lobs sent back seven men at an average of 44.4.

WISDEN 1894

One of WG's batting partners died that year.

OBITUARY

WILLIAM SCOTTON (Notts), who died by his own hand on July 9, was born on January 15, 1856, and was thus in his 38th year. For some time previous to his tragic end he had been in a very low, depressed condition, the fact that he had lost his place in the Notts eleven having, so it was stated at the inquest, preyed very seriously upon his mind… Against the Australian team of 1886 Scotton played two remarkable innings in company with Mr W. G. Grace, the two batsmen scoring 170 together for the first wicket for England at The Oval, and 156 for Lord Londesborough's Eleven at Scarborough.

GLOUCESTERSHIRE

During recent years, Gloucestershire have fared so badly that it was no matter for surprise to find them at the close of the summer at the bottom of the list among the leading counties – a position held by Sussex in 1892 – but on the whole the county did better than in the previous season…

In the latter part of the summer a remarkable young player was introduced into the eleven in the person of Mr C. L. Townsend, a son of Mr Frank Townsend, one of the old school of Gloucestershire cricketers. Both he and Mr W. G. Grace junior – the eldest son of the champion – while still at Clifton College made their first appearance in county cricket, in the match against Middlesex on their own school ground, and for Mr Townsend there is unquestionably a future as a bowler.

Wisden clearly had little confidence in WG junior, whose final figures for the season were eight innings, 72 runs, highest score 18, average 9.00. His bowling analysis for the season was 43–9–108–1. His Clifton College season is recorded in Wisden – 290 runs at 29 and 51 wickets at 11.47. Townsend (WG's godson) scored 310 runs at 28.2, and took 55 wickets at 12.8.

E. M. Grace played 16 matches for Gloucestershire, at the age of almost 52, but only scored 325 runs at an average of 10.15, and took nine wickets at a cost of 22.1 runs each.

Turning to the batting it is pleasant to again find Mr W. G. Grace occupying the post of honour. Though not so successful in county cricket as in 1892, when he scored 802 runs with an average of 36, the champion had a good season, his aggregate being 711 and his average 28. Satisfactory as these figures are, they do not convey an adequate impression of the splendidly consistent batting of the famous cricketer… Outside the county matches Mr Grace was even more successful, the admirable form he displayed in many encounters with the Australians being quite a feature of a busy season. Playing for the Marylebone Club against Kent he made 128, this being his best score in important cricket since 1890. July, with some soft wickets, was a rather bad month for Mr Grace, but while the grounds were hard and firm he fully held his own with the best of the younger batsmen. Altogether in first-class cricket Mr Grace scored 1,609 runs with an average of 35.34, a remarkable record for a player who was at the zenith of his fame when most of his present-day rivals were still at school.

Great cricketer he may still have been, but his captaincy was less successful:

… It is necessary to remark that the team did not work harmoniously together. It was quite an open secret that a spirit of mutiny prevailed and matters went so far that at one time a crisis seemed imminent. Happily, however, good counsels prevailed, and the difficulties that had arisen were smoothed over. There is no doubt that, owing to the cause indicated, Gloucestershire suffered last season, and it is to be hoped that in future a better state of affairs will exist. In the latter part of the season, Mr W. G. Grace wrote to the committee expressing his desire to give up the captaincy of the eleven, but in the autumn he withdrew his resignation.

England v Australia
First Test Match, at Lord's, Monday, Tuesday, Wednesday, July 17, 18 and 19, 1893

Despite the moderate record which the Australians had obtained up to the end of June, the first of the representative matches proved quite as attractive as ever, and there was a great gathering at the St John's Wood ground. On a fast wicket the success of England would have been generally anticipated, but so much rain had fallen on the previous day that the wicket was necessarily very treacherous, and on Monday morning it was known that owing to an injured finger W. G. Grace for the first time since matches between England and Australia had been played in this country would not do battle for the old country.

England v Australia

Second Test Match (for Maurice Read's Benefit), at Kennington Oval,
Monday, Tuesday, Wednesday, August 14, 15 and 16, 1893

England 483 (Jackson 103; Giffen 7–128); **Australia 91** (Lyons 19; Briggs 5–34)
and **349** (Trott 92; Briggs 5–114).
England won by an innings and 43 runs.

Four changes were made from the England team that had gone into the field against the Australians at Lord's, W. G. Grace, W. W. Read, Albert Ward, and Briggs taking the places of Maurice Read, Peel, Wainwright, and Flowers. These alterations undoubtedly strengthened the side, which, although short of.. medium-pace right-handed bowling, was exceptionally powerful in batting, no fewer than seven of the eleven having averages of 33 and over. The game, which was the only one of the three Test matches brought to a definite issue, proved a great triumph for English cricket, the Australians being beaten by an innings and 43 runs… Another admirable commencement was made by Grace and Stoddart, who, beginning the England innings shortly after midday, were still together at the luncheon interval, when the score had been carried to 134 – Stoddart not out 71, and Grace not out 63. Afterwards the total was raised to 151, and then the partnership, which had lasted two hours and a quarter, came to an end.

Stoddart was first dismissed, his innings of 83, although marred by a considerable number of more or less easy chances, including some very fine hits. It may be mentioned that during the first hour the ball now and then got up in an awkward style. Before another run had been added Grace was out for a really admirable innings of 68, in making which the famous batsman had displayed some of his highest skill.

England v Australia

Third Test Match, at Manchester, Thursday, Friday, Saturday,
August 24, 25 and 26, 1893

Australia 204 (Bruce 68; Richardson 5–49) and **236** (A. Bannerman 60; Richardson 5–107);
England 243 (Gunn 102*; Giffen 4–113) and **118–4** (W. G. Grace 45; Trumble 3–49).
Match drawn.

… There was a most disheartening commencement to the England innings, Grace running out Stoddart before a run had been made. This disaster to England had a very prejudicial effect upon the batting, which was afterwards marked by extreme care rather than attractiveness.

… England had 198 runs to get to win, and only two hours and a quarter remained for cricket. Grace and Stoddart were the batsmen, and, making no attempt to hit off the runs, they, by their excellent play, seemed likely for a considerable time to leave the game much in favour of England. Together they put on 78 runs for the first wicket, and within half an hour of the close the hundred went up with only one man out. England then looked like leaving off with an immense advantage, but at this point Grace was dismissed, and shortly before time Trumble bowled out Gunn and Ward with successive balls. Thus at the finish England had six wickets to fall and wanted 80 to win, the draw, in which the match terminated, being rather in favour of the old country.

WISDEN 1895

1894 was a slow climb back to the heights WG would hit in 1895 – the gathering of the storm. His form for his county, however, was poor.

GLOUCESTERSHIRE

A review of Gloucestershire's cricket in 1894 cannot be otherwise than unpleasant reading. From whatever point of view regarded, the state of affairs is most unsatisfactory…

With regard to individual achievements there is little that need be said. There was not a single batting average of 20, Captain Luard just beating Mr W. G. Grace for first place. The champion's record of 567 runs, with an average of less than 19, shows a serious falling-off, and with their great batsman failing to get his customary share of runs, it is small wonder that the other members of the side were not seen at their best. Mr Grace's inability to do himself justice was all the more galling to the supporters of Gloucestershire from the fact that in matches outside the county he did very well. Playing for the Marylebone Club against Cambridge University he scored 139 at Cambridge and 196 at Lord's – this latter score being the highest individual innings in first-class cricket in 1894 – and late in the summer, at Hastings, he obtained 131 for the Gentlemen against a strong bowling side of Players. Altogether in important cricket, Mr Grace scored 1,293 runs, with an average of just under 30, but though he had every reason to be satisfied with his season's labours as a whole, his county record was most disappointing.

MCC and Ground v Cambridge University
At Lord's, Monday, Tuesday, Wednesday, June 25, 26 and 27, 1894

MCC and Ground 258 (Lord Hawke 64; Douglas 4–32) and **595–7** dec (W. G. Grace 196; Candler 3–91); **Cambridge University 262** (Latham 116; W. G. Grace, jun. 6–79) and **217** (Perkins 66; Mead 5–66).
MCC and Ground won by 374 runs.

This, like the last of the Cambridge trials before the University Match, was remarkable for exceptionally heavy scoring – no fewer than three of the ground records, so far as important matches are concerned, being broken. In the first instance, the aggregate number of runs – 1,332 – is the greatest ever obtained at Lord's, in the next the MCC's second total of 595 is the highest ever made there, and in the third Mr W. G. Grace's 196 is the most he has ever scored at the St. John's Wood enclosure. As it happened this brilliant display of the veteran champion's proved the highest individual innings in first-class cricket during the season. All through the match the weakness of the Cambridge bowling was painfully apparent, and though there was some excellent batting by their captain, F. H. Latham, and Perkins, it was small wonder after the Club's big innings, which, by the way, was declared with only seven men out, that the visitors were beaten by the enormous majority of 374 runs.

Gloucestershire's match against the touring South Africans was not afforded first-class status, but WG took the game by the scruff of the neck all the same.

Gloucestershire v South Africans
At Bristol, Thursday, Friday, Saturday, June 28, 29 and 30, 1894

South Africans 185 (F. Hearne 56; W. G. Grace 9–71) and 262 (Halliwell 110; Roberts 4–38);
Gloucestershire 301 (W. G. Grace 129*; Rowe 4–95) and 147–5 (Rice 35; Glover 3–24).
Gloucestershire won by five wickets.

On the occasion of their meeting W. G. Grace for the second time, the South Africans received striking evidence of the great cricketer's powers, both with bat and ball. After taking nine wickets, he played, as will be seen from the score... a not-out innings of 129. Halliwell and Frank Hearne gave a fine display, but Gloucestershire won the match very comfortably by five wickets.

Wisden also published that year an article by "An Old Cambridge Captain" who was, on the whole, very favourably impressed by WG:

CRICKETERS PAST AND PRESENT

Very few persons will agree about the relative merits of past and present cricketers. Wherein do they differ? Were the batsmen of half a century ago equal to those of today? Was the bowling as straight and as difficult then as it is now? These are questions which are not very easy to answer. I do not wish to take the position of a dogmatic umpire upon them, as some of my friends do. "What," they exclaim, "is the good of discussing the subject? Look at the gigantic scores. Look at the batting averages. Look at the bowling feats. Look at the brilliant fielding. Look at the truly magnificent wicketkeeping. The past will not bear comparison with the present in any department of the game." But I venture to think that there is a little, at any rate, to be said on the other side. The cricketers of a bygone age are not to be robbed of their glory without some calm considerations. Are the environments similar? Were the general purposes of the old batsmen the same as those of the modern school? In what respect is the bowling of today superior to that of the best bowlers, say, of the day when W. G. Grace first began to play?

… But it is a little irritating to be told that such a boat was the finest that ever rowed on the Thames; or such an eleven the best that ever left any University; or some particular batsman the best (WG being, of course, condescendingly barred) that ever handled the willow…

There is no stroke in which there is greater variety than the cut. George Parr and W. G. Grace made the cut safe by hitting it on to the ground by chopping it; but that is quite a different stroke from the old-fashioned cut. Felix, Julius Cæsar, C. G. Lyttelton, Carpenter, and many others hit with the bat parallel to the ground with a power that no chop can ever give to the ball…

Turning now to another department of the game, I must confess myself surprised to find that Grace and R. H. Lyttelton both think that the bowling of today is straighter than it was some years ago. WG ought certainly to know, for he has had marvellous experience both of round-arm and "over-hand" deliveries…

One reason why so few bowlers bowl round the wicket now is because they cannot do so safely without a long-stop. I may be wrong, but my opinion is that the ball which beats the batsman inside the leg stump will very often beat the wicketkeeper too, especially if it shoots. Bowlers don't like the balls to go for byes… Of this I am perfectly certain – that the cricket world of today needs a tip-top bowler round the wicket, who would hammer away at the leg stump; and, from a conversation I had some time ago with Earl Bessborough and W. G. Grace, they both think he would be successful. I believe he would "skiddadle" some of our swell players one after the other; but the labour of learning to bowl this way is very great, and all fingers are not suitable for it. Besides, it requires courage to run the risk of byes and to alter the field to the old-fashioned style.

As regards fielding, the difference between ancient and modern players is not very great. The latter, I think, are more skilful in their returns, and certainly more accurate in having a shot at the wickets; but none of them have eclipsed Broughton, Royds, Hornby, and Bell at cover point, Absolom and Kempson at short slip, I. D. Walker at mid-off, Bob Fitzgerald and Smith at long leg, E. M. Grace at point, and Teddy Drake and V. E. Walker to their own bowling and in almost any place in the field.

As time passes it is to me a matter of joy that the game of cricket has become so universal and that it retains its purity and its freedom from those evils which surround some other of our pastimes. No whisper of matches being sold for money is ever heard. No charge of cheating is brought against players. No system of gambling is attached to the greatest of English games.

His concluding paragraph is somewhat Utopian. Cricket started its growth towards its current level of popularity precisely because it afforded a suitable means of gambling for the idle rich of Hambledon and Marylebone 100 years before An Old Cambridge Captain took up his pen.

WISDEN 1896

1895 was WG's greatest year since the 1870s – the full late flowering of his batting skills, a thousand runs before the end of May, the scoring of his 100th hundred and a complete domination of the bowlers of England. Perhaps the fact that he did not travel to Australia during the winter helped him recharge his batteries.

ENGLAND IN AUSTRALIA, 1894–95

It is perfectly safe to say that since the visit of George Parr's eleven in 1863–64 no tour of English cricketers in Australia has been from every point of view more brilliantly successful than that of Mr Stoddart's team. Leaving England in October 1894, the band of players – with three exceptions – returned home in May last, loaded with honours and delighted with their trip. They had abundant reasons for satisfaction, inasmuch as in the series of contests with All Australia they had won the rubber by three matches to two.

... This was undoubtedly a fine side, though in the absence of Mr W. G. Grace, Mr F. S. Jackson, Gunn, and one or two others, it could not be said in October 1894, to fully represent England.

Wisden took the opportunity to celebrate the champion's year, devoting the space that in recent years had gone to the appreciations of the cricketers of the day – what would soon become the settled format of Five Cricketers of the Year – entirely to WG.

W.G. GRACE BY SYDNEY PARDON

It had for some years been intended to publish in *Wisden's Almanack* a portrait of W. G. Grace, and it was felt before the season of 1895 had been many weeks in progress that the most suitable time had arrived. No one interested in cricket will need to be told that Mr Grace last summer played with all the brilliancy and success of his youth. In one respect, indeed, he surpassed all he had ever done before, scoring in the first month of the season a thousand runs in first-class matches – a feat quite without parallel in the history of English cricket. As everyone knows, in the course of the month of May he made, on the Gloucestershire county ground at Ashley Down, Bristol, his 100th hundred in first-class matches, this special circumstance being the origin of the national testimonial which was afterwards taken up with such enthusiasm in all parts of the country, and in many places far beyond the limits of the United Kingdom. It was not to be expected that Mr Grace would be able to quite keep up the form he showed in May, but he continued to bat marvellously well, and it is more than likely that, had the summer remained fine, he would have beaten his best aggregate in important cricket – 2,739 in the season of 1871. The chance of his doing this, however, was destroyed by the wet weather. He could not, at 47 years of age, overcome the difficulties of slow wickets as he might have done in his young days, and, though he again scored well as soon as the sunshine came back, there was no time left in which to break his previous records. Still, despite the severe check that his heavy scoring received, he can look back upon a season of wonderful work. His aggregate number of runs in first-class matches is the third highest in his career – only inferior to those of 1871 and 1876 – and his average of 51 is, with a single exception, the best he has obtained since the last-mentioned year. Moreover, he played nine innings of over a hundred, bringing his number of three-figure scores to 107. The details of Mr Grace's marvellous career are so familiar to all who have any love for cricket that I thought some favourable impressions of the great batsman, contributed by those who had played against him and on his side, would be far more interesting to the readers of *Wisden* than a formal biography. I accordingly wrote to Lord Harris and Mr A. G. Steel, both of whom readily acceded to my wish that they would write something about "W. G." for *Wisden* in 1896. Personally, I would only add a few words. Having known Mr Grace for many years, and seen him make a goodly proportion of his 107 hundreds, I can truthfully say that my feeling of delight when he succeeds, or of disappointment when he fails, has not become less keen with the lapse of time.

W. G. GRACE BY A. G. STEEL

Yielding to none in admiration of the "hero" of a hundred centuries, and to none in love for the game in which he is so proficient, I am bound to say I was not altogether pleased with the *Daily Telegraph* testimonial. A national testimonial in honour of the greatest cricketer the world has ever seen, on his completion of a performance which may be a record for all time, was indeed fitting. Surely the greatest cricket club in the world – the MCC – was the proper initiator of the testimonial to the greatest cricketer. Day after day, as one read of the flood of shillings pouring in, accompanied by such varied correspondence, one could not but feel a little alarm for the dignity of our great game. But whether the means adopted for raising the testimonial were the right ones or not, the fact remains that it was an enormous success, and showed that the personality of W. G. Grace had taken a deep hold upon all classes of the English people. The enthusiasm was such as has probably never before been kindled concerning the exponent of any modern form of athletics.

The first occasion I ever played against WG was at Cambridge in the summer of 1878, and this was also the first time I ever saw him play. I remember being desperately anxious to get him out, but I was disappointed, and on my telling him what pleasure it would give me to get him out, he laughingly replied, "It's only a question of time; if you go on long enough you are bound to get me out." I was not, however, successful on that occasion, but I shall never forget the kindly encouragement I, a young cricketer, received from WG the first time I met him. It was not, however, his batting, oddly enough, which struck me as so wonderful, it was his bowling. Never, as far as I know, did any bowler give the same peculiar flight to the ball as WG does, and well justified is the remark I have often heard him make of a newly-arrived batsman, "Oh, he's a young one, is he? I think I ought to do for him," and he generally does.

WG has, so it goes without saying, a thorough knowledge of the game, and I recollect well in the summer of 1878 an incident which well illustrates the fact. North v South was being played at Lord's. Barlow, the Lancashire professional, was batting, and WG was fielding point. Now Barlow had a trick of tapping the ball away after he had played it, and occasionally, in order to excite a laugh from the onlookers, would scamper down the pitch for a yard or two and then back again. On this occasion he just stopped the ball and it lay by his crease; he then tapped it towards point, and perhaps thinking he would hustle that fielder, he went through his performance of dashing down the pitch and back again. He must have been thoroughly upset by the action of point, who, ignoring the ball, quietly asked the umpire, "How's that for hitting the ball twice?" and out Barlow had to go – a lesson which he never forgot. It was, I think, in that very match that WG hit two consecutive balls from Alfred Shaw clean out of Lord's Cricket Ground. It is true the wickets were pitched slightly on the south side of the ground, but they were both glorious knocks; one went clean over the tavern and the other pitched right on the top of it.

One of the finest innings I ever saw WG play was his 152 against the Australians in the match England v Australia at The Oval in 1880. Certainly he was batting on a good wicket, but his timing of the ball on this occasion was absolutely perfect, and the crispness of his strokes perfection. W. L. Murdoch made 153 in the second innings of this match; a very fine performance it was, too. I afterwards heard a discussion between some of the Australian team as to whether Murdoch was a finer batsman than Grace. A. Bannerman, the little stonewaller of his side, clinched it by saying, in his brusque way, "WG has forgotten more about batting that Billy [Murdoch] ever knew." And A. Bannerman was a very fine judge of the game.

It is during the annual week at Scarborough that WG is, perhaps, seen at his best. The cricket, of course, is good, but there is a sort of holiday aspect about it which is absent from the more serious county and Gentlemen v Players matches that take place earlier in the season. I always used to think that WG hit harder and oftener at Scarborough than elsewhere. I recollect one occasion when he was playing for a team called, I think, the Gentlemen of England against the Zingari. The latter had a good batting side, but were very weak in bowling. The wicket was good and the Gentlemen won the toss. As the Zingari went into the field we all thought we were in for a long day's fielding. WG and C. I. Thornton came in first; H. W. Forster and I began the bowling. I thought it possible that Thornton's hitting might have an effect on Grace, and it did. In the first over Thornton hit me out of the ground, and not to be denied, WG did the same, the very first ball I sent down, but it was too merry to last, and they were both caught in the long field before 30 was up on the telegraph board.

Why has the name of W. G. Grace sunk so deeply into the hearts of all branches of the community? Firstly, because of the national love for the glorious game, and secondly, because of his wonderful skill and the unusual number of years he has maintained the position and name of "champion". It is as a batsman that he has earned this proud title, and it may be of interest to linger for a few moments on the characteristics of his style and play which in their combination have met with such phenomenal success. First of all, W. G. Grace obeys the fundamental rule of batting that is always instilled into young players as the first element of good batting; he keeps his right foot rigid and firm as a rock, and never does he move it during the actual stroke. (Alas! I never could grasp this rule myself or act up to it!) It is an exception, even to slow bowling, for WG to move his right foot. Once I remember (I wonder whether he does) him breaking this rule. During the compilation of one of his hundred centuries, in a match against the Australians at Lord's, he rushed out to hit the slow leg-break bowler (Cooper), missed, and after a somewhat undignified scurry back, just got the benefit from the umpire, a man subsequently not loved by the Australians.

The position WG takes up at the wicket is one eminently calculated to assist him in the marvellous accuracy of his placing on the leg side. The right foot points slightly in front of the crease, thus enabling him to face the leg and body balls and have the greater command over them. If it had been Grace's practice to stand with his right foot pointing backwards or in the direction of his own wicket (as many good batsmen have done and do) we would never have seen the accurate placing on the leg side which, in my opinion, has done more than any other of his great batting qualities to place him in the position he has so long held. Let anyone try for himself, and he will at once see the commanding power that Grace's position on the left side gives, and how cramped and "hunched" up he feels in the other. Grace's defence, of course, is excellent, and his position at the wickets in this relation is worthy of note. He stands with the right leg as near as possible on the line to the leg stump, without, of course, being in front. And every time he plays forward, the left leg and the bat go together so that should the ball not meet the bat there will be no space between the bat and the leg for it to pass through. How often, whilst enjoying that great cricketing luxury of seeing WG in his happiest batting vein, one has occasionally shuddered at the sight of that massive leg coming out straight in front to an off-stump ball.

This art of playing with the left leg close to the bat is one that must be thoroughly mastered before any man can become a really first-class batsman, and W. G. Grace is a master of it. Though using his left leg in this way when playing forward, he is not one of those products of modern days, viz., a batsman who uses his leg on the off side instead of his bat. We should be sorry to think of our great batsman as one of these feeble, faint-hearted players, who, frightened of losing their wickets, dare not use their bats, and who, too timid to try to score, have done so much in many districts to disgust spectators, not with cricket, but with their own wearisome antics. What sort of bowling is W. G. Grace best at? I do not think that any cricketer of experience would hesitate in answering the question. Great, of course, to all styles when at his best, his power of playing fast bowling was the greatest feature of his game. The leg strokes already mentioned, his great height, the quickness of his hand and eye, all combined, gave him at times complete mastery over fast bowling. Bumping balls on the off stump, to a batsman of ordinary height perhaps the most difficult to dispose of, he punishes by hard cuts to the boundary.

What sort of bowling does W. G. Grace like least? I have never asked him this somewhat searching question, nor if I did is it likely that the champion would care to give himself away. His answer, probably, accompanied by a hearty laugh, would be somewhat in this fashion: Like least, indeed? Why, I love them all. Of course he does; but I have an opinion that on a hard, fast, and true wicket, the slower the bowling the less it is to his liking. His great size prevents him getting quickly to the pitch, and a very slow bowler always has terrors to a fast-footed player that do not present themselves to a quick-footed and active batsman. Whilst discussing WG as a batsman, we must not lose sight of another of his great qualities, viz., patience. Never flurried because runs are not coming quite quick enough, never excited because they are coming quicker than usual, he keeps on simply playing the correct game, and even after the 100 goes on the same as before, with his mind fixed upon the 200.

It would be impossible, in a short article such as this is, for me to do anything like adequate justice to the merits of the great William Gilbert Grace. There have been some who for a short period have given reason for the belief that his position as champion batsman was being dangerously assailed. I allude to such names as W. L. Murdoch, A. Shrewsbury, and A. E. Stoddart. That belief was, however, but fleeting. W. G. Grace has proved his batting powers to be immensely superior to every other cricketer. He is, though nigh on 50, still the best, and I sincerely hope he will continue for many years to give us all the pleasure of enjoying his magnificent play.

PERSONAL RECOLLECTIONS OF W. G. GRACE
BY LORD HARRIS

... I well remember the first time I saw the old man – as all cricketers love to call him; it must have been about '67 or '68 that a few of the Eton eleven were taken up to Lord's by Mr Mitchell on a holiday for the express purpose of seeing W. G. bat, and thereby having our own ideas improved. It was a drizzly cold morning, and WG in a thick overcoat had a spirited argument with "Mike" as to the weather and the ground being fit for cricket, the former, caring little about standing as a model for us, thinking it was not; and the latter, caring little as to the particular match, thinking it was. I must have seen but little of WG between then and '72, except in Canterbury in the week, but in '72 I had a two months' experience of his comradeship during the tour in Canada and the States of Mr R.A. Fitzgerald's team, the first amateur eleven that crossed the seas on a cricketing tour, and a right good eleven it was, the best strictly amateur team, I should say, that has ever been made up for that purpose. WG and poor Cuthbert Ottaway went in first, and generally put on 100 before the first wicket fell, a pretty good start, with the "Monkey", Alfred Lubbock, and Walter Hadow to follow on; and then what a bowling side it was, Appleby dead on the off stump every ball, and Billy Rose, about the best lob bowler I ever saw, at the other end, and WG and C. K. Francis as changes. But the history of the tour, is it not all written in *Wickets in the West*, by that prince of cricket reporters, Bob Fitzgerald himself? So I will not reproduce the time-honoured allusion to WG's speeches, but content myself with bearing grateful witness to the kindly sympathetic consideration which characterised his comradeship. That tour commenced and cemented a friendship between us which I value at the highest.

From about '76 to '86 I saw a good deal of the old man's play in the big matches, and I shall never see such all-round play again. There may arise a bat as good, and at point and to his own bowling a field as good, and, of course, there have been and will be bowlers as good, but I doubt one generation producing two such all-round cricketers. And remember, my young friends, that this super-excellence was not the result of eminent physical fitness only, it depended a good deal also on the careful life the old man led. He did not play brilliantly despite how he lived, as some, whose all too brief careers I can remember, did, but he regulated his habits of life with such care and moderation that his physical capacity was always at its best, and has lasted in the most marvellous manner. I shall always hold that WG was the best and pluckiest field to his own bowling I ever saw. The ground he used to cover to the off – and with the legbreak on of course the majority of straight balls went there – made him as good as a 12th man. He used to have his mid-on nearly straight behind the bowler's arm so as to cover the balls hit straight back. I fancy I've noticed that he has not tried for long-leg catches so much since poor dear Fred Grace, the safest catch I ever saw, went home, but it may be only fancy. And then the hot 'uns I've seen him put his hands to, half-volleys hit at ten yards' distance, low down, with all the momentum of a jump in and a swinging bat, catches that looked like grinding his knuckles against the sole of his boot, but I never saw the old man flinch.

I always thought the old man depended rather too much on the umpire for leg-before, particularly when I was on the opposite side. He crossed the wicket so far to the off himself that he could not in many instances judge with any accuracy whether the ball pitched straight or not, and I don't think a bowler ought to ask for leg-before unless he is pretty sure as to the pitch. I remember one day at Canterbury, the wind was blowing pretty strongly across the ground, and WG was lobbing them up in the air to get all the advantage of the wind. I kept on fetching them round to sharp long leg – I never hit him square – or trying to, and every time the ball hit my leg he asked, and every time he asked Willsher shook his head, and the old man was getting almost savage, when, at last, I got my left leg too much to the off, and the ball went through my legs and bowled me. Of course, WG held that was proof positive that all the others would have hit the wicket too, whilst I held that that was possible, but that none of them had pitched straight.

Another reminiscence connecting him with Canterbury Week is that weary day – or day and a half I might say – when he made his 344. We had got a big score in our first and only innings, and had got MCC out for something small. I thought it rather odd, for the wicket was all right, and our bowling was not very deadly, and my forebodings were well founded. It did not matter what we bowled for that day and a half, most balls went quite impartially to the boundary. Mr Foord Kelcey always declared in after years that about five o'clock on the Friday evening, all our bowling being used up, he and poor dear old "Bos" (Mr C. A. Absolom) went on permanently!

On the whole, however, I think in those days we used to get rid of WG pretty luckily when we met him, but he gave us a severe taste of his quality at Clifton one year, over a century each innings. When he had got 98 second innings I thought perhaps a bad lob might produce results. Henty was no longer a member of the Kent team, or he would have gone on, as he always did when we were in serious difficulties, without taking his pads off, but either Mr Patterson or I could bowl quite as bad a lob as he ever did, so one of us, I forget which, went on, and sure enough something did result. The old man hit a fourer, scored his second century in the same match for the second time in his career, and stumps were drawn. Some people said I did this on purpose to let him get his second century, but that allegation was not founded on absolute knowledge, and a bad lob when a man is well set is sometimes luckier than a good ball.

... I do not know whether it is fancy, but I shall always believe that WG's later style of batting is quite different from what it was between '70 and '80. Now he plays the regulation back and forward strokes, but at that time he seemed to me to play every good-length straight ball just in front of the popping crease, meeting it with a perfectly straight bat every time, but a kind of half stroke, only possible when great experience of the bowling, a very clear eye, and great confidence are combined. Remembering how many straight balls he used to place on the on side in those days, and the improbability therefore of the full face of the bat being given to the ball at the moment of impact, his extraordinary accuracy of eye can perhaps be realised.

... I had the opportunity of taking a part in paying him what I know he holds to be as great a compliment as ever was paid him – viz., the decision of the Marylebone Cricket Club to give its support to the National Testimonial which was so enthusiastically started this year. I gave my vote for that decision, not merely because I regard WG as the most prominent exponent there has ever been of the finest and purest game that has ever been played, but also because the old man is the kindest and most sympathetic cricketer I have ever played with. As I said in proposing his health some years ago at a banquet the Kent County Club gave in his honour, I never knew a man make a mistake in the field but what WG had a kind word to say to, and an excuse to find for him, and I doubt if I could conclude with anything in praise of my old friend which would be truer or more gratifying to his feelings than that.

GLOUCESTERSHIRE

In writing of Gloucestershire cricket in 1894, we were compelled by force of circumstances to take a somewhat gloomy view of the situation... There was no disguising the fact that the fortunes of the side were at a very low ebb indeed. Not even the most sanguine of the county's supporters therefore could have been prepared for the many brilliant triumphs that were gained by the team in 1895...

Three men were mainly instrumental in bringing about this welcome change – Mr W. G. Grace, Mr C. L. Townsend and Mr G. L. Jessop. The superb batting of the champion in May had the effect of raising the eleven from their terribly depressed condition and engendering a more hopeful feeling...

Taking part in all the 18 matches the great cricketer scored 1,424 runs, with an average a little under 51. He had not been so successful for Gloucestershire since 1887, when his aggregate was 1,405, and his average a trifle over 63. The month of May found him in remarkable form – indeed it was generally admitted that he had not played such brilliant cricket since 1876 – and while the wickets remained firm and good, he was the most likely run-getter in the country. In the three early successes that fell to the county he played a most important part. Commencing with 288 against Somerset at Bristol – his highest score in a first-class match since 1876 – he obtained 257 and not out 73 against Kent at Gravesend, while in the third match, against Middlesex at Lord's, he scored 169. With this innings, it may be remarked, Mr Grace completed the unprecedented feat of scoring over a thousand runs in first-class cricket during the month of May. An admirable innings of 91 against Sussex at Brighton followed, and then with wickets after a while affected by rain his batting dropped to a moderate level…

With his score of 288 against Somerset, Mr Grace accomplished the unparalleled feat of playing 100 innings of three figures in first-class cricket, and in celebration of the event the champion was subsequently entertained by the county club at a banquet at which the Duke of Beaufort presided, over 400 guests being present. Later in the season the public appreciation of his wonderful ability took a more tangible form in the institution of a national testimonial…

For his brother, now 54, 1895 seemed to mark the end of his career – one which had spanned all 33 editions of Wisden *to date, but* Wisden *was jumping the gun a little:*

For the first time since the formation of the county club, Mr E. M. Grace did not make a single appearance, and we may conclude that a long and distinguished career has at length come to a close. Of the old school of Gloucestershire cricketers, who for eight years were invincible on the home grounds, only Mr W. G. Grace – the greatest of all – remains.

Gloucestershire v Somerset
At Bristol, Thursday, Friday, Saturday May 16, 17 and 18, 1895

Somerset **303** (Fowler 118; W. G. Grace 5–87) and **189** (Woods 47; Murch 8–68);
Gloucestershire **474** (W. G. Grace 288; Tyler 4–160) and **19–1**.
Gloucestershire won by nine wickets.

Though Fowler and Lionel Palairet opened the match by scoring 205 for the first Somerset wicket, Gloucestershire gained a brilliant victory by nine wickets. Everything in the game was dwarfed by Grace's big innings of 288, which was his 100th three-figure score in important cricket. He was batting for five hours and 20 minutes without making a single mistake, his hitting at times being marked by all the vigour of his younger days. He was ninth out at 465, and among his hits were 38 fours, eleven threes, and 29 twos.

Grace took only two more wickets for Gloucestershire all season, after his five-for in the first innings of their first game.

Kent v Gloucestershire

At Gravesend, Thursday, Friday, Saturday, May 23, 24 and 25, 1895

Kent 470 (A. Hearne 155; Murch 3–51) and **76** (A. Hearne 22*; Painter 7–25);
Gloucestershire 443 (W. G. Grace 257; A. Hearne 4–93) and **106–1** (W. G. Grace 73*).
Gloucestershire won by nine wickets.

This was certainly the most remarkable game played last season, affording the only instance in first-class cricket in England of a side winning after having to face a first innings of over 400. Up to luncheon time on the third day only an innings on each side had been got through, and the game looked almost certain to be drawn. The chief credit of Gloucestershire's victory by nine wickets was due to W. G. Grace, who scored 330 runs for once out, and was on the field during every ball of the match.

WG also opened the bowling in the first Kent innings, taking two for 115 in 43 overs. After that he bowled only 15 more overs for the county all summer.

W.G.'s next match for Gloucestershire was against Middlesex at Lord's, in which he scored 169 and completed his 1,000 runs in May. Wisden reports on 'one of his many great innings on last season', but does not mention the fact that he thus reached 1,000 first class runs before the end of May, even though public interest in the possibility of the Champion achieving this unprecedented feat was enormous. WG, incidentally, did not even bother to bat in Gloucestershire's second innings, as they ran out winners by five wickets.

For the Gentlemen against the Players at Lord's in July, the champion was in his element. He was also playing against Tom Hayward, the man who would eventually become the second man to a hundred hundreds, in this fixture for the first time.

Gentleman v Players

At Lord's, Monday, Tuesday, Wednesday July 8, 9 and 10, 1895

Players 231 (Hayward 60; Smith 3–67) and **363** (Storer 93; Dixon 3–44);
Gentlemen 259 (W. G. Grace 118; Peel 4–39) and **303** (Fry 60; Peel 3–51).
Players won by 32 runs.

To do full justice to the match would demand a far larger amount of space than can be spared, and we must be content to dwell on some of the more striking points of the play. At the close of the first day the Gentlemen looked to have a big advantage, their score – in the face of a modest total of 231 – standing at 137 for no wicket. For this favourable position they were indebted first to their generally effective bowling, but chiefly to Grace and Stoddart, who went in at five o'clock and two hours later were not out with 64 and 61 respectively. For nearly half an hour the batsmen were more or less in difficulties, and Stoddart, with his score at six, might have been caught at mid-on from a very tame stroke if Albert Ward had not had the sun in his face. Allowing for some small inequalities, however, the performance of the two batsmen against Richardson and Mold, on a faulty pitch, was one of the greatest of the year. The magnitude of what they had done was not fully realised till the following day, when the Gentlemen's innings was finished off for 259. So difficult was the bowling that, with the out-fielding ground as fast as possible, it took more than two hours and a half to put on 122 runs. Stoddart was first out, his partnership with Grace having in two hours and a quarter produced 151 runs… Grace stayed in till the total had reached 241, and for the first time since the season of 1876 played an innings of over 100 for the Gentlemen at Lord's. Taking into consideration the quality of the bowling and the state of the wicket, we are inclined to think that the innings was the finest he played last season.

And, of course, 1895 was not a great season only for WG. He may have been supreme in many aspects, but others were stealing his records:

MR A. C. MACLAREN

To no one except the brilliant young Indian batsman Ranjitsinhji, did the season of 1895 bring a greater increase of reputation than to Mr Archibald Campbell MacLaren. For Lancashire against Somerset at Taunton in July, he played the record innings in first-class cricket of 424, and in the first-class averages for the year he came out first among those who had played any considerable number of innings, beating Mr W. G. Grace by a fraction.

There was sadness, too, for the Graces:

Dr Henry Grace, the eldest member of the famous cricket family, died on November 13 from an attack of apoplexy. He was born on January 31, 1833, and was thus in his 63rd year. Though never coming prominently before the public, like his younger brothers, EM, WG, and GF, Dr Henry was, in his young days, an excellent cricketer, and but for the calls of his profession would probably have played more frequently in important matches. He is described as having been a vigorous bat, a medium-pace round-arm bowler, and an excellent field – mostly at point. He appeared at Lord's for the first time on July 18 and 19, 1861, and, with a first innings of 63 not out, materially helped the South Wales Club to beat the MCC by seven wickets. The match is a historical one, inasmuch as it introduced Mr E. M. Grace to Lord's ground. Dr Henry Grace was from the formation of the county club an enthusiastic supporter of Gloucestershire cricket, and was never absent from the county matches played at home.

WISDEN 1897

Sydney Pardon chose, as one of his Five Cricketers, the Indian sensation K. S. Ranjitsinhji, who had batted so brilliantly all through 1896. The yardstick of WG's achievements is used to judge any new pretender to his supremacy.

What Ranjitsinhji did last season is set forth in full detail on another page of *Wisden's Almanack*, and there is no need to go twice over the same ground. It will be sufficient to say that he scored more runs in first-class matches than had ever been obtained by any batsman in one season, beating Mr Grace's remarkable aggregate of 2,739 in 1871. While giving the Indian player, however, every credit for his extraordinary record, it must always be borne in mind that while he averaged 57 last season, Mr Grace's average in 1871 was 78.

For WG, the season could hardly have been as spectacular as the year before, but in 1896, he was still a very major batting force.

GLOUCESTERSHIRE

If the general results were scarcely satisfactory, Mr W. G. Grace had every reason to be proud of his own personal efforts on behalf of the side. So far as actual figures are concerned, he even surpassed his splendid record of 1895, when he scored 1,424 runs with an average of just over 50. During the past summer the champion's aggregate was 1,565, and his average only a fraction short of 54. Though the figures are apparently against us, we are disposed to the view that Mr Grace did not play quite such consistently good cricket as in 1895. Four times during the season the Gloucestershire captain scored an innings of three figures, but it perhaps detracts somewhat from the credit of his performances, that two of his great scores – 301 at Bristol, and 243 not out at Brighton – were both made against Sussex, whose bowling was admittedly the weakest among the counties… Making due allowance for the moderate quality of the bowling opposed to him, it was remarkable that after an interval of 20 years he should so closely approach his biggest batting feats… Mr Grace has so long accustomed us to exceptional batting feats that his continued success during the past season was perhaps hardly surprising, but it certainly is an astounding fact that at 48 years of age, he is still able to hold his own with the best of the younger generation of cricketers. His great weight places him at a disadvantage as compared with most other batsmen especially on slow wickets, but on a hard dry ground he is still one of the most dependable run-getters in the country.

His brother EM came out of retirement to play one game for the county, against Warwickshire. He scored 11 and nine, and took one wicket, that of Santall, for 18 runs. W. G. Grace junior played seven times for Gloucestershire, scoring 163 runs at an average of 16.3. He also took three wickets, for 116 runs. He won his Blue for Cambridge, but bagged a pair in the University Match, and Wisden *failed to remark on his abilities one way or the other.*

There is yet another record which WG still holds: the longest elapsed time between first and last first-class triple-centuries – just over 20 years.

Gloucestershire v Sussex
At Bristol, August 3, 4 and 5, 1896

Gloucestershire

Mr. W. G. Grace sen. b Collins 301	Mr. G. L. Jessop lbw b Parris 2
Mr. W. G. Grace, jun. b Hartley 1	†J. H. Board c and b Parris 0
Mr. R. W. Rice c Parris b Ranjitsinhji 84	Mr. S. A. P. Kitcat not out 77
Mr. W. McG. Hemingway c Killick b Hartley . 30	F. G. Roberts c Parris b Killick 2
Mr. C. L. Townsend c and b Tate 30	
H. Wrathall c Parris b Tate 0	B 17, l-b 3 20
Mr. C. O. H. Sewell b Parris 4	551

Tate 65–24–134–2; Mr. Hartley 37–5–115–2; Mr. Collins 24–7–48–1; Parris 63–30–103–3; Killick 32.2–11–57–1; Bean 13–4–34–0; Ranjitsinhji 12–1–40–1.

Sussex

F. W. Marlow c Hemingway b Townsend 57	c and b Townsend 21
E. H. Killick b Jessop 13	b Jessop 20
K. S. Ranjitsinhji b Roberts 38	c W. G. Grace, jun. b Jessop 54
Mr. W. L. Murdoch b Townsend 12	run out 9
Mr. W. Newham not out 63	lbw b W. G. Grace 11
G. Bean c Jessop b Townsend 8	c Wrathall b W. G. Grace 6
Mr. A. Collins c and b Roberts 23	not out 14
Mr. J. C. Hartley c W. G. Grace b Roberts 0	b W. G. Grace 0
F. Parris c Townsend b W. G. Grace 1	b Roberts 3
F. W. Tate b Roberts 4	lbw b Roberts 30
Mr. R. W. Fox b Roberts 9	lbw b Townsend 0
B 13, l-b 5, w 1, n-b 3 22	B 6, l-b 1, n-b 3 10
250	178

Mr. Townsend 27–4–88–3; Roberts 27–7–50–5; Mr. Jessop 19–4–52–1; Mr. W. G. Grace sen. 10–3–30–1; Mr. W. G. Grace, jun. 4–0–8–0.
Second innings—Mr. Townsend 26.3–3–67–2; Roberts 24–10–38–2; Mr. Jessop 14–7–40–2; Mr. W. G. Grace sen.19–11–23–3.

Umpires: A. Chester and G. W. Littlewood.
Gloucestershire won by an innings and 123 runs.

At Brighton in Whit week, W. G. Grace scored 248 not out, and in the return he surpassed that achievement, playing a remarkable innings of 301. This was the highest individual score of the season, and the third-best ever made by Grace in first-class matches. On Monday he scored 193 out of 341 for three wickets, and he was ninth out with the total at 548. He was at the wickets for eight hours and a half, and so grandly did he play, that he gave no actual chance.

The Australians played three Tests in 1896, and the 48-year-old WG was there to do battle with them once again:

England v Australia
First Test Match, at Lord's, Monday, Tuesday, Wednesday, June 22, 23 and 24, 1896

Australia 53 (Darling 22; Richardson 6–39) and **347** (Trott 143; J. T. Hearne 5–76);
England 292 (Abel 94; Eady 3–58) and **111–4** (Brown 36; Jones 2–42).
England won by six wickets.

The first of the three Test matches proved an enormous attraction, the official return showing that on the opening day no fewer than 25,414 people paid for admission, The full attendance was estimated at nearly 30,000, but while this great crowd was in itself a compliment to the Australians it had a grave disadvantage. The field of play was seriously encroached upon, and it is to be feared that a good many of the people saw very little of the cricket. Under the circumstances it would hardly be fair to criticise the conduct of those present, but there was certainly an absence of the quiet and decorum usually characteristic of Lord's ground... The match was the most sensational of the whole tour, its fortunes changing from time to time in a fashion that was quite bewildering. England won by six wickets, but before that gratifying end was reached some startling things happened. Trott had the good fortune to beat W. G. Grace in the toss for innings, and when the Australians went in to bat on a perfect wicket a score of at least 250 was confidently expected. To the amazement of everyone on the ground, however, the Australians failed in a fashion that has seldom been seen on a dry true pitch, being all got rid of by Richardson and Lohmann in an hour and a quarter for 53 runs.

The Surrey bowlers did wonders, but lack of nerve on the part of the Australians must have been largely answerable for such an astounding collapse...

England went in to bat soon after half past one, and when time was called at the close of the afternoon, they had scored 286 for eight wickets. This was a very fair performance but at one time something much bigger seemed in prospect, 250 being on the board with only four men out. It must be admitted, however, that the Australian bowlers were far from fortunate in the support they received, Abel being palpably missed in the slips when he had scored nine, and W. G. Grace let off at long-on at 51... Jackson, who in brilliant style scored 44 out of 69, palpably gave away his innings. The encroachment of the crowd prevented Darling catching him on the on side, and at once, he gave the fieldsman a second opportunity.

The attendance on the second day was only half as large as on Monday, a great many people evidently thinking the match as good as over. Those who stayed away, however, had reason to regret their want of faith in the Australians, as they missed seeing some of the finest cricket of the whole season. England's innings was quickly finished off for 292, and then the Australians, with a balance of 239 against them, went in for the second time...

On Giffen's dismissal, Gregory joined Trott, and a partnership commenced which as long as cricket is played will cause the match to be remembered. Getting together before one o'clock, the two batsmen resisted the England bowling for nearly two hours and three quarters, putting on in that time no fewer than 221 runs. Both played superbly, their cricket leaving no room whatever for adverse criticism... Gregory hit 17 fours in his 103, and Trott, who was batting nearly three hours and a half, struck 24 fours in his 143. When Gregory left at 283 the Australians were 44 runs ahead with six wickets to fall, and the position of England was certainly an anxious one.

England v Australia
Second Test Match, at Manchester, Thursday, Friday, Saturday,
July 16, 17 and 18, 1896

Australia 412 (Iredale 108; Richardson 7–168) and **125–7** (Gregory 33; Richardson 6–76);
England 231 (Lilley 65*; McKibbin 3–45) and **305** (Ranjitsinhji 154*; McKibbin 3–61).
Australia won by three wickets.

The second of the three great Test matches was in many ways one of the most remarkable matches of the season, for though the Englishmen were defeated at the finish, the two best performances of the game were accomplished for them, Ranjitsinhji playing perhaps the greatest innings of his career, and Richardson bowling in a style he has seldom approached.

... Trott changed his bowling with remarkable skill and judgment, and it was quite a stroke of genius to go on first himself with Jones. He had the satisfaction of easily getting rid of Grace and Stoddart, thus giving his side the good start they so needed.

England v Australia
Third Test Match, at Kennington Oval, Monday, Tuesday, Wednesday,
August 10, 11 and 12, 1896

England 145 (Jackson 45; Trumble 6–59) and **84** (Abel 21; Trumble 6–30);
Australia 119 (Darling 47; J. T. Hearne 6–41) and **44** (McKibbin 16; Peel 6–23).
England won by 66 runs.

Statements in certain newspapers as to the allowance made for expenses to amateurs caused great irritation, and for a time there was much uncertainty as to how the England eleven would be finally constituted. In the end matters were smoothed over, but not until a definite statement – which will be found in another portion of this Almanack – had been made public as to the financial relations between Mr W. G. Grace and the Surrey Club.

This statement read:

Mr W. G. Grace and The Surrey Club

Various rumours having gained currency as to the amount of money allowed to Mr Grace for expenses when playing for England at The Oval, the following official statement was made public on August 10 – the opening day of the Third Test match.

The Committee of the Surrey County Cricket Club have observed paragraphs in the Press respecting amounts alleged to have been paid, or promised, to Dr W. G. Grace for playing in the match England v Australia. The Committee desire to give the statements contained in the paragraphs the most unqualified contradiction. During many years, on the occasions of Dr W. G. Grace playing at The Oval, at the request of the Surrey Committee, in the matches Gentlemen v Players and England v Australia, Dr Grace has received the sum of £10 a match to cover his expenses in coming to and remaining in London during the three days. Beyond this amount Dr Grace has not received directly or indirectly, one farthing for playing in a match at The Oval.

Signed on behalf of the Committee

August 10, 1896 C. W. Alcock

The Editor, Sydney Pardon, in a forerunner to the now essential Notes By The Editor, wrote of this matter in his article, "Some Current Topics":

Into the thorny question of amateurs' expenses I do not propose to enter, for the good and sufficient reason that I do not possess the necessary information. No doubt there are some abuses, but as a famous cricketer – a county captain and quite behind the scenes – has assured me, he does not know more than half a dozen men, playing as amateurs, who make anything out of the game, the evil would not seem to be very widespread. Mr W. G. Grace's position has for years, as everyone knows, been an anomalous one, but "nice customs curtsey to great kings" and the work he has done in popularising cricket outweighs a hundredfold every other consideration.

Happily, the match, which had been preceded by all these storms and troubles, passed off in the pleasantest fashion, and proved a complete success. Played on a wicket ruined by rain, it produced some startling cricket, and was in the end won by England by 66 runs, the Old Country thus securing the rubber.

WISDEN 1898

After his successes in the 1897 season, G. L. Jessop was selected as one of the Five Cricketers of the Year. The comparisons were inevitable.

Mr Jessop is one of the most enthusiastic of cricketers, and it was certainly a fortunate day for Gloucestershire when his ability was discovered. Barring the Graces themselves, the county has never had such an all-round player.

GLOUCESTERSHIRE

The county had a good year in 1897, finishing fifth in the table.

Mr W. G. Grace and the fine band of young cricketers he has gathered round him may be congratulated on the result of their labours during the summer of 1897…

    An important factor in Gloucestershire's improved fortunes was the fact that the side were not so largely dependent in batting on the individual efforts of Mr W. G. Grace as they had been in some recent years, and indeed, before the famous cricketer ran into form, the western eleven had gained three wins as against two defeats. Putting on one side the big average of 61 by Mr Kitcat, who only took part in three matches, Mr Grace again comes out at the head of the batting, with an aggregate of 1,079 and an average only a run short of 40. Excellent as this record is, it falls considerably short of what the champion accomplished for the county in the two preceding seasons… The appreciable drop in Mr Grace's figures is not in any way attributable to any falling-off in skill. It was brought about by a strange lack of judgment during the early part of the season. For several weeks the great batsman laboured under the impression that it was imperative upon him to make runs at a quick rate. The result was, that though playing several bright innings, he frequently lost his wicket at a time when he might have been considered well set, and so long did he continue to play in a manner quite foreign to his normal methods as to create a feeling of dismay. However, a finely played 66 for the Gentlemen against the Players at Lord's apparently convinced him of the error of his ways, as from that point he recovered his patience and returned to his proper game. No sooner had he done so than he at once resumed his old place among batsmen, again becoming one of the most dependable run-getters in the country. In addition to scoring 113 against the Philadelphians, he obtained 126 against Notts at Trent Bridge, 116 against Sussex at Bristol, and 131 against Notts at Cheltenham. He thus gave ample proof that when content to take his time over his runs and thoroughly play himself in, he was still a great batsman, and it was unfortunate that he should, through some misapprehension as to his powers, have allowed May and June – two months of hard wickets – to slip by without making one really big score. As a consequence Mr Grace, in first-class cricket, was far from approaching his performances of 1895 and 1896, when he scored respectively 2,346 and 2,135 runs. Still, on the whole, he had a thoroughly successful season, obtaining 1,532 runs, with an average of 39. This record, of which the best batsmen might well be proud, becomes remarkable indeed when one reflects that the great cricketer is now in his 50th year.

Though WG continued to dominate Gloucestershire's statistics, his 24-year-old son WG junior had a more modest summer, making just 96 runs at an average of 12 in his seven matches for the county, and taking eight wickets for 203 runs. EM did not play first-class cricket in 1897. His career was at last over, at the age of 55.

WISDEN 1899

FIVE GREAT PLAYERS OF THE SEASON

Mr C.L. Townsend

Except Mr Grace himself, and Ranjitsinhji, there is no more interesting figure in the cricket field at the present time than Mr C. L. Townsend... Barring the Graces, Gloucestershire has produced no such remarkable cricketer.

Townsend was WG's godson and a schoolfriend of WG junior.

It was another good year for Gloucestershire – they finished third.

In connection with county cricket in recent years there has been nothing more remarkable than the revival in the fortunes of the Gloucestershire eleven...

For Mr Townsend the season of 1898 was one of conspicuous all-round success, as in the 20 county matches, in addition to taking 130 wickets for less than 20 runs each, he scored 1,072 runs with an average of 38. This is a record worthy of Mr Grace himself in his best days...

Once more, Mr W. G. Grace is at the head of the batting tables and the famous cricketer may be congratulated upon a highly successful season. He did not do so well as in 1895 and 1896, but his record was an improvement upon that of 1897... Last summer he raised his aggregate to 1,141, and his average to 47... He played three innings of over 100 [but] his highest score in a home match was 93 not out against the Sussex bowlers at Bristol, and on that occasion he declared the innings of his side closed. The explanation of this seemingly curious proceeding was to be found in the fact that with the exception of 93 he had previously made in first-class cricket every score from 0 to 100, and was desirous of obtaining this particular number. As a bowler Mr Grace occasionally met with success, his most notable achievement in this direction being accomplished at Taunton when he obtained 12 Somerset wickets. In the match at Leyton he had a great personal triumph, as after taking seven wickets in Essex's first innings for 44 runs, he went in and scored 126. In the matter of all-round work, Mr Grace had done nothing so remarkable as this in first-class cricket since his wonderful performance at Oxford in 1886, when he scored 104 and in the University's second innings obtained all ten wickets for 49 runs.

Essex v Gloucestershire
At Leyton, Thursday, Friday, Saturday, July 7, 8 and 9, 1898

Essex **128** (Mead 34; W. G. Grace 7–44) and **250** (Perrin 81; Wright 4–32);
Gloucestershire **231** (W. G. Grace 126; Kortright 5–41) and **151–9** (W. G. Grace 49; Kortright 7–57).
Gloucestershire won by one wicket.

Mr Grace had never before appeared at Leyton in a county match, and he marked the occasion by giving an astonishing display of all-round cricket on the opening day, taking seven wickets for 44 runs and then playing an innings of 126, with which not the slightest fault could be found. He was batting for three hours and ten minutes and scored his 126 out of a total of 203. The close of the game was intensely exciting, two runs being wanted by Gloucestershire when Roberts, the last man, went in. Next to Grace's all-round cricket, Kortright's terrific bowling was clearly the feature of the game.

WG junior played only four times for the county in 1898, scoring 51 runs at an average of 12.75. He did not bowl.

In all cricket in 1898, WG senior scored 1,513 runs, at an average of 42.02 and with a highest score of 168, for Gloucestershire against Notts. He took 36 wickets at 25.47 each.

WISDEN 1900

WG shocked the cricket world in 1899 when he left the county club that he had helped to form.

In connection with Gloucestershire cricket in 1899, the most important fact was the secession of Mr W. G. Grace from the eleven. Mr Grace took part in four games in May, his last appearance for the county being against Middlesex at Lord's. It then became known that he had resigned the captaincy and retired from the team. It was understood that his relations with the county committee had been somewhat strained, and there is not much doubt that his acceptance of the position of manager to the new London County Club, organised by the Crystal Palace authorities, was a source of irritation. It would be idle, even if one were in a position to do so, to enter into the merits of the dispute, but the upshot was that Grace withdrew from a post he had held since the formation of the Gloucestershire county club 30 years ago. When interviewed on the subject, Mr Grace said that he had not refused to play for Gloucestershire, but as he was not seen in the eleven after May, it may fairly be assumed that his connection with the county has finally ceased. It is a matter of regret that his county career should have ended in such an unfortunate manner, for whatever the real rights of the quarrel, his retirement marked the close of a great and glorious chapter in cricket history. Though not playing in first-class cricket to anything like the same extent as in former years, Mr Grace took part in several important games, scoring 515 runs at an average of 23. He represented England against the Australians in the first Test match at Nottingham and played for the Gentlemen against the Players both at The Oval and Lord's. At the Surrey ground he scored 28 and 60, and at Lord's 78, this being his highest score in a first-class match. On this last occasion he had the misfortune to be run out when apparently well set for his hundred. It is difficult to say whether or not there was any deterioration in his powers as a batsman as he did not have a sufficiency of first-class practice to keep himself in form.

WG had been appointed secretary and manager of the newly formed London County club at the end of 1898. He moved from Gloucestershire to Sydenham to be near the ground, but intended to carry on playing for Gloucestershire when his duties with his new club permitted. Somehow his amateur status was not affected.

The break with Gloucestershire came when the county committee wrote a letter to WG asking him to tell them exactly which games he intended to play. Given that other Gloucestershire amateurs, notably C. L. Townsend and G. L. Jessop, had also played for the London County club at WG's invitation, without being sent such letters, and given that the secretary of the Gloucestershire club was his elder brother EM, Grace took offence and, on May 28, wrote to the committee, stating that: "I had intended to play in nearly all our matches, but in consequence of the resolution passed and other actions of some of the Committee, I send in my resignation as captain." He concluded his letter abruptly: "I have the greatest affection for the county of my birth, but for the Committee, as a body, the greatest contempt." Wisden reported none of this.

The Australians toured England again in 1899. WG, who turned 51 that July, felt he was still ready for the challenge.

England v Australia
First Test Match, at Nottingham, Thursday, Friday, Saturday, June 1, 2 and 3, 1899

Australia 252 (Hill 52; Rhodes 4–58) and **230–8** dec (Hill 80; Jackson 3–57);
England 193 (Fry 50; Jones 5–88) and **155–7** (Ranjitsinhji 93*; Trumble 3–39).
Match drawn.

In picking the England team for the first of the five Test matches the committee had rather a thankless task. It was early in the season for such a big event, and so many of the matches in May had been played on wickets damaged by rain that there had not been a really fair chance of discovering what men were in form. The great difficulty, however, lay in the question of fast bowling. Lockwood had broken down at the Crystal Palace in the first match of the Australian tour; Richardson was obviously not himself, and Mr Kortright, owing to a bad strain, was quite incapacitated... Making the best of a bad job, they decided, in the event of the weather proving fine, to let Hirst, for this one occasion, be the England fast bowler. It cannot be said that the experiment was in any way a success. Hirst worked hard for his side, his fielding indeed being perfection, but as a bowler he did not cause the Australians any trouble.

As everybody knows, the match ended in a draw, time alone saving the English eleven from defeat. When stumps were finally pulled up on the Saturday afternoon they wanted 135 runs to win and had only three wickets to go down. Ranjitsinhji saved the side with a superbly played 98 not out, his best innings against the Australians during the whole of the season. Never probably did a batsman, in the endeavour to save a match against time, play such a free and attractive game as he did during the last 40 minutes he was at the wickets ...

The team went in after luncheon with nothing to hope for but a draw, and at the end of 55 minutes four wickets were down for 19 runs, the four men out being Grace, Jackson, Gunn and Fry. Grace and Jackson were bowled by Howell in one over with beautiful breakbacks ...

The Australians' first innings had been finished off for 252, and Grace and Fry were together with England's score at 70 for no wicket. Just after this, however, Grace lost his wicket in his over-eagerness to score from Noble on the off side, and from the moment of his downfall to the finish of the game the Englishmen were completely outplayed.

After this game, WG decided to call an end to his England career. As a batsman he might still have been worth his place, but his bowling had fallen away and, in particular, he felt that his fielding was no longer good enough.

ENGLAND V AUSTRALIA (SECOND TEST MATCH)

The second of the Test matches was the only one of the five brought to a definite conclusion, and its result was heavy blow to English cricket, the Australians gaining a brilliant victory on the third afternoon by ten wickets. They played a winning game all the way through, fairly beating the Englishmen at every point. The match, indeed, furnished one of the most complete triumphs gained by Australian cricketers in England since Gregory's team came over and astonished us in 1878. Without in any way attempting to make excuses for an overwhelming defeat, it must be said that the committee in picking the England eleven laid themselves open to obvious criticism. They made no fewer than five changes from the side that had done duty at Trent Bridge a fortnight before, A. C. MacLaren, Townsend, G. L. Jessop, Lilley and Mead taking the places of W. G. Grace, William Gunn, Hirst, Storer and J. T. Hearne. As regards batting, they were probably right to leave out Grace and Gunn, but having done that they ought assuredly to have invited Shrewsbury to play. The Nottingham batsman had given conclusive evidence that he was in form, and with Grace standing down there would have been no difficulty about his fielding at point.

By the 1900 edition "Some Cricket Records" was becoming an ever more important part of the Almanack, and WG's achievements were dotted throughout. Among the most impressive of his records at that date was:

Three hundreds in succession in first-class cricket have been scored by Mr W. G. Grace in 1871, 1872, 1873 and 1876, while in 1874 three innings of over a hundred by him were divided by a match against odds for the United South of England XI; by Mr A.C. MacLaren in 1895; in 1896 by Abel, Storer and K. S. Ranjitsinhji; in 1897 by Tyldesley and in 1899 by Major Poore.

For 24 seasons, WG was the only man to have accomplished this feat, and by the time anybody repeated it once, he had done it five times. But others were catching up:

Mr C. L. Townsend in 1899 scored over 2,000 runs and took over 100 wickets in first-class matches, a feat only performed before by Mr W. G. Grace in the season of 1876.

EM, never a shrinking violet, felt in 1900 (in which year he would celebrate his 60th birthday) that his deeds on the cricket field, in both first-class and less important cricket, should be noted. Wisden's *editor obliged:*

E. M. GRACE IN THE CRICKET FIELD BY SYDNEY PARDON

During the autumn Mr E. M. Grace was kind enough to send me – to do what I liked with – the statistics of his career in the cricket field from the time when, as a lad of less than ten years old, he played his first match in 1851 down to the end of the past season. Without going into details or separating big matches from small ones, he sent a concise statement of the runs he had scored and the wickets he had taken in 49 years, and very wonderful the figures looked. They struck me as so interesting that after seeing to their immediate publication in several news papers I thought I could not do better than find a place for them in *Wisden's Almanack*. At the time Mr Grace wrote to me I feared he had determined to give up cricket, but in answer to my enquiry he wrote that he had no such intention and should go on playing as long as possible. It is of course unreasonable to expect him at 58 years of age to equal his old feats with either bat or ball but as he is full of vigour and capable of hunting four days a week he will probably be seen in the Thornbury eleven for several seasons to come.

I never look at E. M. Grace's scores in old Almanacks and newspapers without wondering what would have been thought of him if he had not found in his own family a greater than himself. He was the biggest run-getter in the world when he went out to Australia with George Parr's team in 1863, and was a greater force on a side than any other player of that day – V. E. Walker not excepted. When he returned home, however, in the following year WG appeared on the scene and it was readily seen that the younger brother would soon be the finer bat of the two. E. M. Grace had by sheer force of genius for the game risen to the top of the tree in defiance of orthodox rules, for with all his great qualities he never played with a bat as straight as Fuller Pilch's. While WG went on from strength to strength – at 18 he was clearly the best bat in England – EM dropped to some extent out of public matches, his medical work taking up a good deal of his time. However, with the formation of the Gloucestershire County Club, EM started what I may call the second half of his career. He was still quite a young man and, always playing plenty of local cricket, he had kept himself in thorough practice. He helped to lift Gloucestershire in 1876 and 1877 to the very top of the tree and kept his place in the team down to quite recent years. Perhaps he played for a season or two longer than he ought to have done, but one can well understand his reluctance to finally withdraw from an eleven with which he had from its start been so closely associated. During all those long years he did many big things for Gloucestershire but never was his skill as a batsman shown in a brighter light than when he played against the first Australian teams in 1878 and 1880. At Clifton in 1880, though he did not succeed in winning Gloucestershire the match, he astonished Spofforth by hooking to the boundary some of the best balls that greatest of bowlers sent down. His success on that occasion – he scored 65 and 41 – led to what I have always regarded as the crowning triumph of his career. Seventeen years had passed away since he reached his highest point as a batsman, and yet, purely on his merits, he was picked for the first England and Australia match ever played in this country. It was an eventful moment in the history of modern cricket when on that September day in 1880 he and WG opened England's innings at The Oval. They scored 92 runs together for the first wicket, and so laid the foundation of England's score of 420. A melancholy interest will always in the Grace family attach to the match as it was the last one – or at any rate the last one of any public interest – in which the three brothers took part together. On September 22 Fred. Grace was dead.

It is a thousand pities that E. M. Grace has never been induced to write and publish his recollections of the cricket field. It is not at all right that the endless good stories he tells with such racy humour should all be lost to the world. More than that, he would, I think, be able to give us a fuller and better comparison of the great players of his youth with those of our own day, than has yet appeared. He has enjoyed an almost unique experience, making as he did big scores against Jackson, Tarrant, and Willsher, and playing in his later days against Spofforth,

Palmer, Turner, Ferris, Lohmann, and Richardson. As a batsman, E. M. Grace may fairly be described as the great revolutionist. When he came before the public, batting was a very orthodox science indeed, the pull with which we are now almost too familiar being regarded as little less than a sin. E. M. Grace changed all that. Disregarding the protests of the purists he scored where he could and thought nothing of taking the ball from wide of the off stump round to the on side if by so doing he could score four runs. More than anyone else he enlarged the scope of batting, and those who on the perfectly prepared wickets of these days pull with such certainly, should modestly remember that E. M. Grace, playing under far less favourable conditions, first showed more than five and thirty years ago how the thing could be done. In regard to his personal characteristics E. M. Grace is very happily hit off in a phrase in the seventh volume of *Scores and Biographies*, Mr Haygarth describing him as "Overflowing with cricket at every pore, full of lusty life, cheerily gay, with energy inexhaustible." The words were written of Mr Grace when he was 20, and though he is now 58 they still hold good. I am not without hope that the famous cricketer may yet embody his experiences in book form. At one time, at any rate, he was not averse to writing, for he tells me that when returning from Australia, in 1864, he wrote a full account of the doings of George Parr's team, intending to publish it when he got back to England. For some reason, however, the project fell through, and the matter, covering ten quires of foolscap, remains in manuscript. The last page, as giving Mr Grace's impressions of Australia five and thirty years ago, will be read with no little interest:

"I saw what I have told. Australasia was hung with flags and clothed in purple and fine linen. Senators, cheers, complimentary speeches, and brass bands met the Eleven everywhere. But I have no reason to believe that there were hid beneath this glittering surface those festering sores – poverty, ignorance, and injustice which are corroding the vitals of so many older states. In all the enjoyment there was nothing forced or unnatural, it was the healthy pleasure-taking of men in at least comfortable circumstances. We did not see the Australians in their business life, but we were sure that when they returned to the ordinary cares of business, though the laugh and frolic might have passed, they would still possess comfort and prosperity. I do not say that suffering never visits the homes of Sydney, Melbourne or Dunedin, nor do I wish to convey the idea that even want is actually unknown – sickness, disappointment, care, anxiety and bereavement cast shadows as dark in the Southern Hemisphere as in the Northern. The widow and the orphan, the victims of disease and accident, the aged and infirm, all these find that even in the golden land there and are privations. But the charities of the people are large and the helpless are few in number. I can say with truth that I have not tried to colour this sketch."

… I will leave the record of Mr E. M. Grace's career to speak for itself, merely adding that though the figures let us know how many runs he has made and how many wickets he has taken, they cannot tell us that he was, by universal consent, the most brilliant and daring field at point the world of cricket has ever seen.

Year	Wickets taken	Runs scored
1851	22	256
1852	26	370
1853	35	431
1854	89	446
1855	73	563
1856	82	579
1857	76	628
1858	69	870
1859	173	1121
1960	189	1372
1861	286	1747
1862	312	2190
1863	339	3074
1864	370	2054
1865	246	1626
1866	196	1738
1867	166	1218
1868	128	1300
1869	163	1979
1870	194	1100
1871	186	1538
1872	239	2628
1873	298	2493
1874	312	2052
1875	369	2426
1876	262	2020
1877	268	1351
1878	260	2114
1879	239	2048
1880	250	1384
1881	253	2770
1882	201	2726
1883	250	3166
1884	231	2556
1885	Did not play owing to an injured knee.	
1886	175	1179
1887	214	1422
1888	224	2016
1889	223	1139
1890	278	1221
1891	203	1173
1892	232	1284
1893	217	1464
1894	223	1320
1895	240	973
1896	205	864
1897	227	990
1898	241	831
1899	252	672
	10,006	72,482

CHAPTER 5

THE TWENTIETH CENTURY

"An idea of what his batting was like in his prime"

It was astonishing, even in those days, to find a leading sportsman still worth his place among the very best at the age of 50-plus, but WG's right still to be considered one of the great players of his day was not disputed as the new century arrived. There were signs that his powers were waning – in 1899, WG recognised after the Trent Bridge Test against Australia that, at the age of 50 years and 320 days, his Test career was over. But he still had centuries to score and wickets to take in first-class cricket, and his London County side to manage, captain and play for.

The London County experiment, similar in many ways to the earlier attempts of clubs like Prince's to set themselves up as rivals to MCC, was no doubt financially attractive for WG, but it was not a popular success. Attendances were low, even when the great man himself was playing. And the matches, although billed as first-class, were of little significance. After the 1905 season, London County disbanded, and with it, the Champion's career faded to a close. He played his final first-class match at the beginning of the 1908 season, at the age of 59 years and nine months

Even in these final seasons, when he was far less mobile than he had been in his youthful prime three decades earlier, he still showed flashes of his old brilliance. His final innings for the Gentlemen against the Players at The Oval in 1906 was worth 74 runs, an achievement which Wisden put into perspective: "The magnitude of the performance could only be realised when one bore in mind that WG made his first appearance for the Gentlemen both at The Oval and at Lord's in 1865." Almost every year for 42 seasons, Grace had been the dominant figure in the leading match of the season. It is an achievement that is unthinkable now.

His brother EM had finally given up the first-class game, but was still playing regularly for Thornbury, and WG's eldest son, William junior, died after an operation for appendicitis, in 1905 at the age of just 30. So WG was the last of his family still playing top-class cricket.

WISDEN 1901

By this time, the obituary section of Wisden contained almost as many references to the Grace family as did the scorecards.

Richard Daft, died on July 18. His death, which took place at Radcliffe-on-Trent, removed from amongst us one of the greatest cricketers of the last generation... Coming out as an amateur, he made his first appearance at Lord's, for North against South, in 1858, and quickly established a reputation as one of the best batsmen of his day. He took to cricket as a professional in 1859, but played again as an amateur when his career in public matches was nearly over. It is a noteworthy fact that he and the Warwickshire cricketer, Diver, are the only men who have played on both sides in the Gentlemen and Players match... He came before the public at about the same time as Robert Carpenter and the late Thomas Hayward, and for three or four seasons it was a disputed point as to which of the three was the finest bat in England. George Parr was on the wane, and they had no rival until E. M. Grace appeared on the scene. Whether Daft was as good or better than Hayward or Carpenter is purely a matter of opinion, but there can be no question that in their day all three were very great indeed.

Mr William Yardley, whose sudden death occurred at Kingston on October 28, will be remembered as one of the greatest cricketers of his day... Few batsmen, either of his own day or any other time, have been better worth looking at than Mr Yardley, his style being free and commanding and his hitting brilliant in the extreme... It is no flattery to say that in 1870, 1871, and 1872, his only superior as a batsman was Mr W. G. Grace. In those days when he and Mr Grace played on the same side they always had a small wager on their scores and, long after he had retired from first-class cricket, Mr Yardley was fond of recalling the fact that in the Gentlemen and Players match at Lord's, in 1871, he beat the great man in both innings.

WG no longer played for Gloucestershire, and although the London County side was not part of the County Championship, Wisden *allotted a chapter to their first-class matches. WG also played for other teams as the fancy took him:*

North v South (Philip Need's Benefit)
At Lord's, Thursday, Friday, Saturday, September 13, 14 and 15, 1900

South 474 (W. G. Grace 126; Briggs 6–135) and **142–6** dec (Warner 62*; Smith 3–76);
North 405 (Hirst 89; Jephson 7–132) and **130–7** (Lord Hawke 48; Jephson 5–66).
Match drawn.

Among several fine batting performances, that of W. G. Grace stood out as the highest and nearly the best. The veteran was in wonderful form, scoring 126 out of 274 in about three hours – his biggest innings of the season. His innings was faultless and his hits included 15 fours, six threes and six twos.

WG is described as "nearly the best", but Wisden *does not give an opinion as to who batted better. At the age of 52, he seemed indefatigable:*

Cambridge University v London County Club
At Cambridge, Thursday, Friday, Saturday, May 31, June 1 and 2, 1900

London County 311 (W. G. Grace 86; Dowson 4–92) and **128–3** dec (W. G. Grace 62);
Cambridge University 253 (Taylor 98; W. G. Grace 5–99) and **90–4**
(Taylor 27*; Quaife 2–8).
Match drawn.

W. G. Grace was in great form, batting finely in both innings, and taking five wickets. In getting his 86 he was at the wickets two hours and three-quarters.

THE LONDON COUNTY CLUB

Captain and Secretary: Mr W. G. Grace

With all their matches against prominent elevens officially recognised as first-class and counted in the averages, the London County Club started its second year of existence with a fairly promising outlook, and the results, if not brilliant, were at least as good as could reasonably have been expected... Beyond everything else, the season's cricket was remarkable for the success of Mr Grace's batting. In far better form than he had been in the previous year the great cricketer played many fine innings and twice got into three figures. With an aggregate of 982 runs he had an average of over 46.

He also took 30 wickets for his team, at an average of just under 30 apiece.

Over the whole season, Grace batted 31 times, scoring 1,277 runs at an average of 42.56, placing him 12th in the first-class averages. Ranjitsinhji was top, with the unheard aggregate of 3,065 runs at an average of 87.57. Four other batsmen – Fry, Abel, Hayward and Jessop – scored over 2,000 runs. The young guns of the golden age of cricket were achieving what even WG might once have thought impossible.

Grace's 32 wickets at 30.28 each were excellent figures for a man of 52, but meant he was three-quarters of the way down the final averages lists.

WISDEN 1902

The old order was beginning to pass by 1901. E. M. Grace was still secretary of Gloucestershire, but there was no other family connection. WG played for London County, for the Gentlemen against the Players, for An England XI against Yorkshire, and also for MCC, for whom his batting average was a mere 12, compared with Dr Arthur Conan Doyle's 30.66. He did, however, take five wickets in the second innings of MCC's match against Leicestershire, finishing with 12 wickets at 17.50 for the Marylebone Club.

THE LONDON COUNTY CLUB

In the course of the 13 matches, a great number of players assisted the London County, but interest usually centered in the doings of Mr W. G. Grace. In his fielding the great cricketer showed more than ever the effect of advancing years, but he was in capital batting form, scoring 761 runs in 20 innings, with an average of 38. He would have made a good many more runs had he been able to travel quicker between the wickets. His best scores were 132 against MCC and 108 against Cambridge University*, both innings being played at the Palace. During the first half of the season he bowled with a great deal of his old skill, and though he did not manage to keep up his form during July and August, he came out with a record of 39 wickets for 21 runs each... Mr Grace is excusably proud of the opportunities he has given at the Palace to cricketers who would otherwise have had no opening in first-class matches.

This is a rare mistake by Wisden. *It was not W. G. Grace who scored 108 against Cambridge University, it was his opening partner W. G. Quaife. Grace scored 72 in a partnership of 163.*

London County v MCC and Ground
At the Crystal Palace, Thursday, Friday, Saturday, August 8, 9 and 10, 1901

London County 633 (I. Walker 222, W. G. Grace, sen. 132; Atfield 3–102);
MCC and Ground 501 (Doll 224*, G.G. Hearne 115; W. G. Grace, sen. 5–159).
Match drawn.

London County scored 309 for six wickets on the first afternoon, their veteran captain making his first and only hundred in first-class cricket during the season, and Walker, the Surrey amateur, compiling 209 not out. While the pair were together they added 281 in less than three hours... It will be noticed that the bowling was absurdly weak on both sides.

W. G. Grace junior opened with his father in this match, and made 32.

W. G. Grace senior ended the season with 1,007 runs at an average of 32.48. He also took 51 wickets at 21.78 each. C. B. Fry and J. T. Tyldesley both scored over 3,000 runs. Wilfred Rhodes took 251 wickets.

OBITUARIES

George Lohmann
Born in June 1865, he was only in his 37th year. He first played for Surrey in 1884, and did enough to convince good judges – W. G. Grace among the number – that an all-round cricketer of no ordinary promise had come forward... As

a match-winner we have in this generation had no one greater except W. G. Grace, and, possibly, A. G. Steel. To him more than to anyone else was due the restoration of Surrey to its old place at the head of the counties.

Robert Carpenter
One by one the great professional cricketers of the last generation are passing away. Richard Daft, Thomas Hearne, and R. C. Tinley died in 1900, and on July 13, 1901, Robert Carpenter passed away… [Tom Hayward and Carpenter] went to America with an English eleven in the autumn of 1859, and in conjunction with E. M. Grace were the great stars of the splendid eleven that toured in Australia under George Parr's captaincy in the winter of 1863–64… Carpenter was essentially a back player, and rarely went forward except when he meant hitting. No one in the old days of rough wickets at Lord's could come down on a shooter with greater certainty, and W. G. Grace himself scarcely possessed a stronger defence… Mr E. M. Grace says of Carpenter as a batsman that there never was a finer back player.

Robert Clayton, for many years past one of the groundstaff at Lord's and formerly a member of the Yorkshire eleven, died on November 26 at Gainsborough. He was born at Caley, near Otley, in Yorkshire, on January 1, 1844, and was thus nearly 58 years of age. Though he assisted Yorkshire for several seasons in the seventies, it cannot be said that he ever fulfilled the promise of his earliest performances… [In 1871] at Lord's he played for Yorkshire against the MCC, and met with great success, bowling W. G. Grace in the first innings, and securing in all ten wickets for 94 runs. His form was so good that in the Whit Monday match, between North and South, he was, in the absence of the late George Freeman, given a place in the Northern eleven. Once more he did well, for though the South scored 328 (W. G. Grace making 178), six wickets fell to him for 77 runs.

WISDEN 1903

In 1902, at the age of 54, WG scored 1,000 runs in a season for the 28th and final time. There were several flashes of his old brilliance:

MCC and Ground v Derbyshire
At Lord's, Monday, Tuesday, June 23 and 24, 1902

Derbyshire 208 (Wright 41; Trott 7–84) and 88 (Wright 31; Mead 6–36);
MCC and Ground 148 (Bohlen 39; Hulme 3–11) and 151–4 (W. G. Grace 74*).
MCC and Ground won by six wickets.

After being outplayed on the opening day, when with an innings apiece decided the MCC were headed by 60 runs, the club, thanks to the bowling of Mead and the batting of W. G. Grace, not only recovered their lost ground, but gained a handsome victory by six wickets... Derbyshire's second attempt only amounted to 88, which left the club 149 to make. Grace was in superb form and, helped by Crawford and Hawke, the veteran made 74 not out, out of 151, in two hours and ten minutes and won the match.

London County v MCC and Ground
At Crystal Palace, Monday, Tuesday, Wednesday, July 14, 15 and 16, 1902

MCC and Ground 235 (Geeson 44; May 6–72, Grace 4–89) and **290** (Rawlin 122; Odell 6–114); **London County 568** (Wood 176, Poidevin 161, Grace 131; Trott 5–173). London County won by an innings and 43 runs.

On the opening day the game pursued a quiet course, but on Tuesday some remarkable hitting was seen, London County, in four hours and 20 minutes, increasing their overnight score of 111 for two wickets to 568. This huge total was mainly the work of Wood, Poidevin and Grace, who, between them, made no fewer than 468 of the number. Poidevin played irreproachable cricket, his cutting and placing to leg being exceedingly fine, and his off-driving brilliant to a degree... Wood and Grace, both of whom made most of their runs by clean hard driving, were also seen to the very best advantage.

WG's other century of 1902 was for London County against Warwickshire, 129 in a drawn game which closed London County's season. Wisden was less than complimentary, reverting to its earlier rather grudging attitude towards Grace's run-scoring:

For London County, Grace and Braund played finely, on the opening day scoring 164 between them in an hour and 20 minutes for the second wicket. Braund's innings was faultless, but Grace owed a good deal to fortune, Davey missing him at long-on before he had scored.

WG ended the season with 1,187 runs at an average of 37.09, placing him 11th in the averages, above such names as Fry, Foster, Jessop, Murdoch, Hayward and Jackson – a remarkable achievement. He also took 46 wickets at 23.34 in 406 overs, which hardly compares with Rhodes's 213 wickets at 13.15, in 1,306.3 overs of left-arm spin. But WG's average put him well ahead of Tom Richardson, whose 106 wickets cost 24.59 each.

OBITUARIES

Mr Thomas William Lang died on May 30. Mr Lang (a brother of Mr Andrew Lang, the well-known writer) had long ago dropped out of first-class cricket, but during his brief career he earned great distinction... While still at Clifton he played under the residential qualification for Gloucestershire, and in August 1872, during the absence in Canada of Mr W. G. Grace, who was touring with the late Mr R. A. Fitzgerald's team, he helped to win for the County, on the Clifton College Ground, a remarkable match against Sussex. Gloucestershire followed on against a majority of 101, and won the game by 60 runs. Sussex only wanted 153 in the last innings, but poor Fred Grace and Mr Lang, bowling unchanged, got them out for 92, the former taking seven wickets for 43 runs and Lang the other three for 42.

WISDEN 1904

There were strong signs that the life of the London County Club would not be a long one.

LONDON COUNTY

Secretary and Captain: Mr W. G. Grace

For the season of 1903, Mr Grace arranged a more ambitious programme than he had previously ventured upon. Had the summer been fine, it is highly probable that cricket at the Crystal Palace would have attracted greater attention from the general public than in any other year... As it happened, however, the wretched weather completely ruined three of the six home engagements and the appearance of Gloucestershire without Jessop aroused very little interest... Of the 11 matches actually played, four were won, four lost and three drawn – a season's work with which Mr Grace had no reason to feel dissatisfied. Depending as largely as he does on what may be called outside help, Mr Grace, in London at any rate, was able to get together sides that were surprisingly strong considering the heavy demands now made upon players by county matches...

In the course of the season some 50 cricketers took part in the London County matches, and as so few had anything more than limited opportunity the averages are of small value. Grace alone took part in all the matches, but the batting of the great cricketer showed a marked falling-off as compared with the two previous seasons. He started the season well, and in the match with Gloucestershire in June played an innings of 150, but in the later engagements he was by no means himself. The wet wickets doubtless had something to do with his want of success, but Grace is now 55 years of age and it is only natural to expect that the process of time must mark a decline in his powers... G. W. Beldam is nominally at the head of the bowling, but the honour rightly belongs to Posthuma who at times proved quite deadly and had a fine record of 23 wickets for just over 15 runs each. Odell and Grace bore the brunt of the work with Posthuma, but whereas Odell took 24 wickets for 21½ runs apiece, Grace only obtained eight at a cost of over 50 runs each. Except when the Australians are in the country, the interest of the cricket enthusiast centres chiefly in County Championship matches, but having regard for the delightful conditions under which the game is played at the Palace it is surprising, and much to be regretted, that so little public support is accorded the London County Club.

London County v Gloucestershire
At Crystal Palace, Thursday, Friday, Saturday, June 4, 5 and 6, 1903

Gloucestershire 397 (Fowler 114; W. G. Grace 6–102) and **61** (Spry 14; Prichard 6–31);
London County 311 (W. G. Grace 150; Spry 5–67) and **150–3** (Douglas 54; Langdon 2–39).
London County won by seven wickets.

This was quite a remarkable match, Gloucestershire losing by seven wickets after having scored 397 in their first innings. When play ceased on the opening day the London County were in a bad position, as in face of Gloucestershire's big total they had lost two wickets for 21 runs. On the Friday however, Grace gave one of his very best displays, and thanks to his efforts and the excellent batting of Poidevin and Douglas the score in the end reached 311. Gloucestershire on going in a second time failed dismally, and in an hour and a quarter were all out.

In this match, WG scored his first century against his old county, the 12th county against whom he had hit a hundred. He never scored a hundred against Derbyshire, Hampshire or Leicestershire of the first-class counties he played.

He also became the oldest man ever to score a century and take five wickets in an innings in the same match. At the time he was nearly 55 years old.

At the end of the season, the averages showed that he scored 593 runs at 22.80, and took ten wickets at 47.90 each. He was last but one in the bowling averages.

OBITUARIES

Arthur Shrewsbury
As everyone interested in cricket is aware, Arthur Shrewsbury shot himself on the evening of May 19. Illness which he could not be induced to believe curable, together with the knowledge that his career in the cricket field was over, had quite unhinged his mind…

It may fairly be claimed for Shrewsbury that he was the greatest professional batsman of his day. As a batsman he had a style of back play peculiarly his own, and his judgment of the length of bowling was almost unequalled. It was said of him that he seemed to see the ball closer up to the bat than any other player. More than that, there was such an easy grace of style and such a suggestion of mastery in everything he did that, whether he scored slowly or fast, his batting, to the true judge of cricket, was always a delight. Excepting of course W. G. Grace, it may be questioned if we have ever produced a more remarkable batsman.

Robert Thoms

For some time before he passed away on June 10 there had been such very bad accounts for Bob Thoms' health that no one was at all surprised when the announcement of his death appeared in the papers... In him there has gone a remarkable and interesting personality. No one had a more thorough knowledge of cricket, or could speak with greater authority about all the leading players of the last 60 years... He came out at Lord's when Fuller Pilch was the best bat in England, and it was his privilege to watch the triumphs of George Parr, Hayward, Carpenter, Richard Daft, Jupp, Tom Humphrey, E. M. Grace, W. G. Grace, and all the other great run-getters down to Ranjitsinhji and C. B. Fry. Even in the season of 1902 he saw Victor Trumper bat at the Hastings Festival, and complimented him on his splendid innings of 120 against the South of England.

The Graces, as cricketers, had no more fervent admirer than Thoms, and he was fond of saying that if W. G. Grace had not been such a marvellous bat he would have been the best slow bowler in England, his head work being so remarkable and his command of length so perfect. Of E. M. Grace's all-round capabilities, too, and especially his fielding at point, Thoms would never weary of talking.

This is a rare reference in Wisden *to the style of W. G. Grace's bowling – slow. Not even Cricinfo today tells us how and what the great man bowled. In fact, when he first began playing important cricket, he was trying to be a fast bowler, but with age and experience he became a very canny slow-medium bowler.*

WISDEN 1905

In 1904, WG scored his 126th and final first-class century, on his 56th birthday. A phenomenal first-class career was coming to an end.

LONDON COUNTY

Though less attractive than in the previous year, neither Lancashire nor Gloucestershire renewing their fixtures, the programme of first-class fixtures arranged for London County last season was an interesting one. Relying so largely on outside help, however, Mr Grace was not often able to put into the field a team strong at all points, and it was therefore not surprising that the failure outnumbered the successes... As in previous years, the cricket at the Crystal Palace received but a small amount of public support, Mr Grace's presence in the field naturally not being the potent attraction it once was. The expense of carrying through a regular programme of out and home matches having proved too heavy, London County will in 1905 cease to be a first-class team, but some interesting cricket, including an Australian match, will be seen at the Palace.

London County v MCC and Ground
At Crystal Palace, Monday, Tuesday, Wednesday, July 18, 19 and 20, 1904

MCC and Ground 189 (A. Hearne 42; Ranjitsinhji 4–63) and **185** (Harrison 42; Braund 5–50); **London County 392** (W. G. Grace 166; A. Hearne 5–101). London County won by an innings and 18 runs.

The MCC practically lost the match on the opening afternoon, as they were all out on an excellent wicket in less than three hours, for 189, and when stumps were drawn, London County had got to within 72 of this total without loss… Everything else in the match was dwarfed by the batting of Grace who gave an exceedingly fine display, hitting with great power in all directions. He made one or two faulty strokes, but gave no actual chance during the five hours and a quarter he was at the wickets. He hit 14 fours. This was the only occasion in first-class cricket last season in which Grace played a three-figure innings.

Ranji and Fry dominated the batting averages, and WG finished the season with 637 runs at 25.48, and 21 wickets at 32.71.

OBITUARIES

Mr Herbert Jenner-Fust, the oldest of cricketers, passed away on July 30. The veteran, who played his first match at Lord's for Eton against Harrow in 1822, was born on February 23, 1806, and was thus in his 99th year. He was the last survivor of the first Oxford and Cambridge match in 1827, and, owing to the calls of his profession, retired from first-class cricket the year before Queen Victoria came to the throne. Still, though nothing was seen of him in great matches after 1836, he played cricket in a more modest way for a long time, and made his last appearance in the field very late in life… Herbert Jenner, to speak of him as he will always be known in cricket history, was President of the MCC in 1833, and was for many years President of the West Kent Cricket Club, holding this position to the end of his long life. It is a curious fact that though he retained a keen interest in cricket he never took the trouble to see W. G. Grace play.

Did Wisden *relish or deplore Jenner-Fust's lack of interest in WG?*

The character of E. M. Grace comes strongly through in another obituary

Mr Frederick Aitken Leeston-Smith, who had played for Brecknockshire and Somerset, died during 1903. He was a powerful hitter, a middle-paced round-armed bowler, and generally fielded at point. In 1881 he played an innings of 204 for Weston-super-Mare v Clevedon… In a match between Weston-super-Mare and Thornbury, he once hit E. M. Grace for four sixes from consecutive balls, a performance which the latter has described as follows: "F. L. Cole made one off my first ball, F. A. Leeston-Smith six off the second, six off third, six off fourth, six off fifth, when the umpire said, 'I am afraid it is over, Doctor.' I said, 'Shut up, I am going to have another,' and off this one he was stumped. Weston-super-Mare had to follow their innings. Leeston-Smith came in first, and the first ball I bowled him he hit for six. The second also went for six, but off the third he was stumped again."

WISDEN 1906

With the demise of London County as a first-class team, WG's appearances in top cricket halved, so that he played just eight times in 1905. His brother was still playing for Thornbury.

"Some Cricket Records" includes this statement:

Mr E. M. Grace, in all matches in which he has participated during his extraordinary career, has scored 76,098 runs and obtained 11,395 wickets. He was born in 1841, and for the Thornbury Club in 1904, he took 277 wickets. In 1905 he took 303 wickets.

WG played for The Gentlemen of England against the Australians at Crystal Palace, the opening match of their tour, but only made five. This was, however, more than Trumper, Warner, MacLaren and Gregory combined, in the first innings of the drawn game.

Oxford University v Gentlemen of England
At Oxford, Monday, Tuesday, Wednesday, May 22, 23 and 24, 1905

Oxford University 349 (Norris 72; W. G. Grace 4–121) and **273** (Wright 67; Marshall 5–50); **Gentlemen of England 181** (Kenward 43; Henley 4–39) and **391** (Marshall 94, W. G. Grace 71; Branston 4–41).
Oxford University won by 50 runs.

The side that W. G. Grace got together certainly should not have been given such a high-sounding name as Gentlemen of England. Still, they made a very fine fight and only lost the game by 50 runs. They were set to get 442 in the last innings, and at the end of the second day Grace and Marshall had scored 143 without being separated. Marshall was out next morning at 168 and Grace, after batting for three hours, left at 192.

The Gentlemen of England played several matches at Crystal Palace, enjoying the first-class status that London County had relinquished. WG appeared in most of the matches, but did not make much impression.

For "Gentlemen of the South" against "Players of the South" at Bournemouth, Grace top-scored in the Gentlemen's first innings, with 43, but as his team was thoroughly beaten, Wisden *made no comment on his play.*

His season ended with a tally of 250 runs at 19.23, with a highest score of 71. He took only seven wickets, and thus was not included in the season's averages.

OBITUARY

Mr William Gilbert Grace, Jun., eldest son of the greatest of cricketers, died suddenly at three o'clock on the morning of March 2, at East Cowes, after an operation for appendicitis. As he was born on July 6, 1874, he was under 31 years of age at the time of his death. He was in the Clifton College XI in 1891–92–93, being captain in his second year, and assisted Cambridge against Oxford in 1895 and 1896. His first pronounced success was gained in the Reigate Festival of 1894, when he played a not-out innings of 148 for his father's XI against Mr W. W. Read's XI. At Cambridge on June 1, 1896, he and G. S. Graham-Smith made 337 together for the first wicket of Pembroke College v Caius College, and at the Crystal Palace on September 16, 1901, he and W. L. Murdoch (who carried out his bat for 200) put up 355 for the first wicket of London County v Erratics. In these matches his scores were respectively 213 and 150. As a bowler he frequently did well, and for London County v Bromley Town, at the Crystal Palace on August 25, 1902, he obtained all ten wickets in an innings. From 1897 until 1903 he was an assistant-master at Oundle, and during the last two years of his life he occupied a similar position at the Royal Naval College, Osborne. He was buried at Elmers End Road Cemetery on March 6.

WISDEN 1907

WG showed he had some progressive if unpopular ideas.

NOTES BY THE EDITOR

No season goes by without producing some discussion as to the County Championship, and 1906 was no exception to the rule. It was rather surprising, however, to find a proposal to arrange the Championship in two divisions, after the style of the Football League, emanating from W. G. Grace. I am, as everyone must be, quite conscious of the anomalies inevitable in a competition in which 16 counties play an unequal amount of matches, but for the two-division suggestion I have no liking whatever. I cannot bring myself to look with any favour on a scheme which might, as the result of one unlucky season, involve the most famous counties being put down into the second rank. The traditions of cricket are against such a system.

Gentlemen v Players

At Kennington Oval, Monday, Tuesday, Wednesday, July 16, 17 and 18, 1906

Players 365 (King 89*; Crawford 4–105) and **335** (Hardstaff 104; May 4–89,
W. G. Grace 1–23); **Gentlemen 258** (Wood 68; Lees 5–84) and **277-7**
(W. G. Grace 74; Quaife 2–9).
Match drawn.

After three days of heavy run-getting, the Gentlemen and Players' match at The Oval ended in a draw, the Gentlemen at the finish wanting 166 to win with only three wickets to go down. As has been the case for many years past the match had nothing like the importance of the corresponding fixture at Lord's, but for all that it proved a genuine attraction... In one respect the match was memorable, W. G. Grace, who completed his 58th year on the Wednesday celebrating the occasion in a most appropriate way with a score of 74. Though he tired towards the end of his innings, his play while he was getting his first 50 runs was good enough to give the younger people among the crowd an idea of what his batting was like in his prime. The magnitude of the performance could only be realised when one bore in mind that WG made his first appearance for the Gentlemen both at The Oval and at Lord's in 1865. He was naturally delighted at his success and received numberless congratulations.

WG dismissed J. H. King, c Colbeck b Grace for 88, in the second innings, his final wicket in first-class cricket.

The end of season averages showed WG made 240 runs at 26.77, in the season in which Tom Hayward scored a record 3,518 runs at 66.37. His bowling figures were excellent – 13 wickets at 20.61 – the last wickets he was to take in first-class cricket. Eight of these came against the touring West Indians in their first match in England.

The efforts of George Hirst in scoring over 2,000 runs and taking over 200 wickets that year established a record that even WG had been unable to achieve.

WG's performances were by this time always the yardstick when assessing the merits of others.

OBITUARIES 1907

Mr W. W. Read died on Sunday, January 6, at his residence, Colworth Road, Addiscombe Park. More than nine years have passed away since Mr Read dropped out of the Surrey eleven and gave up first-class cricket, but his wonderful play during a long career is vividly remembered. Beyond question he was one of the greatest batsmen the game has known, holding a high place among those nearest in merit to W. G. Grace.

Mr George Gilbert, who died at Summer Hill, New South Wales, on June 16, at the age of 78, was a cousin of the Graces, and in his time played no mean part in the cricket field. He was born in Gloucestershire, and appeared several times for the Gentlemen of Surrey, and, in 1851, for the Gentlemen against the Players at Lord's. He went to Australia in 1852, and four years later captained New South Wales in the very first match that state ever played against Victoria. He also played for the New South Wales XXII against the first English team which visited Australia – in 1861–62 – and to the last took a great interest in the game. At The Oval, in 1851, he played a single-wicket match against Mr F. P. Miller, the Surrey captain, in which a curious occurrence took place. The latter cut a ball which went round the boundary stump. Gilbert threw the ball at the wicket but, as it did not pass within bounds, was told to fetch it back and try again. During the argument Mr Miller ran 13 for the hit.

WISDEN 1908

WG played only one first-class game all summer – an early-season match:

Surrey v W. G. Grace's XI
At Kennington Oval, Thursday, Friday, May 2 and 3, 1907

W. G. Grace's XI **78** (Crawford 22; Lees 5–29) and **98** (Wood 26; Lees 5–35);
Surrey 155 (Holland 64; Brearley 8–71) and **22–1** (Smith 16*).
Surrey won by nine wickets.

WG's 16, opening the first innings, was the ninth-highest score of the match; Jack Hobbs made two. In the second innings WG made three, and he played no more first-class cricket that summer.

WISDEN 1909

Alfred Lubbock, clearly what C. B. Fry would have called 'laudator temporis acti', wrote an article for the 1909 Wisden, *entitled*

CRICKET IN THE SIXTIES AND AT THE PRESENT DAY

Comparing the cricket in the sixties with that of the present day is not easy, for many reasons; namely, that it is played under very different conditions and on totally different wickets. I consider that the Cricket County Championship has also made a difference in the game. It has made it more a matter of business than pleasure, and it is played in a far more serious manner than formerly. In the sixties the chief matches were, Gentlemen v Players, North v South, Gentlemen of the South v Players of the South and a few suchlike games… As regards the actual players, I consider there are more good players and this, no doubt, has been caused by the County Championship rivalry… Now as for the Gentlemen batsmen in the sixties there were a few quite as good as any of the present day, and I have heard it said more than once that had W. G. Grace had the present wickets when in his prime he never would have been got out at all. I myself can't go quite so far as this, but still it would have been a job. I consider there were others quite as good and with better style than WG, but not so safe and sure. One of the reasons why WG made more hundreds than other Gentlemen was because he always played so carefully and never took risks. In fact often after he had made a hundred or even two hundred he would play on quite as steadily as when he first went in, and being very strong and always in good trim he never seemed to tire. Many other amateurs after they got a hundred would slog out at everything, and so almost get out on purpose. This I never saw WG do. One of the chief reasons for it was because everything was then run out, and batsmen had often had about enough of it and didn't care to run any more. Now a man can go in and get a hundred by tapping balls to the boundary, and be just as fresh and strong as he was when he started. One batsman of the old school had he had the present wickets to bat on would I think have been quite as good, if not better, than any of the present bats. That was Bill Yardley. He was a wonderfully fine bat all round and fast run-getter and had quite as good a defence as WG, but not the steadiness or patience WG had…

I think you will find that most old cricketers will say they were quite as good as any same number at the present day. E. M. Grace was a most brilliant all-round man, quite as likely to make a hundred as anybody, a splendid field anywhere, especially at point – where he always stood close up, not about 20 yards off like many do now and a very tricky bowler.

Owing to the placing balls to leg and the leg glide you never see the fine leg-hitting you used to see; no doubt the new style is the safer game, but not so ornamental. WG chiefly started this and Ranji brought it to perfection… On the whole, although I consider that now there are six good cricketers where formerly there were only one or two, they are not actually better than they were 40 years ago, but they have more advantages, and from an onlooker's point of view I do not think the game (unless Jessop is in and scoring) quite so attractive or interesting as it was in the sixties.

An update on the amazing E. M. Grace:

Mr E. M. Grace, in all matches in which he has participated during his extraordinary career, has scored 76,705 runs and obtained 11,959 wickets. He was born in 1841, and for the Thornbury Club in 1904, he took 277 wickets. In 1905 he took 303 wickets, and in 1906 as many as 352. In 1907 he obtained 212 wickets for 2,382 runs, and had 208 catches missed off his bowling. He did not play in 1908, owing to lameness.

The record of the precise number of catches dropped, a figure submitted to Wisden by the player himself, tells us much about EM's competitive streak.

What proved to be WG's final first-class match took place before winter had had its final say.

Surrey v Gentlemen of England
At Kennington Oval, Monday, Tuesday, Wednesday, April 20, 21 and 22, 1908

Surrey 390 (Lees 97; Cameron 5–83); **Gentlemen of England 219** (Crawford 91;
Busher 3–51) and **130** (Wilkinson 39; Crawford 4–21).
Surrey won by an innings and 41 runs.

Contested in bitterly cold weather, this Easter Monday match possessed a sentimental interest inasmuch as it was the only first-class contest in which W. G. Grace appeared during the season. The famous veteran kept up his wicket for two hours on Tuesday and played very well indeed in the follow-on, but his side suffered defeat by an innings and 41 runs… Early on Monday morning The Oval was covered with snow.

His final two innings read:

W. G. Grace b Busher ……. 15   b Busher ……. 25

WG was second-top-scorer in the second innings. He also bowled two overs for five runs, but took no wickets in his final first-class spell.

WISDEN 1910

NOTES BY THE EDITOR, BY SYDNEY PARDON

One fact in connection with the season I must not allow to pass unnoticed. W. G. Grace was not seen in a first-class match, his career, which practically began in 1864, thus coming to an end. As he only played in 1908 in the Easter Monday match at The Oval the difference between one year and the other was trifling, but one did not know till last summer that, so far as public cricket was concerned, he had done with the game. Dropping out in this gradual way he took no formal farewell. Perhaps, like many famous actors and singers, he kept on a little too long, but everybody could understand his reluctance to leave the scenes in which for so many years he was supreme. I shall always think that his career really terminated in 1906, when, on his 58th birthday, he played such a remarkable innings for the Gentlemen against the Players, at The Oval. He made his first appearance for the Gentlemen at Lord's and The Oval in 1865, his association with the representative match at The Oval thus extending over a period of 41 years. He played for the Gentlemen at Lord's for the last time in 1899, and, but for an unhappy run-out, when firmly set, would very likely have finished with a hundred. There will be great cricketers in the future as there have been in the past, but it is safe to say that we shall never see another W. G. Grace.

Apart from his unequalled genius as a player, he had an enthusiasm for the game that never waned and, in his prime, a stamina that few men have possessed. It is a curious coincidence that in the year in which for the first time WG is missing from the scores in *Wisden*, E. M. Grace should have retired from his position – held since the formation of the County Club of secretary to Gloucestershire. Thus for the time being the name of Grace disappears from cricket. Opinions differ on the point, but I think that, as match-winner and a personal force on a side, E. M. Grace never had a superior among English cricketers except his own brother. To realise what he was at his best one must look up his doings in 1862 and 1863.

Wisden 1911 is the first edition since the Almanack was first published in 1864 with nothing new to say or report about any member of the Grace family.

CHAPTER 6

THE AFTERLIFE OF THE GRACES

"A land mark, a figure head, a giant, a master man"

After WG retired from playing, there were still many thousands of words to be written in the pages of Wisden about the remarkable Grace family. Many of the references come in obituaries, as those who played with WG grew older and died, but the use of Grace as a yardstick for those who followed him was a regular feature of Wisden.

When Grace himself died, in 1915, the Almanack, which was devoted mainly to the stories of those cricketers who died in the Great War, took up many pages with its obituary, memories and recollections of the great man. The 1916 edition, which also includes obituaries of A. E. Stoddart, whom some would describe as the greatest all-round sportsman to have represented England at cricket (with Grace and C. B. Fry, to name but two, following close behind), and Victor Trumper, the sublime Australian batting genius, both of whom died young, has become probably the most sought after edition of the Almanack by collectors, not only for its contents but also for its rarity value, given the limited print run of the wartime editions.

The tributes to his prowess seemed to include ever more superlatives the more that first-hand recollections faded. Hubert Preston in 1949, to mark the centenary of his birth, described him as "the greatest figure who ever trod the cricket field", which a century after his death is perhaps harder to justify. But by the time anybody who must have seen him play was dead and buried, attitudes began to change, in the pages of Wisden at least. In 1998, Geoffrey Moorhouse wrote a long article to mark the 150th anniversary of WG's birth, but the tone was very different from what Hubert Preston had written 50 years earlier. "He was notorious for employing, in order to pursue victory or personal achievement, a variety of wiles and tricks that may be thought of as, well, hardly cricket," wrote Moorhouse. "He was also, throughout his career, quite breathtakingly grasping when his eye caught the glint of hard cash." By the time that Craig Spearman broke WG's record for the highest score ever made for Gloucestershire, in 2004, Wisden records that "even umpire Kitchen shared his pleasure. 'Get rid of the old man,' he said. 'He used to pick up the bails and put them back on the stumps.'" Urban myth was becoming reality.

WISDEN 1912

In 1911, the second-greatest cricketer produced by the Grace family died.

Mr Edward Mills Grace died on May 20 after a long illness at his residence, Park House, Thornbury, Gloucestershire. But for the accident that his own brother proved greater than himself, E. M. Grace would have lived in cricket history as perhaps the most remarkable player the game has produced. Barring WG, it would be hard indeed to name a man who was a stronger force on a side or a more remarkable match winner. Primarily, he was a batsman, but his value in an XI went far beyond his power of getting runs. As a fieldsman at point – at a time when that position was far more important than it is in modern cricket – he never had an equal, and, though he did not pretend to be a first-rate bowler, he took during his career thousands of wickets. In his young days he bowled in the orthodox round-arm style, but his success in club cricket was gained by means of old-fashioned lobs. Fame came to him early in life. Born on November 28, 1841, he made his first appearance at Lord's in 1861, and a year later he was beyond question the most dangerous bat in England. It was in the Canterbury Week in 1862 that, playing as an emergency for the MCC against the Gentlemen of Kent, he scored 192 not out, and took all ten wickets in one innings. This was a 12-a-side and one man was absent in the second innings when he got the ten wickets. He reached his highest point as a batsman in 1863, scoring in all matches that year over 3,000 runs.

After the season was over he went to Australia as a member of George Parr's famous team, but it cannot be said that in the Colonies he did all that was expected of him. He was handicapped by a bad hand, but, as he himself stated, there was another reason for his comparative lack of success. At the start of the tour he fell into rather a reckless style of batting, and, try as he would, he could not get back to his proper method. Still, he did some good things, scoring, for example, 106 not out in a single-wicket match. He had not been back in England more than two years before WG, as a lad of 18, began to put him in the shade. The two brothers were in the Gentlemen's eleven together in 1865 – WG's first year in the representative match – and had a share in gaining for the Gentlemen their first victory at Lord's since 1853. While he was qualifying as a surgeon E. M. Grace to a certain extent dropped out of first-class cricket, but he came very much to the front again on the formation of the Gloucestershire County Club in 1871. He was secretary from the start, and held his post without a break till his resignation in 1909.

In Gloucestershire's early days he renewed the successes of his youth, batting especially well in August 1872, when WG was away in Canada with the amateur eleven captained by the late R. A. Fitzgerald. It is matter of common knowledge that chiefly through the efforts of the three Graces – G. F. died in 1880 – Gloucestershire rose to the top of the tree, being champion county in 1876 and again in 1877. Not till the first Australian team played at Clifton in 1878 did the Gloucestershire eleven know what it was to be beaten at home. One of the greatest triumphs of E. M. Grace's career came in 1880, when, strictly on his merits, he was picked to play for England at The Oval in the First Test match with Australia in this country. After an extraordinary game England won by five wickets, the task of getting 57 runs in the last innings against Palmer and Boyle costing the side five of their best batsmen. EM and WG opened England's first innings, and scored over 90 runs together. WG made 152, and in Australia's second innings W. L. Murdoch just beat him by scoring 153 not out. Never has a finer match been seen.

E. M. Grace continued to play for Gloucestershire for many years, dropping out of the eleven after the season of 1894. Thenceforward his energies were devoted to club cricket, chiefly in connection with his own team at Thornbury. Lameness gradually robbed him of his old skill as a run-getter, but even in 1909, 119 wickets fell to his lobs. As a batsman E. M. Grace was unorthodox. Partly, it is thought, through using a full-sized bat while still a small boy, he never played with anything like WG's perfect straightness, but his wonderful eye and no less wonderful nerve enabled him to rise superior to this grave disadvantage. He was perhaps the first right-handed batsman of any celebrity who habitually used the pull. In his young days batting was a very strict science, but he cared little for rules. If an open place in the field suggested runs the ball soon found its way in that direction. Personally, EM was the cheeriest of cricketers – the life and soul of the game wherever he played. It was a great misfortune that he could never be induced to write his recollections of the cricket field. His good stories could be numbered by the hundred, and in conversation he told them with immense vivacity.

WISDEN 1913

OBITUARIES 1912

The Australian giant George Bonnor's obituary included an anecdote about G. F. Grace's famous catch in 1880 that had not seen the light of day before.

George John Bonnor, born at Orange (N.S.W.), February 25, 1855; died at Orange (N.S.W.), June 27, 1912. Though he was last seen on an English cricket ground more than 20 years ago, George Bonnor had not in one sense outlived his fame, his doings being constantly recalled and talked about. He was, indeed, far too striking a personality to be forgotten in less than a generation. Australia has sent to England many finer batsmen, but no other hitter of such extraordinary power… A famous catch to which Bonnor was out was in the England and Australia match at The Oval in 1880 – the first Test match in England. The ball was hit to such a tremendous height that the batsmen had turned for the third run when Fred

Grace caught it. That great cricketer, who died a fortnight after the match, said he was sure his heart stopped beating while he was waiting for the ball to drop.

Mr W.L. Rees, a cousin of W. G. Grace, died at Gisborne, New Zealand, on May 13, aged 76. A good all-round cricketer, he played for Victoria v New South Wales in 1857, 1858, and 1865, and later on a few occasions for Auckland. He was chosen captain of the East Melbourne CC upon the formation of that Club over 50 years ago, and in his early days in New Zealand defeated single-handed an eleven in Auckland. He was a Member of Parliament in the Dominion, and once made a stonewalling speech of about 20 hours.

WISDEN 1915

On the outbreak of war, W. G. Grace was one of the leading advocates of an immediate curtailment of the cricket season, but the Championship title was nevertheless awarded.

NOTES BY THE EDITOR

Turning to the past season, it was pleasant to find Surrey winning the Championship, a distinction that had not fallen to them since 1899. Some people thought that when, in deference to public opinion – W. G. Grace himself was the chief spokesman – Surrey cancelled their last two matches, the Championship would have to remain in abeyance for the year, but this view received no countenance from the MCC. It would have been iniquitous if Surrey had been robbed of the position they had so fairly won. When, at Surrey's own request, the question was brought before the MCC committee, the matter was promptly settled, Middlesex disclaiming any notion of objecting.

WISDEN 1916

DEATHS IN 1915

Sydney Pardon wrote the obituary of the Grand Old Man.

W. G. Grace
William Gilbert Grace, born at Downend, near Bristol, July 18, 1848
   Died at his home, Fairmount, Eltham, Kent, October 23, 1915
   In no branch of sport has anyone ever enjoyed such an unquestioned supremacy as that of W. G. Grace in the cricket field. In his great days he stood alone, without a rival. Not even George Fordham and Fred Archer as jockeys, or John Roberts as a billiard player, had such a marked superiority over the men who were nearest

to them in point of ability. Whatever may be in store for the game of cricket in the future, it seems safe to say that such a player will never be seen again. A rare combination of qualities went into the making of W. G. Grace. Blessed with great physical advantages, he united to a strength of constitution that defied fatigue a devotion to the game which time was powerless to affect. When he was in his prime, no sun was too hot, and no day too long for him. It is on record that when, for a cricketer, he was no longer young, he spent the whole night by the bedside of a patient, and on the following day stepped onto the Clifton College ground and scored over 200 runs.

Mr Grace's career on the cricket field – almost unexampled in point of length – can be sharply divided into two portions. His early fame as a batsman culminated in the season of 1876, when in the month of August he scored in three successive innings 344 against Kent at Canterbury, 177 against Notts at Clifton and 318 not out against Yorkshire at Cheltenham. Soon after that, having passed his examination at Edinburgh as a surgeon, he thought of gradually retiring from cricket and settling down, like his elder brothers, to the busy life of a general practitioner. As a matter of fact he did for many years hold a parish appointment at Bristol, a locum tenens doing his work in the summer months. There can be little doubt that his change of plans was mainly due to the appearance in England in 1878 of the first Australian eleven…

Mr Grace had never been in such poor batting form as he was in 1878, and on the few occasions that he met the Australian bowlers he did nothing in the least degree worthy of his reputation. I have no exact knowledge on the point, but I feel tolerably certain that the success of the Australians revived Mr Grace's ambition… This second part of his career as a batsman began towards the end of the season of 1880. Following some fine performances for Gloucestershire he played, as everyone will remember, a great innings of 152 at The Oval in the first match in this country between England and Australia. Even then, however, though only in his 33rd year, he laboured under one serious disadvantage. In the four years following his triumphs of 1876, he had put on a lot of weight and was very heavy for so young a man…

He kept up his batting, however, in a marvellous way, the success of what one may call his second period in the cricket field reaching its climax when in 1895 he scored 1,000 runs in first-class cricket in the month of May. His batting at the time has never been approached by a man of the same age; he was nearly 47…

Of Mr Grace's cricket from the time of his first appearance at Lord's in July 1864, for the South Wales Club against the MCC, columns could be written without exhausting the subject. He was picked for the Gentlemen, as a lad of 17, both at Lord's and The Oval in 1865, the honour being conferred upon him quite as much for his medium-pace bowling as for his batting. A year later, however, he proved himself, beyond all question, the best batsman in England, two wonderful innings at The Oval establishing his fame… An attack of scarlet fever interfered with his cricket in 1867, but after that he never looked back. His best seasons as a batsman were, I fancy, 1871, 1873 and 1876. His play in 1871 far surpassed anything that had ever been done before...

With Mr Grace's characteristics as a batsman I must deal rather briefly. He was, in the main, quite orthodox in style, his bat being as perfectly straight as Fuller Pilch's, but he greatly enlarged the domain of orthodoxy, playing a far more aggressive and punishing game than any of the classic batsmen who came before him. It should be explained here that E. M. Grace, who first made the family name famous, played a game of his own and was a little outside comparisons. WG developed the art of batting to an extraordinary degree, but he was not, like EM, a revolutionist. There is his own authority for stating that he did not indulge in the pull till he was 40. A splendid all-round hitter, he excelled all his predecessors in his power of placing the ball on the on-side. A story is told of a cricketer who regarded Fuller Pilch as the last word in batting, being taken in his old age to see Mr Grace bat for the first time. He watched the great man for a quarter of an hour or so and then broke out into expressions of boundless delight. "Why," he said, "this man scores continually from balls that old Fuller would have been thankful to stop." The words conveyed everything...

Mr Grace's batting from 1868 onwards quite overshadowed his bowling, and yet during his career he took many hundreds of wickets. Indeed, old Bob Thoms, the umpire, always contended that if he had not been such a wonderful batsman he would have been the best slow bowler in England. Even as it was he held his own very well with such masters as Alfred Shaw and Southerton. He bowled medium-pace with a purely round-arm action in his young days, but slackened his speed about 1872... He did not rely much on break, only turning in a little from leg, but he had a great command over his length and very seldom indeed pitched short. His chief strength lay in head work. No one was quicker to find out the weak points of a batsman or more certain to lure an impetuous hitter to his doom. In Gloucestershire's great days he was much helped by brilliant fielding, Fred Grace, in particular, at deep square leg, being invaluable to him. When he first appeared for the Gentlemen, Mr Grace was a splendid outfield, capable of throwing a ball 100 yards, but as time went on he took to fielding near the wicket and for many years he had no superior at point except his brother EM.

Personally, WG struck me as the most natural and unspoiled of men. Whenever and wherever one met him he was always the same. There was not the smallest trace of affectation about him. If anything annoyed him he was quick to show anger, but his little outbursts were soon over. One word I will add. No man who ever won such worldwide fame could have been more modest in speaking of his own doings. Mr Grace was married in 1873 to Miss Agnes Day. His domestic life was unclouded except for the death of his only daughter in 1899 and of his eldest son in 1905. Mrs Grace and two sons – Captain H. E. Grace, RN, and Captain C. B. Grace, KFRE – survive him.

There then follow 34 pages of statistics. Among the mass of numbers and small print can be found:

1868 – At the athletic sports at The Oval, during the visit of the Australian Aboriginals, WG, in three successive attempts, threw the cricket ball 116, 117 and 118 yards and also threw it 100 yards one way and back 105. He once threw it 122 yards at Eastbourne.

1874 – In a match, W. G. Grace's XI v F. Townsend's XI, at Cheltenham, the arrangement was that WG should use a broomstick, each of the other players being allowed a bat. Even so handicapped, he made the second-largest score (35) in the game.

1913 – His last match for MCC – v Old Charlton, at Charlton. He scored 18.

It is estimated that during his career WG made about 80,000 runs and took about 7,000 wickets.

Sydney Pardon asked Lord Harris to lead the tributes.

For a personal tribute to W. G. Grace, whose death, even apart from the War, would have made the year one of sad memories, I have to thank Lord Harris – a comrade of the great cricketer in many a famous match.

W. G. Grace
A Tribute
By Lord Harris

It is 30 years since I ceased to play regularly with "WG" and a period such as that plays havoc with one's memory of particulars; but as one of the few left who played with him in the great matches of the seventies and eighties I feel that though one's thoughts are concentrated on a far different field, I ought to try, before it is too late, to leave on record my recollections of him and his play.

I suppose it has been difficult for the present generation, who have seen occasionally at Lord's or in some country match his massive form, to realise that in the seventies he was a spare and extremely active man. My old comrade, Mr C. K. Francis, reminded me when we attended his funeral, that in 1872, when Mr Fitzgerald's team of Gentlemen visited Canada and the United States, WG's playing weight was no more than 12 stone seven pounds; he was a magnificent field in any position, but more especially in fielding his own bowling he was unsurpassed.

For a long time during his career he fielded regularly at point, and though those who had seen both considered his brother EM far the better of the two in that place, he was quite first rate. He was a long thrower in his earliest days, but quite early in his career, when he sometimes went long field, preferred to bowl the ball up to throwing it. He was always when at point on the lookout for a batsman being careless about keeping his ground, and you would see him occasionally face as if about to return the ball to the bowler, and instead send it under-arm to the wicketkeeper, but I never saw him get anyone out that way.

He was originally a medium-paced bowler without peculiarity, meeting occasionally with considerable success, but in the seventies he adopted the delivery, slow with a legbreak, by which he was known for the rest of his great career, and added to his otherwise extraordinary capacity as a cricketer. He must have been by nature a great bat and field, but he made himself, by ingenuity and assiduity, a successful bowler: and though I never knew anyone keener on having his innings, I am by no means sure he did not prefer the other department of the game; at any rate, it was very difficult to take him off once he had got hold of the ball. It was "Well, just one more over," or "I'll have him in another over or two," when one suggested a change. The chief feature of his bowling was the excellent length which he persistently maintained, for there was very little break on the ball, just enough bias to bring the ball across from the legs to the wicket; not infrequently he bowled for catches at long leg, and when his brother Fred was playing was often successful in trapping the unwary, for with a high flight and a dropping ball it is difficult to avoid skying a hit to leg.

… The success of WG's bowling was largely due to his magnificent fielding to his own bowling. The moment he had delivered the ball he took so much ground to the left as to be himself an extra mid-off, and he never funked a return however hard and low it came. I have seen him make some extraordinary catches thus; he had also the additional chance of the umpire making a mistake over an appeal for lbw. He crossed over to the off so far and so quickly that he could not possibly see whether the ball would have hit the wicket, but he generally felt justified in appealing.

On one occasion at Canterbury with a high wind blowing down the hill he was having much success, and asking every time he hit the batsman's legs. He could not get me caught at long leg for I always hit him fine, but he asked every time I missed the ball; I kept remonstrating, and he kept responding indignantly until at last I put my left leg too far to the left, the ball passed through my legs and hit the wicket, upon which he argued that all the previous balls would have done the same, whilst I argued that that and all the others had not pitched straight. He always had his mid-on very straight behind him to make up for his crossing to the off. He seemed quite impervious to fatigue, and after a long innings would gladly, if allowed to, bowl through the opponents' innings. It is right to dwell thus much on his bowling for though not a brilliant he was a decidedly successful bowler, and with a wind to help him actually difficult. But, of course, he will go down to fame as the greatest batsman that ever played, not as the greatest bowler; and I should judge that that description of him is justified. I happen to have seen and played on the average wickets we had to play on before the days of the very heavy roller, and also on the wickets batsmen now enjoy and bowlers groan over. I was too long after his time ever to see Fuller Pilch bat, but I fancy it would be a very fair comparison to pit WG's performances against Fuller's, and great batsman as the latter was, I cannot believe he was as great as WG.

I have elsewhere dilated, at such length as to prohibit repetition here, on the difference between the wickets of my earlier and of my later experience, the far lower level of batting averages in the seventies, as compared with those of the nineties and subsequently, is ample proof of the improvement of wickets, for the bowling has certainly not deteriorated, and it should be remembered that WG was making as huge scores on the more difficult wickets as his successors have done on the easier.

…WG could hit all round, he used every known stroke except the draw which had become all but obsolete when he commenced first-class cricket; and he introduced what was then a novel stroke, and one more adaptable to the break-back bowling which he had as a rule to meet, than the leg-break bowling which was common in Pilch's time, viz., the push to leg with a straight bat off the straight ball, and his mastery of this stroke was so great that he could place the ball with great success clear of short leg and even of two short legs. It was not the glide which that distinguished cricketer Ranjitsinhji developed so successfully, or a hook, but a push and a perfectly orthodox stroke.

In his prime he met the ball on the popping crease, neither the orthodox forward nor the back stroke; it was a stroke entirely unique in my opinion needing remarkable clearness of eye and accurate timing: it is easy enough to play thus when one's eye is in, but when at his best he commenced his innings with it. He stood very close to the line from wicket to wicket and made great use of his legs in protecting his wicket, not be it understood, by getting in front of the wicket and leaving the ball alone, for no batsman left fewer balls alone, but bat and legs were so close together that it was difficult for the ball to get past the combination. So much so that the unfortunate umpires of those times were constantly being grumbled at either by the bowlers for not giving him out, or by him for being given out. J. C. Shaw, in particular, who remarked once: "I puts the ball where I likes, and that beggar he puts it where he likes," was constantly appealing to heaven – as he had failed in his appeal to the umpire – that he had got him dead leg-before; and WG remonstrating in that high-pitched tone of voice, "Didn't pitch straight by half-an-inch."

I cannot remember his ever – when in his prime – slogging: he seemed to play the same watchful, untiring correct game as carefully towards the close as at the commencement of a long innings: and there was no need for he had so many strokes and could place them so clear of the field, and with such power that when runs had to be made fast his ordinary style was enough to secure all that was wanted.

He was quite untiring during the longest innings, and just as anxious and watchful for every possible run whether he had got to save his duck or had already made 200 and he was very fast between the wickets, and just as reluctant to leave the wicket whatever his score was as was Harry Jupp, but more observant of the rules, practice and etiquette of the game than that stolid player, of whom a story was told that playing in a country match he was bowled first ball. Jupp turned round, replaced the bails, and took guard again; "Ain't you going out, Juppy?" said one of the field. "No," said Jupp, and he didn't.

Lord Harris attributes this to Harry Jupp, but it has also been told about WG himself.

WG was desperately keen for his side to win, and consequently was led, in his excitement, to be occasionally very rigid in demanding his full rights, but he was so popular, and had the game so thoroughly at heart that such slight incidents were readily forgiven him and indeed more often than not added to the fund of humorous stories about him. When the luck of the game went against him his lamentations were deep, and his neighbourhood to be temporarily avoided, except by the most sympathetic. Alfred Lyttelton used to tell a delightful story of how in a Middlesex v Gloucestershire match WG, having been given out for the second time caught at the wicket for a small score, he retired to the dressing tent with his shoulders so humped up and his whole aspect so ominous that the rest of the Gloucestershire XI were to be seen sneaking out of the back of the tent to avoid an interview.

His ability to go on playing in first-class cricket when age and weight had seriously increased was quite remarkable. He was a most experienced and skilful anatomist of his own body, and knew how to save the weak points, but in addition he was always a most plucky cricketer. Standing up, as he had to, to the fiercest bowling sometimes on most fiery wickets, and putting his hand to everything within reach no matter how hard hit, he had of course at least his share of painful contusions, but I cannot in the years that I was playing with him remember his ever standing out or flinching: and I have seen him playing with badly bruised fingers.

... He was then and always a most genial, even-tempered, considerate companion, and of all the many cricketers I have known the kindest as well as the best. He was ever ready with an encouraging word for the novice, and a compassionate one for the man who made a mistake.

The soubriquet "Old Man", and it was a very affectionate one, was an abbreviation of "Grand Old Man", copied from that given to Mr Gladstone by his admirers, and indeed he was the Grand Old Man of the Cricket World and the Cricket Field. It is I suppose natural if the present generation who have never seen him play cannot realise what he was to the cricketers of mine. He was a land mark, a figure head, a giant, a master man, and to most of those who are left I imagine it must be as difficult as it is to me to imagine cricket going on without WG. He devoted his life to it, and was perhaps as well-known by sight to the public as any man in public life; for he played all over England, in his younger days with the United South of England Eleven – managed, if I remember right, by Jim Lillywhite – against odds; later as county cricket increased the Gloucestershire matches took him to all the great cricketing counties; but I think he would have said that his home in first-class cricket was Lord's; he was a most loyal supporter of MCC cricket, and the admirable likeness of him by Mr Stuart Wortley shows him batting on that historic ground, the combination of man and place surely most appropriate: the greatest cricketer in the history of the game batting on the most celebrated ground in the world.

He has gone and it is difficult to believe that a combination so remarkable of health, activity, power, eye, hand, devotion and opportunity will present itself again; if not then the greatest cricketer of all time has passed away, and we who saw his play, were encouraged by his invariable kindness, and gloried in his overwhelming excellence, may well think ourselves fortunate that a few of our cricketing years fell within his long cricketing life. It was a shock to hear that WG was no more; the crowd at his funeral, at a time when many of his greatest admirers were occupied with war work, was the best proof of the respect, admiration and affection he had won. The well-known lines in remembrance of Alfred Mynn pray that the Kentish Turf may lie lightly on him; it now provides a calm and honoured home to the remains of W. G. GRACE.

WISDEN 1917

OBITUARY

Dr Alfred Grace, the last of the famous brotherhood, who was born at Downend on May 17, 1840, died in a nursing home in Bristol on May 24, and was buried at Chipping Sodbury. He never appeared at Lord's, but was a very useful cricketer, his usual post in the field being long-stop. As a player he at no time ranked with his brothers, but in local cricket he scored several hundreds, and when only 15 years of age formed one of the Gloucestershire XXII which met the All England Eleven at Bristol. Although he was not in the front rank of cricketers, he stood out as one of the finest horsemen in England, and for many years followed the Duke of Beaufort's hounds three or four times a week. He was known as The Hunting Doctor. For many years he practised as a surgeon at Chipping Sodbury, Gloucestershire. He never got over the tragic death of his son, Dr Gerald Grace, in South Africa.

WISDEN 1920

NOTES BY THE EDITOR, SYDNEY PARDON

The Memorial Biography of W. G. Grace duly appeared during the year, publication having been delayed till after the war. Though the book gives a faithful record of all that WG did in the cricket field it would have been all the better if the recollections furnished by many famous players had not had to be so severely condensed, and in some cases left out altogether. Sir Home Gordon tells me he had sufficient material to fill a far larger volume but that the restriction as to size was unavoidable. One omission is much to be regretted. There is no portrait of WG in his young days except in a group of the amateur team that went to Canada in 1872. We are in danger of forgetting that WG was not always bulky of figure. He put on weight very rapidly before he was 30 but it was not until after 1876 – one of his greatest seasons – that the burden of the flesh began to trouble him. Not the least wonderful thing about him was the way he played when weighing considerably over 16 stone.

WISDEN 1922

Sydney Pardon, in his notes, took to task those who focussed only on Test cricket, especially after a season in which England had been thoroughly beaten by Warwick Armstrong's touring Australians:

Reading much that is written about our great game I am struck by the tendency to regard English cricket as having been more or less negligible till the first visit of the Australians. Young people not versed in cricket history might well gather from what they are told that nothing of real importance happened prior to 1878. This, of course, is an utterly fallacious view. The absurdity of it is proved by the fact that W. G. Grace had passed his best before the Australians came here. They gave a fresh spur to his ambition but, though he did brilliant things against them and was their most formidable opponent in many tours, he was never, by reason of increased weight, in the same physical condition as in his younger days. In comparing the past with the present Lord Harris, with his long experience and undiminished interest in the game, is a safe guide, and in his book *A Few Short Runs* he maintains strongly that the great batsmen of a past generation – R. A. H. Mitchell, Yardley, Ottaway, and A. P. Lucas among others – would on the wickets of today have easily held their own, with W. G. Grace as unrivalled as he always was.

In what was largely a diatribe against the lack of adventure among post-war batsmen, the former Cambridge Blue and Malvern College schoolmaster Charles Toppin invoked the spirit of WG:

MODERN BATTING BY C. TOPPIN

Teach the boys the real amateur type of batting, teach them strokes, let them know that the *raison d'être* of a batsman is that he should get runs, and that, with discretion, the sooner he gets them the better. Don't let a batsman go to the wicket with the intention of playing himself in, let him learn to deal at once with each ball on its merits, at the same time never forgetting that in cricket as in everything else the surest defence is offence, and in particular bearing in mind the immortal W. G. Grace's maxim that in dealing particularly with a fast bowler "it is good to get at him before he gets at you". *Pace* his revered memory I should like, as a principle, to apply his dictum in facing every type of bowling, and I believe that he would have been the first to acquiesce.

Wisden *that year also published the MCC's plans for a W. G. Grace Memorial.*

The following was sent out by the MCC in December:

The Committee of MCC, after consideration of several designs, have decided – as authorised by and at the General Meeting of May 5, 1920 – that the Memorial of Dr W. G. Grace shall take the form of handsome Iron Gates at the Members' Entrance to Lord's, and these will be adapted to harmonise with certain improvements at that entrance which the Committee feel it necessary to make.

The Gates being thus in public view the Committee feel that it is legitimate to offer to the friends and admirers of the late Dr Grace, and to Cricket Clubs, the opportunity of being connected with the Memorial by making donations to the extent of one half of the cost of the gates, the Club contributing the balance.

A tender has been accepted amounting to £2,268, and donations of any amount can be sent to the Secretary of MCC, Lord's, St. John's Wood.

Should the amount received as above be in excess of one half of the cost, the Committee will hand over such excess sum to the Cricketers' Fund Friendly Society.

WISDEN 1925

OBITUARY

Gilbert, Mr Walter Raleigh, was born in London on September 16, 1853, and died at Calgary, in Alberta, Canada, on July 26, aged 70. A steady batsman, a very useful slow round-armed bowler, and a very good field at long leg and cover point, he played for Middlesex by birth in 1873 and 1874, for Gloucestershire by residence 1876 to 1886, and four times for the Gentlemen v Players between 1874 and 1877. He also appeared in a few stray matches for Worcestershire and Northants. In 1873–74 he toured Australia under the captaincy of his cousin, W. G. Grace, and he took part in a very large number of minor matches, especially for the United South of England Eleven, which he managed after the death of G. F. Grace in 1880. His fielding at deep leg to W. G. Grace's bowling was always excellent, for he covered much ground and was a sure catch. Although overshadowed by his famous cricketing cousins, he played a prominent part in the victories gained during Gloucestershire's greatest years. For Thornbury v Sneyd Park in 1874 he made 254 not out, but in a match of note his highest innings was 205 not out for An England Eleven at Cambridge against the University in 1876, when he batted for about seven hours without a mistake and carried his bat through; he hit a five, nine fours and as many as 66 singles, and batted on each of the three days. At Canterbury later in the same season he scored 143 for Kent and Gloucestershire against England, and at Gloucester in 1885 made 102 v. Yorkshire. In the match with Notts at Clifton in the last-mentioned year he took 70 minutes to obtain four runs in his first innings, and two hours and three-quarters to score 21 in his second. Against Sussex at Brighton in 1878 he took four wickets for 12 runs and in the return, at Cheltenham, four for eight, while in the match with Lancashire at Clifton in 1878 he and W. G. Grace bowled unchanged through both innings. At the beginning of 1886 he became a professional, and the season was not far advanced before his career in first-class cricket ended abruptly. He then left England for Canada. He kept up the game in the Dominion and made hundreds in both Halifax and Montreal.

Gilbert's career "ended abruptly" when he was caught stealing from team-mates' clothing in the dressing-room. He was sentenced to 28 days' hard labour and then sent to Canada to begin a new life, which happily proved to be honest and successful.

WISDEN 1926

When Jack Hobbs overtook WG's record total of first-class centuries, it was "forever memorable":

Somerset v Surrey
At Taunton, Saturday, Monday, Tuesday, August 15, 17 and 18, 1925.

Somerset 167 (Young 58; Lockton 4–36) and 374 (MacBryan 109; Fender 5–120);
Surrey 359 (Hobbs 101; Young 3–9) and 183–0 (Hobbs 101*).
Surrey won by ten wickets.

This was the match rendered forever memorable by the triumph of Hobbs, who, by playing innings of 101 and 101 not out, equalled on the Monday morning

W. G. Grace's aggregate of 126 centuries in first-class cricket, and on the Tuesday afternoon beat the "Grand Old Man's" record. Circumstances generally combined to invest the occasion with exceptional excitement. During the early part of the season Hobbs had been so phenomenally successful that by July 20, when he completed a score of 105 at Blackheath, there were a dozen hundreds standing to his credit and the three-figure innings of his career numbered 125. There, as it happened, his extraordinary run of triumphs temporarily ended. He made many substantial scores but in match after match the century needed to bring his total up to that of W. G. Grace eluded his efforts...

Wanting only nine for his hundred on Monday morning, Hobbs did not keep the large company long in suspense. Three singles, a four off a no-ball and another single brought him to 99, and then placing a ball from Bridges to square leg, he attained the object of his great ambition, the total then standing at 167. Tremendous cheering, of course, greeted the accomplishment of the feat; indeed so pronounced was the enthusiasm that the progress of the game was delayed some minutes...

Fortunately for Hobbs, Somerset played up so well at the second attempt that Surrey were set a task substantial enough to furnish that batsman with the chance of making a second hundred. Of that opportunity he duly availed himself, and so less than 30 hours after equalling W. G. Grace's record, he surpassed it.

It was not until the 1940 edition that Wisden *first printed a list of leading career run scorers and leading career wicket takers. Thus nobody was aware when Hobbs overtook Grace's total runs scored, nor indeed when his record total of wickets was passed, probably first by J.T. Hearne. But his record of 126 centuries was firmly in the public consciousness.*

For the record, Hobbs passed Grace's total of 54,896 runs on 9 August 1930, during his innings of 40 for Surrey v Middlesex at The Oval. J.T. Hearne overtook WG's total of 2876 first-class wickets while taking 5 wickets for 34 runs during Warwickshire's first innings against Middlesex at Lord's in the match beginning on 22 July 1912. Nobody noticed.

Exactly when Frank Woolley overtook WG's total of 887 catches is more difficult to pinpoint, because both Woolley's and Grace's fielding statistics have been revised over the years. We can, however, be sure that Woolley became the leading catcher during the 1935 season.

WISDEN 1927

Recollections of F. R. Spofforth, who died in 1926, included memories of the Grace family.

Lord Harris

I was playing for ten years abroad and at home against those great medium-pace Australian bowlers, Allan, Garrett, Palmer, Giffen, Turner, and Ferris, as well as Spofforth, and I have of course also played such great English medium-pace bowlers as Alfred Shaw, Watson, Jim Lillywhite, Lohmann, C. T. Studd and W. G. Grace, and I am quite satisfied and always have been, that Spofforth was the most difficult of them all, because he concealed so well the pace of the ball.

C. I. Thornton

To get Spofforth and E. M. Grace on a side was to ensure a pleasant day's cricket if not necessarily a successful one. Spofforth was at his happiest at country matches where his stories – always told with an air of sincerity – used to amuse people immensely. One special one that never failed to please used to be given in the following circumstances. I would say to him at lunch, "How did you learn to be such a fine short slip, Spoff?" And he would reply, "When I was quite young I made a boy, when out for a walk, throw stones into a hedge, and as the sparrows flew out, I caught 'em."

WISDEN 1931

OBITUARIES

Grace, Mrs Agnes Nicholls, widow of WG, died at Hawkhurst, Kent, on March 23, aged 76. Mrs. Grace possessed a rare fund of reminiscences of the game. Her memory will be cherished by many cricketers.

Grace, Dr Alfred Henry, born at Chipping Sodbury on March 10, 1866, died at Iron Acton, near that town, on September 16, 1929, aged 63. He was son of Dr Alfred Grace and, therefore, nephew of W. G., E. M. and G. F. Grace. His appearances for Gloucestershire were very few, although in good-class club cricket he was a free and successful bat, often going in without pads against all types of bowling and playing a dashing innings. He was also a good change bowler, similar in style to WG, and an excellent field. For Thornbury, Chipping Sodbury and British Medicals he made many hundreds. He was educated at Epsom College, where he gained a place in the Eleven.

WISDEN 1935

To mark the retirement of Jack Hobbs, the editor, Sydney Southerton, asked him to put a few thoughts and memories on paper. Like everybody else, he assumed that WG would have been the Champion of any era.

THE HOBBS ERA, BY JACK HOBBS

Shortly after I began to play first-class cricket came the googly, known in Australia as the "bosie" because it was first discovered by B. J. T. Bosanquet. The South Africans were quick to realise the deadliness of this ball once a command of length had been gained. On the matting wickets in their country they soon perfected it and in G. A. Faulkner, A. E. Vogler, Gordon White and R. O. Schwarz they produced the finest array of googly bowlers ever seen together in one team. W. G. Grace did not, I think, play in an important match against googly bowling but obviously he must have been so very good that he, like many of us later on, would have mastered it. He would have played every ball on its merits.

WISDEN 1938

In 1937, Wisden's *obituarist recorded the death of the man who, together with WG bore the brunt of the bowling for Gloucestershire in the 1880s.*

Woof, William Albert, the old Gloucestershire slow left-hand bowler, died at Cheltenham on April 4, aged 77. Born at Gloucester on July 9, 1859, he was educated at Bedford Grammar School with the intention of becoming an engineer. He played for the Gloucestershire colts in 1878 and took five wickets for 78 runs, among his victims being W. G. and G. F. Grace. When tried for the County, he failed and next year, accepting an engagement on the groundstaff at Old Trafford, he decided to make cricket his career. Then A. N. Hornby persuaded him to change his pace from fast to slow with very beneficial effect. W. G. Grace, hearing of this, got him a post as bowler at Cheltenham College and in 1882 recommended him for the groundstaff at Lord's where he made a name in MCC matches and remained for four seasons. Appointed coach at Cheltenham in 1885 he retained the position until 1925 and on his retirement he received £1,200 as a testimonial from past and present Cheltonians.

Altogether in first-class cricket Woof took 752 wickets at less than 17 and a half runs apiece. His best seasons were 1884, when he dismissed 116 men for 18 runs each, and 1885 when 100 wickets fell to him at an average cost of less than 18 runs. After this, owing to his duties at Cheltenham, he could not give much time to help his county until the vacation, and he retired from first-class cricket in 1894, but four years later for East Gloucestershire he took seven MCC wickets for 28 runs.

WISDEN 1939

OBITUARY

Grace, Mr Charles Butler, the last surviving son of W. G. Grace, died while playing in a cricket match at Hawkhurst, on June 6, aged 56.

WG's other son, Admiral Henry Edgar Grace, had died in 1937, but his death was not recorded in Wisden.

WISDEN 1945

OBITUARY

Grace, Captain Edward Mills, RAMC, a grandson of the great hitter and lob bowler, Dr E. M. Grace, "The Coroner", of Gloucestershire and England after whom he was christened, died of typhoid fever on March 14, the illness being caught when on active service in Italy. A useful cricketer, left-handed with both bat and ball, he played for Wrekin College and Bristol University, for whom he did well in a good innings of 96 against Birmingham University. In 1935, when a substitute for Worcestershire Gentlemen against Gloucestershire Gipsies, a club of which his father, Dr Edgar Mervyn Grace, was captain, he made 82 not out at Cirencester, and in recognition was elected a member of the club! In build he resembled his illustrious grand-uncle W. G. Grace, and fielded finely close to the wicket – a characteristic of his grandfather as described in *The Cricketer*. He was aged 28.

WISDEN 1948

In his Notes by the Editor, Hubert Preston notes an old Test player's memories of WG:

S. P. Jones, born on August 1, 1861, [is] strong and hearty, as my son, Norman Preston, when touring with the England team last winter, found him at Auckland, New Zealand. Sam Jones… came to England in 1882, 1886 and 1888, having first played for Australia in February 1882 at Sydney, when the England team, captained by Alfred Shaw, lost by five wickets. Talking to my son, Jones said he disliked modern batsmanship, even deploring the methods of Hobbs and Hammond compared with the old masters, Grace and Trumper. On his first visit to England he played in the historic Oval Test which Australia won by seven runs. The sole survivor of that match, he remembers vividly how W. G. Grace, fielding point, ran him out. Of Grace, whom he described as a great sportsman and cricketer, he said, "I never saw him leave alone any ball outside the off stump. He either cut or drove them."

WISDEN 1949

To mark the centenary of WG's birth, Wisden's *editor, Hubert Preston, who had seen WG play, wrote a long tribute. It is interesting to modern eyes to read the tributes to his character, especially the view that "He insisted on the closest possible adherence to the laws, so preventing any attempts at sharp practice by fieldsmen to distract the batsman's attention from the bowler." Today's more cynical commentators, who never saw him play, might subscribe to a different view.*

W. G. GRACE, BY HUBERT PRESTON

When W. G. Grace passed away in 1915, Sydney Pardon, then Editor of *Wisden*, paid the highest eulogy possible to the greatest figure who ever trod the cricket field, and after the centenary of his birth one may assert confidently that no one has risen to equal fame in the world of cricket. As batsman, bowler and fielder he remains supreme, while to those who knew his attributes from watching many of his wonderful performances his position stands out with all the more clearness. My personal knowledge of his greatness by means of eyesight commenced in 1884 at The Oval Test match in which Australia scored 551. How WG kept wicket and caught Midwinter off the Hon. Alfred Lyttelton, who, with his pads on, bowled lobs from the Vauxhall end and finished Australia's innings by taking the last four wickets for eight runs, remains a clear picture to me. When England batted, W. L. Murdoch, the Australian captain, tried the experiment of putting on G. J. Bonnor, the six-foot-four giant, to open the bowling with the pavilion behind him. How WG calmly played forward and turned the good-length ball to the leg boundary was a matter of perfect timing and subtle wrist-work. WG made 19 and then was run out. He played a ball to cover point, and Blackham, the brilliant wicketkeeper, fourth bearded man in the match, receiving a splendid return, whipped off the bails as Grace slid his bat over the crease. It was a sad disappointment when the umpire signalled out. The stubborn Scotton and free-hitting Walter Read in a ninth-wicket stand of 151 saved England.

I can see the bearded giant at a distance two years later making 170 for England against Australia at The Oval on drying turf. He was second out at 216; he hit splendidly, his on-drives over the boundary from Spofforth arousing much delight. And so by various pictures on to 1895 at Gravesend, where he came to the Press tent during lunch time and wrote a telegram. To my delight, Edgar Pardon, my chief, introduced me to the Doctor, so making the occasion still more memorable to me – though unforgettable for anyone present. That was the match in which WG scored 257 out of 443 before being last out on the Saturday. Then after lunch Kent were dismissed for 76. Of the 106 runs which gave Gloucestershire victory by nine wickets WG scored 73, while to complete the remarkable three days, during which he was on the field while every ball was bowled, he trotted from the dressing tent in his tweed tail suit and hard felt hat, carrying his heavy cricket bag to a four-wheeled cab which took him to the station. Nothing legendary – a word misapplied to him by some writers who cannot have seen him – about this, but honest fact. This was the first instance in first-class cricket in England of a side winning after facing a total of over 400 – Kent began the match with 470. WG was then 47.

Next season came another triumph – the last match in which WG led England to victory. In this encounter at The Oval in 1896 the dismissal of Australia by Robert Peel and J. T. Hearne for 44 established what is still a Test record for The Oval, eight less than the total for which the home country fell last season on that sad Saturday, August 14. In that innings of 44, nine wickets were down for 25 when McKibbin joined Hugh Trumble and hit up 16 before a grand catch at slip by Abel completed the collapse. WG scored 33 runs in the match, an aggregate exceeded only by F. S. Jackson, Robert Abel and Joe Darling, the Australian captain, who equalled Jackson's 47.

So we may look back with thanks to WG for one Test match record, and remember that when the Australians came in 1878 he decided not to give up all his time to medicine as he had intended, but to continue participation in the game taught him by his father, uncle and other relations from the time that he could run with a bat in his hands. In 1880 I felt surprise when W. L. Murdoch, with 153 not out, just beat WG's score in the first England v Australia match at The Oval; and then came The Ashes match – a doleful day for a boy worshipper of cricket even at home as I heard the news.

These are merely memories of what I saw, and are small items in his wonderful life. From the many books on WG one gathers an amazing panorama of astonishing events. In 1865 he first appeared for Gentlemen against Players at Lord's, and in this connection it is good to quote the Hon. Robert H. Lyttelton, whose tribute hangs at Lord's by the side of a small copy of the W. G. Grace picture, which is placed prominently in the National Portrait Gallery: The Champion in flannels, wearing the MCC red and yellow cap, as he always did on the cricket field.

William Gilbert Grace
1848–1915

The greatest of the world's cricketers, as a batsman, supreme; as a bowler, great. In his prime he towered above his contemporaries. From 1850 to 1866 the Professionals won 23 out of 26 matches against the Amateurs. In the next series of 26 matches the Amateurs won 19, the Professionals one. This remarkable change was entirely due to the black-bearded hero 'WG'. A terror to bowlers, he was worshipped by the crowd.

Arranged as customary for the third week in July, the Gentlemen and Players match at Lord's came opportunely for celebrating the Centenary, and MCC appropriately marked the anniversary.

On entering the ground one saw that laurel leaves surrounded the panels on each side of the gates, on which the exact inscription is:

TO THE MEMORY OF

WILLIAM GILBERT GRACE

THE GREAT CRICKETER

1848–1915

THESE GATES WERE ERECTED BY THE MCC AND OTHER FRIENDS
AND ADMIRERS

"The Great Cricketer" was decided upon as the simplest and best description at the suggestion of Sir Stanley Jackson.

The scorecard was headed: In celebration of the 100th anniversary of the birth of Dr W. G. Grace, and on the back was printed:

DR W. G. Grace
The Great Cricketer
July 18th, 1848 – October 23rd, 1915.

In 44 seasons of first-class cricket – 1865 to 1908 – he scored 54,896 runs, took 2,876 wickets, and made 126 centuries.

… In prowess and personality alike he dominated the cricket field; he was the kindest of men and no Englishman was better known.

In Wheatstone Hall, Gloucester, Colonel D. C. Robinson, a former captain of the County team, presided at a meeting, and C. L. Townsend, a fine all-rounder, opened an exhibition of trophies used by WG and other players in memorable games. Among the company was Paish, another contemporary of Grace: Gilbert Jessop wrote that WG was his hero as a boy and remained so still. Walter Hammond sent a menu card of the banquet held in 1895 to celebrate Grace's 100th century, and the Gloucestershire XI, headed by B. O. Allen, signed a letter of good wishes. As *The Times* correspondent wrote, "This exhibition shows how W. G. Grace in this century year of his birth is remembered with pride and affection."

Interesting Events
W. G. Grace established a name in the West Country before the Gloucestershire County Club was formed, and he first played at Lord's in 1864 for South Wales against MCC. Just 16 years of age, he was then, as stated in *Scores and Biographies*, an inch or two taller than six feet and weighed 14 stone five pounds. He scored 50, a week after making 170 and 56 not out against Gentlemen of Sussex at Brighton. Yet it was as a bowler that he first attracted attention in first-class cricket. In 1865 at The Oval he and I. D. Walker bowled unchanged through both innings of Players of the South; WG took 13 wickets for 84 runs.

When 18 years of age he scored 224 not out for England against Surrey at The Oval. On the second afternoon he was allowed by V. E. Walker, the England captain, to go to Crystal Palace for the National Olympian Association 440 yards hurdle race, which he won over 20 hurdles in 70 seconds.

Also in 1866, for Gentlemen of South against Players of South, he scored 173 not out and took nine wickets for 108 runs. These performances earned him the description The Champion.

In August 1868 he scored 130 and 102 not out for South of Thames v North of Thames at Canterbury – the first instance of two hundreds being made by a batsman in a first-class match. The season of 1871 brought wonderful performances. WG scored 2,739 runs in first-class matches when the over was four balls and every stroke run out except a hit out of the ground for six; he made ten centuries and twice passed 200, average 78.25; also he took 79 wickets at a cost of 17.03 each.

Besides his phenomenal batting in August 1876, when he scored consecutive innings of 344 out of 546 in six hours 20 minutes for MCC against Kent at Canterbury, 177 out of 262 in three hours ten minutes for Gloucestershire against Nottinghamshire at Clifton, and 318 not out against Yorkshire at Cheltenham, carrying his bat through the innings of 528, which lasted eight hours, he took four wickets against Kent, nine against Nottinghamshire, eight in the second innings for 69 runs, and two wickets for 48 against Yorkshire. The Sunday intervening between the first two matches was the only break in these stupendous performances. His aggregate runs for the season was 2,622, average 62.42, and he took 129 wickets at 19.05 apiece.

Regarding these wonderful innings, the tale has been handed down that the Nottinghamshire team leaving Clifton met the Yorkshiremen on their way to Cheltenham. "What did the black-bearded blighter do?" asked a Tyke, and, on being told, said, "Thank goodness we've got a chance." The reply came next day – 318.

… Although a splendid athlete – he won more than 70 prizes on the track – he gradually put on weight, and was a very heavy man for his age when, in 1880, he played the only three-figure innings against the powerful Australian side captained by W. L. Murdoch in a season when run-getting generally was low.

… It is related that on one occasion when young strangers were in his side he asked one hopeful: "Where do you go in?" "I'm always No. 1." "No. 11 today. And you, my lad, where do you go in?" "Where I'm put, sir." "Then come in first with me."

WG was a strict disciplinarian; his presence kept everyone intent on the game, and it would be for the good of cricket if such an example was with us now. He insisted on the closest possible adherence to the laws, so preventing any attempts at sharp practice by fieldsmen to distract the batsman's attention from the bowler.

W. G. Grace, in his last match – Eltham v Grove Park on July 25, 1914 – when 66 years of age, scored 69 not out in a total of 155 for six wickets declared; the next-best score was 30 not out by E. F. Tyler. Grove Park lost eight wickets for 99 and the result was a draw.

The figures given are taken from the book by F. S. Ashley-Cooper, published by John Wisden & Co on July 18, 1916, and these quotations are worthy of inclusion in a lasting memorial of The Champion.

F. R. Spofforth, the Australian Demon bowler, said: "He seems different from all other cricketers – a king apart. I never see him in the field but I am reminded of my boyish days when our schoolmaster used to join in the game and teach us the way. W. G. Grace is like a master among his pupils; there may arise pupils who will be no less skilful with the bat and ball, but they never will command the permanent and worldwide reputation of the man who first taught us to play."

Lord Harris, England captain, contemporary with Grace, wrote: "He was always a most genial, even-tempered, considerate companion, and, of all the many cricketers I have known, the kindest as well as the best. He was ever ready with an encouraging word for the novice, and a compassionate one for the man who made a mistake."

A National Testimonial organised by MCC raised £1,458, besides a handsome clock, and the presentation was made at Lord's during the Over 30 v Under 30 match in 1879. In 1895, as an appreciation of WG's rejuvenation, the MCC initiated a Grace Testimonial Fund, which amounted to £2,377 2s. 6d., and a National Testimonial organised by the *Daily Telegraph* produced £5,000 in shilling subscriptions.

WISDEN 1952

The secrets of WG's success appear in the most unexpected places.

Odd, Mr Montagu, who died at Sutton, Surrey, on June 11, aged 82, used to make cricket bats by hand for Dr W. G. Grace at a guinea apiece. He was at work in his little shop a few days before his death.

WISDEN 1954

OBITUARIES

Grace, Mr Edward Sidney Henry, who died at his home at Cheltenham in April, aged 79, was the eldest son of Dr E. M. Grace, a nephew of the famous Dr W. G. Grace. E. S. H. Grace appeared with his father and WG in a team composed entirely of members of the Grace family.

Wright, Mr Levi George, who died at Derby on January 11, four days before his 91st birthday, was one of the finest batsmen who ever appeared for Derbyshire... Of his fielding, E. M. Grace used to relate how on one occasion when a batsman kept poking at the ball and cocking it up, Wright crept in closer and closer till he was only a yard or so away from the striker. Soon the fieldsman thought he saw his chance of a catch. He made a grab and the crowd cheered, but it was the bat he held, not the ball!

WISDEN 1955

Sir Pelham Warner, in an article called "Twilight Reflections", had a new story of WG to tell:

Selection of England teams is obviously of the highest importance. Before 1899 there were only three Test matches – v Australia at Lord's, The Oval and Old Trafford. The teams were chosen by the authorities of MCC, Surrey and Lancashire. This system seems to have worked well, and so far as Lord's was concerned Mr Henry Perkins, Secretary of MCC, told me that "Gilbert" – he was one of the very few men who called W. G. Grace by his Christian name – "and I chose the teams and we did not lose any matches." In the main this is true, for we lost only one match, that of 1888, of the first six played at Lord's.

WISDEN 1957

Norman Preston liked county histories. Every year, a different county's past would be spotlighted, and in 1957 it was the turn of Gloucestershire. The article taught us a little more about WG's bowling action:

THE GREAT MEN OF GLOUCESTERSHIRE, BY H. F. HUTT

... The feats of WG, who died in 1915, aged 67, are legendary. He led Gloucestershire from 1870 to 1899 and did more to popularise cricket than anyone else. As a batsman he achieved almost everything of distinction – two centuries in a match, three hundreds in succession, 2,000 runs in a season and three scores of over 300. A bowler of medium-pace, with round-arm action and a little break from leg, he took all ten wickets in an innings, and he did the double on eight occasions. WG hit 126 centuries, 51 of them for Gloucestershire, with a highest score for the county of 318 not out, and the remarkable average of 40.80 spread over 30 years with the club. In 1895, when 47 years old, he scored 1,000 runs in May – an amazing performance.

WG himself gave his recipe for success. "I aim," he said, "at placing every ball, however straight and good the length of it, for that is the only way to score at all rapidly against crack bowlers who can bowl over after over every ball on the wicket." As a bowler, no one was quicker than the Doctor to find out the weak points of a batsman, and in Gloucestershire's heyday the brilliant fielding of G. F. (Fred) Grace was invaluable to him. WG began as an alert outfield, despite his bulk, capable of very long throws, but in later years he fielded near the wicket and only E. M. Grace, his other brother in the Gloucestershire Eleven, was his superior at point.

THE BEARD LEGEND

Inevitably there have been many stories told about The Champion, and there are several versions of the one about the bumping ball which flew through his beard. Ernest Jones, the Australian fast bowler, was the man concerned, but Sir Stanley Jackson, who was at the wicket with WG when the incident occurred, has put on record that he does not think the ball actually touched Grace's beard. Sir Stanley, who died in 1947, said that he believed he was responsible for the beard-parting story as on his return to the pavilion he jocularly cried to his team-mates: "Did you see that one go through WG's beard?" So history is written.

There have been many memorials to W. G. and the cradle in which he was rocked in his home at Downend more than 100 years ago is now in Bristol Museum.

WISDEN 1959

Herbert Strudwick, the great Surrey and England wicket-keeper of the early part of the 20th century, wrote an article about his career, entitled "From Dr Grace to Peter May". He included his memories of WG:

I have known nearly all the famous cricketers of the 20th century, from Dr W. G. Grace to Peter May, the present Surrey and England captain. One recollection I have of Grace was when I played for Surrey against London County at the Old Crystal Palace ground in 1902. On the day that WG bowled me for my second duck of the match, Southampton and Sheffield United were fighting out the FA Cup Final, also at the Crystal Palace. As I passed the Doctor on my way out, he said to me: "Why didn't you tell me you got a duck in the first innings, youngster? I would have given you one to get off the mark." "Never mind, sir," I said. "I want to see the second half of that Cup Final." And away I scampered.

WISDEN 1963

SIX GIANTS OF THE WISDEN CENTURY BY NEVILLE CARDUS

I have been asked by the Editor of *Wisden* to write appreciations of six great cricketers of the past 100 years. I am honoured by this invitation, but it puts me in an invidious position. Whichever player I choose for this representative little gallery I am bound to leave out an important name. My selection of immortal centenarians is as follows: W. G. Grace, Sir Jack Hobbs, Sir Donald Bradman, Tom Richardson, S. F. Barnes and Victor Trumper.

... I'll give reasons why my six have been picked. There have been, there still are, many cricketers who possess the gifts to bat brilliantly, skilfully and prosperously. There have been, there still are, many bowlers capable of wonderful and destructive arts. But there have been a few who have not only contributed handsome runs and taken worthy wickets by the hundred, but also have given to the technique and style of cricket a new twist, a new direction.

These creative players have enriched the game by expanding in a fresh way some already established method. One or two of them have actually invented a technical trick of their own... My immortal six were at one and the same time masters of the old and initiators of the new.

W. G. Grace

In recent years his great bulk has seemed to recede. Others following long after him have left his performances statistically behind. In his career he scored 54,896 runs, average 39.55. He also took 2,876 wickets, average 17.92. He scored 126 hundreds in first-class matches, a number exceeded by Sir Jack Hobbs, Hendren, Hammond, Mead, Sutcliffe, Woolley and Sir Leonard Hutton.

None of these, not even Sir Jack, dominated for decades all other players, none of them lasted so long, or wore a beard of his commanding growth. In the summer of 1871 his aggregate of runs was 2,739, average 78.25. The next-best batsman that year was Richard Daft, average 37.

A Hobbs, a Bradman, a Hutton, a Compton might easily any year amass more than 2,000 runs, averaging round about the 70s. But some other batsmen will be running them close, as far as figures go, averaging 50, 60 and so on.

Grace, in 1871, achieved an average which was proof that he stood alone in consistent skill, twice as skilful as the next best! His career ranged from the age of 17, in 1865, until 1908, when he was nearing 60 years. He had turned the 50th year of his life when for the Gentlemen v the Players at Kennington Oval he scored 82 and one of the attack he coped with magisterially was none other than S. F. Barnes, approaching his best.

All these facts and figures tell us no more of the essential WG than we are told of Johann Sebastian Bach if all his fugues, cantatas, suites, and even the B Minor Mass, are added up.

In a way he *invented* what we now call modern cricket. His national renown packed cricket grounds everywhere. He laid the foundations of county cricket economy. The sweep of his energy, his authority, and prowess, his personal presence, caused cricket to expand beyond a game. His bulk and stride carried cricket into the highways of our national life.

He became a representative Victorian, a father figure. People not particularly interested in cricket found the fact of WG's eminence looming into their social consciousness. The Royal family (in those days too) inquired from time to time about his health – a formal request, because WG was seldom, if ever, unwell.

We must not remember him as the Grand Old Man of his closing years. He was an athlete, a champion thrower of the cricket ball, a jumper of hurdles. Yet, though I have seen portraits of him taken in early manhood, in his late teens in fact, I have never seen a portrait of a beardless WG. Is such a one in existence anywhere?

Ranjitsinhji wrote in his Jubilee book (or C. B. Fry wrote it for him) that "WG transformed the single-stringed instrument into the many-chorded lyre", which, translated, means that WG elaborated batsmanship, combined back-and-forward play for the first time, and perfected the technique of placing the ball.

When he began to play cricket, round-arm bowling had been the fashion for some 30 years. He inherited a technique formed from an obsolete attack and soon he was belabouring over-arm fast bowling at ease – often on rough wickets. He murdered the fastest stuff right and left.

He kept his left leg so close to the ball when he played forward that an old professional of the late 1900s told me (long after his retirement) that "WG never let me see daylight between pads and bat. Ah used to try mi best to get 'im out on a good wicket, then suddenly summat 'give' in me, and we all knew it were hopeless." If WG kept religiously to a rigid right foot in his batting, we must take it for granted, from the greatness he carved out of the game, that this principle suited all the needs and circumstances of cricket as he had to meet them.

It is stupid to argue that he couldn't have scored heavily against bowlers of 1963. He mastered the bowling problems presented in *his* period. Logically, then, we can demonstrate that he would have mastered those of today.

WG's mastery over speed compelled bowlers to think again. Thus, ironically, he was the cause of the first extensive developments of spin. A. C. M. Croome played with Grace (later he became cricket correspondent of *The Times*, one of the most learned). "The first season I saw Grace play," he wrote, "was 1876. In August he scored 318 v Yorkshire. Earlier in the week he had made 177 v Nottinghamshire, and on the previous Friday and Saturday 344 at Canterbury v Kent. He scored 1,200 runs in first-class cricket during that month of August, yet he found time before September came to run up to Grimsby and score 400 not out for United South against 22 of the district. That would be a normal month for him if he could begin again today, knowing that even bowlers and wicketkeepers know now all about the 'second line of defence', and enjoy the advantages of true wickets, longer overs and shorter boundaries."

He conquered the entire world and range of the game – 15 centuries v the Players, so that in 18 years of his reign the Players won only seven times. He scored 1,000 runs in May 1895, within two months of his 47th birthday, scored two hundreds in one match v Kent; took 17 wickets in one and the same match v Notts; and took all ten wickets in an innings v Oxford University.

He was cricket of his period personified; he was one of the eminent Victorians; he had the large girth and humanity of the foremost Englishmen of his epoch. Nobody before him, nobody following greatly in his train, has loomed to his stature or so much stood for cricket, or done as richly for it.

WISDEN 1966

NOTES BY THE EDITOR, BY NORMAN PRESTON

Remembering W. G. Grace

The 50th anniversary of the death of Dr W. G. Grace occurred on October 23, 1965. To commemorate the occasion a service was conducted by the Rev. A. N. B. Sugden at Elmers End Cemetery, Kent, where the remains of the greatest of all cricketers are buried. Mr Sugden, chaplain at the cemetery, some weeks earlier drew attention to the neglected state of the grave and with Mr Ray Ingelse, from Holland, organised a Memorial Fund which received support from various parts of the world. A new plaque was unveiled and a laurel wreath, bearing the MCC colours, including red and yellow roses, was placed on the grave. Mr A. E. R. Gilligan read the lesson. Mr Sugden reminded the congregation that in 1948 Donald Bradman brought some of his Australian side to honour "WG" on the 100th anniversary of his birth, and laid a wreath. "Cricket is a fine game; with some it is a religion," said Mr Sugden, "and if it continues to be played in the spirit in which W. G. Grace played it – he put the bat to the ball and hit it – then the future is in good hands."

WISDEN 1971

The story of how the Grace family enticed Billy Midwinter to leave his Australian team-mates at Lord's and play for Gloucestershire, the county of his birth, at The Oval in 1878 was unravelled by Grahame Parker.

THE MIDWINTER FILE, BY GRAHAME PARKER

W. E. Midwinter has a unique place in cricket history. He was Gloucestershire's first full-time professional, the only cricketer to have played for Australia and

England in Test matches against each other, eight for Australia and four for England, and the first of the inter-hemisphere cricket commuters.

… And so we come to a fateful day. On Monday, June 20 the Australians were playing at Lord's. They had lost the toss and had been put in to bat. Their opening pair, Bannerman and Midwinter, were padding up, unaware that a storm was approaching them through the cloudless summer sky. On the other side of London at The Oval, W. G. Grace had found his Gloucestershire team a man short. The Champion, 6ft 2 in, wicketkeeper J. A. Bush, 6ft 2½ in and The Coroner, E. M. Grace, 5ft 8in – to do the talking, no doubt – burst into Lord's, persuaded Midwinter he should be playing for Gloucestershire, bundled him into the waiting carriage and were gone. Much later Midwinter regretted what had been done, but before they had reached the Edgware Road he must have wondered how fate had dropped him into that hot, uncomfortable seat. The dust had hardly settled in the St John's Wood Road when an Australian posse set off in pursuit of the Gloucestershire hijackers. In the posse were the Australian manager, John Conway, Midwinter's friend Harry Boyle, and David Gregory, the captain. An unhappy altercation took place at The Oval gates where WG, in front of bystanders, called the Australians a damn lot of sneaks.

The Australians were deeply hurt. Letters of increasing acidity passed between them and the County during the following weeks. The first was despatched by John Conway on June 22 from the Horse Shoe Hotel, Tottenham Court Road, and was read at the Gloucestershire Committee meeting of July 1: Unless Mr W. G. Grace apologises for his insulting behaviour… we shall be compelled to erase the Gloucestershire fixture from our programme. The Committee drafted a reply regretting this fact, but added Mr W. G. Grace did not for a moment intend his remarks to apply to Mr Conway and Mr Boyle. This brought a stinging reply from David Gregory at the Albion Hotel, Manchester. They still refused to play at Bristol. "I may state that he (WG) publicly insulted the whole of the Australian Eleven in most unmistakable language." He now introduced for the first time the initial cause of the storm, "… moreover we are averse to meeting Midwinter, whose defection from us we regard as a breach of faith."

The long Gloucestershire reply tried to spread some oil on the disturbed waters, but set out their version of the Midwinter affair:

"Midwinter is a Gloucestershire man, he returned to England last year and played in all the matches which were played by Gloucestershire after his arrival in England. This year he has already played in the Colts match at Bedminster and had promised Mr Grace to play in all our County matches. This engagement of his was well known all over England, and can hardly fail to have been known to you. Mr Bush discussed this with Mr Conway at Prince's on Monday and Tuesday, June 17 and 18. With the knowledge of Midwinter's engagement staring you in the face you attempted to induce him to break his promise, desert his County, and play for you by offering him a much larger sum than we could afford to pay him.

Such proceedings are to say the least uncommon and go far, in our judgment, to palliate Mr Grace's stormy language at The Oval."

The Australians would not leave it there. In a letter from Leicester dated July 15, David Gregory still refused to bring his team to Bristol, but was "willing to overlook Midwinter's defection though they consider they have first claim to him, as before he came to England he asked Mr Conway to keep a place for him in the team. We started from Australia relying upon his joining us."

E. M. Grace, as Secretary, dutifully transcribed all those letters in the Minutes Book, but the page continuing WG's eventual letter of apology contains only the heading "Mr W. G. Grace wrote a letter apologising to David Gregory and the Australians"! After a long search the contents of this letter came to light in an Australian report of the tour:

The Cottage,
Kingswood Hill,
Bristol.
July 21.

Dear Sir,

I am sorry that my former expression of regret to the Australian cricketers has not been considered satisfactory. Under the circumstances, and without going further into the matter, I wish to let by-gones be by-gones. I apologise again, and express my extreme regret to Conway, Boyle and yourself, and through you to the Australian cricketers, that in the excitement of the moment I should have made use of unparliamentary language to Mr Conway. I can do no more but assure you that you will meet a hearty welcome and a good ground at Clifton.

Yours truly,
W. G. Grace.

The matter closed with WG's apology.

WISDEN 1973

SHILLINGS FOR WG, BY SIR COMPTON MACKENZIE

Wisden is privileged to have received the last article by Sir Compton MacKenzie. It arrived a week before he died in Edinburgh on November 30, aged 89. In the last few years of his life Sir Compton was almost blind and only last summer he had a spell in hospital which left him with periodic fatigue. During his life he wrote about 100 books.

Cricket is a pastime I have always enjoyed. I do not suggest that I was ever a good cricketer. I suffered, in my opinion, from the handicap of being a left-handed bowler and a right-handed batsman. I could bowl without disgracing myself, but as a batsman I was hopeless.

… The year 1895 was to become a remarkable one in the history of cricket. The prodigious performance of W. G. Grace in scoring over 1,000 runs in 22 days in the month of May inspired the whole country with a tremendous interest in cricket and cricketers. There had been nothing like it and, moreover, more than 30 years passed before it was repeated by another Gloucestershire stalwart, W. R. Hammond, in 25 days.

There must have been three or four periodicals produced in 1895 devoted to cricket records and the personalities of the various cricketers. It may have been due to this interest at this time that, as I remember, five were promoted to first-class counties that year. These were Hampshire, Derbyshire, Warwickshire, Leicestershire and Essex.

It was a batsman's year. W. G. Grace was in his 48th year and he had taken considerable pains to get himself into the best physical condition possible. He was by far the heaviest player taking part in the great matches and he was in his 31st season in first-class cricket. Moreover, he played many long innings without a mistake: 288 against Somerset at Bristol in five hours, 20 minutes; it was his 100th century; 257 against Kent at Gravesend, and The Champion was on the field during every ball of the match.

Enthusiastic crowds flocked to see him wherever he appeared and he finished that memorable summer in making 2,346 runs, the largest aggregate of the year. He was entertained at banquets in London and Bristol; a National Testimonial was organised and the *Daily Telegraph*, the paper with which I was later to have some connection, collected £5,000, by means of a shilling subscription. Schoolboys all over the country were invited to contribute. I can still recall from 80 years ago our determination not to let our pocket money of sixpence per week be given to cigarettes until we had the necessary shilling for WG.

One summer's evening in mid-July of this year of WG, when I was in the Recreation ground a friend came along Gliddon Road and shouted to me to open the gate for him.

"Archie MacLaren has made 424 against Somerset," he announced as he passed through the gate.

"You liar!"

"No, really he has, and Lancashire have made 801."

Even in the year of Grace, not every record was his.

WISDEN 1975

OBITUARY

Grace, Dr Edgar Mervyn, of Hilltop, Alverston, Bristol who died on November 24, aged 88, was the son of Dr Edward Mills Grace, known in his cricketing days as The Coroner. He was a nephew of W. G. Grace and G. F. Grace. Dr Edgar made his first appearance for the Thornbury club at the age of nine when he came in as a substitute against Cinderford and took six wickets for 24 with innocent-looking lobs. He went on to become captain of Thornbury for 37 years and altogether served the club for 79 years. In 1920, his best season, he scored well over 1,000 runs and took 146 wickets for only seven runs each. Dr Edgar's son, Gerald (G. F.) and grandson, (E. M.) now carry on the family association with Thornbury.

WISDEN 1976

OBITUARY

Grace, Capt. Norman Vere, RN (retired), who died on February 20, aged 80, was a son of the famous E. M. Grace and thus a nephew of WG. A useful all-rounder, he was a member of the Free Foresters and had played for the Royal Navy.

WISDEN 1977

Major James Gilman, who played with WG for London County, reminisced with Jack Arlidge shortly before he died, aged 97, in September 1976.

TALES OF W. G. GRACE – JAMES GILMAN RECALLS THE PAST, BY JACK ARLIDGE

The legendary Dr W. G. Grace strode across the dressing-room and said to a solemn-faced young man, "I'm taking you in with me to open the innings," and thus began a phase in the sporting life of James Gilman which he was able to recapture in thrilling detail until his death at the age of 97 late last summer...

"I was sitting in that dressing-room, with famous players all round me, and the first time Grace spoke to me he asked, 'Are you nervous?', and then his eyes twinkled when I replied, 'I'm terrified, sir.' He then went out to toss for innings, and it was when he came back that he told me to get padded up and open with him. It was a kind and very shrewd move, because he could see I'd have been reduced to a jelly if I'd had to wait to bat. It was typical of WG – his bark was worse than his bite."

Major Gilman... chuckled to remember that his famous partner was out shortly after lunch for 71.

"This wasn't at all surprising," he said. "The 'Old Man' was very keen on the catering and we had a sumptuous lunch, with hock and claret on the table. He had a real whack of the roast, followed by a big lump of cheese. He also tackled his whisky and selzer, which was always his drink"...

"He was not very happy in a match at Derby that same season of 1900 when the home side caught us on a gluepot. A slow bowler named Hulme had the 'Old Man' leg-before in the first innings – for 2, and Bestwick in the second for 0, also leg-before. I was batting at the other end and so had a seat in the stalls, so to speak, to observe his reaction. The first decision did not seem a good one. Grace stalked off to the dressing-room and when I went back there soon afterwards there was a rare old rumpus. Grace had one leg out of his flannels and kept saying, 'I won't be cheated out, I've a good mind to go home.' We tried to calm him down and a whisky and selzer came to the rescue. But the real hero was that same umpire who gave him out again."

… "He might not have had the shots of Bradman nor the flowing strokes of Hammond, but he had a shot for every ball. WG was an orthodox batsman whether driving, pulling or cutting. No 'shouldering arms' to a ball for him. He went out for his shots and my old friend Herbert Strudwick… always maintained that he was a very easy batsman to keep wicket to. He rarely missed a ball!"…

As a bowler, Grace did not turn the ball very much, Major Gilman remembered, but relied on length and flight. If he wasn't batting he liked to be bowling. He had amazing stamina, even in his fifties… The wickets of those days were "not too bad", but Grace might have found run-getting a little easier on modern pitches. He would certainly have become a sporting millionaire had he been playing today, for, as his old opening partner recalled with a smile, "He did not do too badly as an amateur."

… His epitaph for WG was: "He had a great sense of mischief, but a twinkle in the eye."

WISDEN 1988

John Lawson looked back on a century and a half of cricket at Trent Bridge, and at the first Test match ever played there, in 1899.

150 YEARS OF TRENT BRIDGE, BY JOHN LAWSON

Australia were the visitors, and with around 40,000 people watching the three days' play – the ground capacity in those days was between 20,000 and 25,000 – Test cricket was off to a satisfactory start. The match itself was drawn, with Ranjitsinhji saving England with a fine unbeaten innings of 93, and it saw the farewell Test appearance, at 50 years and 320 days, of W. G. Grace, who in 1871 had scored the first Championship hundred at Trent Bridge. Making his Test debut in this same match was Wilfred Rhodes, who was to become the oldest Test cricketer.

WISDEN 1992

It took Wisden *the best part of 130 years to acknowledge that women played cricket as enthusiastically as men, but Teresa McLean understood the importance of the distaff side of the Grace family in their astonishing success.*

WOMEN IN CRICKET, BY TERESA MCLEAN

"What is human life but a game of cricket?" asked the 3rd Duke of Dorset, fervent cricket fan and supporter of the Hambledon club, in a letter to "a circle of Ladies, his intimate Friends" in 1777. "And if so, why should not the ladies play it as well as we?"

Unreliable though he was in most of his dealings with the female sex, the 3rd Duke was unfailingly generous towards women's cricket. He liked his women sporty and rangy, in the outdoor mode, and his support for women's cricket was only one of his many efforts to help women play the game, however much opposition they met.

At this early stage in the life of cricket there was little concerted opposition to women taking part in the game. The standard attitude was of ignorance, with a vague predisposition to believe that cricket was, as W. G. Grace still considered it more than a century later, "not a game for women, and although the fair sex occasionally join in a picnic game, they not constitutionally adapted for the sport!"

… Martha Grace was an amazon among cricket enthusiasts, watching, coaching and commenting on her five sons' performances on the field of play. Three of them, EM, GF and WG, played for England in the first Test in England against Australia, at The Oval in 1880. The late 19th century was a high point of female efforts to improve men's cricket and a starting point of serious women's cricket, played as a sport rather than being an amusing spectacle.

WISDEN 1995

Wisden *noted that it was 100 years since WG's astonishing season in 1895. Even from such a distant viewpoint, it still seemed to be a golden summer.*

YEAR OF GRACE, 1895

This year marks the centenary of one of the most remarkable cricket seasons ever, when the Golden Age of the game was close to its zenith and the greatest of all cricketers reached previously uncharted peaks. Dr W. G. Grace had been in poor form, by his standards, for some years before 1895, which was not surprising since he was about to celebrate his 47th birthday that July.

He did not play a first-class match until May 9, for MCC against Sussex when he made 103, his 99th century. After failing twice for MCC against Yorkshire, he returned home to Bristol for Gloucestershire v Somerset. In weather so cold that tradition says he batted with snowflakes in his beard, Grace not merely became the first man to score 100 hundreds but went on to make 288. He followed this a week later with 257 against Kent and, on May 30, hit 169 against Middlesex at Lord's to become the first man to score 1,000 runs in May, a feat emulated only twice since.

The years had rolled away, wrote Bernard Darwin later, and for this one year WG once more stood supreme as in the 'seventies… the unbeatable, the unbowlable. Three national testimonials were launched, raising more than £9,000 between them; and *The Times* suggested, unavailingly, that he ought to be in the Birthday Honours.

A fine spring meant that batting records were broken all over England. As Grace was scoring his 288, Nottinghamshire were making 726 against Sussex, the highest total in county cricket. This, however, was surpassed in July when Lancashire made 801 at Taunton and A. C. MacLaren scored 424, which remained the highest first-class score in the world for almost three decades. It was also the summer when K. S. Ranjitsinhji first batted, brilliantly, for Sussex. It was still possible to bowl: Tom Richardson of Surrey took 290 wickets. In September, *Punch* marked the season in verse:

> Yet ne'er before three heroes have I seen
> More apt and splendid on the well-rolled green;
> Men of one skill, though varying in race –
> MacLaren, Ranjitsinhji, Grand old Grace.

WISDEN 1998

To mark the 150th anniversary of WG's birth, Wisden *asked the distinguished writer and historian Geoffrey Moorhouse to write an appreciation of WG and his place in cricket's pantheon. It was not the usual paean of praise.*

W. G. GRACE: 150 YEARS ON, BY GEOFFREY MOORHOUSE

On July 18, it will be 150 years since W. G. Grace was born, but there are other ways of measuring how distant he is in time. For one thing, no one still alive, not even Jim Swanton, can remember seeing him play (although in *Sort of a Cricket Person*, EWS notes that "I am supposed to have watched [him] from my perambulator on the Forest Hill ground around 1910"). Eight decades have passed since Grace died, yet he dogs us still, demanding our attention at regular intervals.

The statistics of his career are alone enough to explain why – more than 54,000 first-class runs (there are at least two different versions of the precise figure, so let's leave it at that) spread across 44 seasons, including 839 in just eight days of 1876, when he hit a couple of triple-centuries, and only one other batsman managed to top 1,000 runs in the entire season; a thousand in May in 1895, when he was nearly 47; and 2,800-odd wickets costing less than 18 runs apiece. I suppose we might wonder why his bowling average wasn't even more impressive, given the ropey pitches on which Dr Grace played. No modern cricketer would deign to turn out on them, which makes his batting all the more wondrous, and comparisons with Bradman or anyone since quite pointless.

But there was not that much to Grace apart from these skills and his devotion to his family. A hand of whist appears to have marked the limit of his capacity for cerebration, and if one wished to be rude to suburbia one might identify Grace as suburban man incarnate, fluctuating mentally as well as physically between the fringes of Bristol and the London Counties, ultimately coming to rest in Eltham. His one inherited asset was that he came from a clan which was dotty about a great game and dutiful (but in some cases no more) about the general practice of medicine, with no doubt in its collective mind which came first at all times and in all places. His brother E. M. Grace, who was a coroner, once had a corpse put on ice until he could attend to it at close of play, and WG himself must have had one of the most prolonged medical trainings in history because he so frequently interrupted it in order to exercise his major talent at the crease. He began to study as a bachelor of 19, and was a father of three in his thirties before taking his final qualification at Westminster Hospital. His most conspicuous act as a doctor is thought to have occurred when an unfortunate fieldsman impaled himself on the boundary fence at Old Trafford.

It was simply because the cricketing Grace totally dominated his own era that an exasperated C. L. R. James could not understand why standard history books of the period never mentioned him. This man, for heaven's sake, opened for England at the age of 50 – and at the age of 18 he had scored 224 not out for England against Surrey, in a match which he left halfway through in order to win a quarter-mile hurdles championship at the Crystal Palace! No wonder he was the best-known Englishman apart from Mr Gladstone, so much so that Evelyn Waugh's friend, Monsignor Ronnie Knox, waggishly suggested that Gladstone and Grace were really one and the same celebrity.

Athletic is not a word that obviously comes to mind when contemplating Grace in his prime, though a slim young man did precede the pot-bellied genius who in middle age was far too heavy for any horse to bear. I have often wondered how stylishly he played his strokes, ever since I saw some film in which he appeared to be brandishing his bat as though he was about to poke the fire with it. Something tells me that he never hit the ball as gracefully as Victor Trumper did in the famous photo of his straight drive; Grace, I suspect, was much more about power than aesthetics.

That, at any rate, would fit what we know of his character in general. Apart from tenderness to his relatives and a generous soft spot for children, he was not, I think, a particularly attractive man, though he could sometimes (and it is usually recorded as remarkable) encourage a young player on his own side with – as the saying went in his day – bluff good humour. After the Australians had experienced him for the first time, a commentator Down Under observed that, "for so big a man, he is surprisingly tenacious on very small points." He was notorious for employing, in order to pursue victory or personal achievement, a variety of wiles and tricks that may be thought of as, well, hardly cricket. He was also, throughout his career, quite breathtakingly grasping when his eye caught the glint of hard cash.

It was the social historian Eric Midwinter who, some years ago, pointed out that on Grace's first tour of Australia in 1873–74 (when he was a medical student simultaneously enjoying his honeymoon) he extracted a fee of £1,500 from the organisers, which would be well over £100,000 at present values. On his second tour in 1891–92, one-fifth of the entire cost of transporting 13 English cricketers across the world, supporting them in Australia and paying them for what they did there, went into Grace's pocket. He regularly collected testimonials – one, worth £1,458, was organised by MCC so that he might buy a medical practice – and overall probably took something like £1million in today's currency out of the game; and, remember, there was no sponsorship nor endorsements in those days to inflate a star's income. This was in a period when the prosperous middle classes were earning no more than £1,000 a year, a highly skilled artisan £200, and a labourer half as much if he was lucky. A good professional county cricketer in the second half of the 19th century saw his wages rise from £100 to £250. No wonder it cost twice as much to get into some English grounds if Grace was playing than if he was not.

The astonishing thing about the mercenary Grace, of course, is that he was classified and has ever since been glorified as an amateur. Nothing more exposed the humbug that used to smother the entire topic of Gents v Players than an examination of Grace's financial rewards from the game; and nothing more reveals the intellectual dishonesty at the heart of the humbug than something Grace once said when trying to argue the Gloucestershire committee into playing more amateurs than professionals.

He declared his fear for the future of cricket if it became wholly professional. "Betting and all kindred evils will follow in its wake, and instead of the game being followed up for love, it will simply be a matter of £ s d." Prophetic words, perhaps; but it ill became W. G. Grace to mouth them.

It will be gathered from the above that he has never been a hero of mine, not since the day in adolescence when I discovered that he was sometimes a shameless cheat in a game that, I was being asked to believe, was wholly honourable. I shall nevertheless drink to his memory on July 18 because his tremendous gifts, especially his phenomenal batting, were largely responsible for the elevation of cricket from just another 19th-century game, which had become popular partly because it lent itself to gambling.

Grace's towering presence, more than any other single factor, transformed it into the unrivalled spectator sport of summer, first of all in England, subsequently in other lands spread widely across the world. I would even suggest that a true measurement of WG's unique stature is that he is instantly identifiable, even by some who are uninterested in his vocation, by his initials alone. I cannot think of another human being in any sphere, not even W. C. Fields, of whom this is also true.

WISDEN 1999

The Book Review section, written this year by Mark Lawson, includes a review of Simon Rae's biography of WG:

W. G. Grace: A Life marked the 150th anniversary of the birth of a man who has become the touchstone for discussion of cricket much as Olivier became in acting and Lincoln in politics…

It intrigued me that many of the cricket writers who reviewed Rae's book, particularly those correspondents of the older school and the venerable broadsheets, seemed keen to treat Grace's cheating and financial deceit as a bit of fun, and unsurprising for the time. But – rather as Thomas Jefferson's sex life provides a useful historical counterpoint to Bill Clinton's – part of the importance of Rae's work is that, at a time when international cricketers are being held to very high moral standards by the media, it usefully questions the existence of a golden age of integrity and fairness.

WISDEN 2002

An excerpt from Don Bradman's obituary compares two of the giants of the game.

Other cricketers, said C. L. R. James, "had inhibitions Bradman never knew". The sole tiny bow to convention lay in his rarely opening the batting, although it seldom seemed to diminish him if a wicket fell immediately and he had perforce to take centre stage. W. G. Grace would have scorned the wasted time of an inferior being permitted to replace him at the top of the order. None the less, no one has matched what Neville Cardus called Bradman's "cool deliberate murder or spifflication of the bowling".

Under the pressure of such attainment, one feels forced to seek counter-arguments. It has been suggested that Bradman rarely played against what, by the statistics of wicket-taking, bowling average and strike-rate, might be regarded as England's top bowlers of all time. One statistician, Peter Hartland, has calculated that W. G. Grace, when aged 25 and having scored some 10,000 first-class runs at an average of 61, was at that moment twice as good as any contemporary batsman – a dominance not even Bradman could match. It might be cavilling to recall that Don Bradman was not a great cricketer but a great batsman. He was an unassuming leg-spinner with a mere 36 first-class wickets to his name; a highly competent out-fielder who took 131 catches, plus a solitary stumping; and a hard-nosed, shrewd captain. But this did not make him an all-round cricketer in the Garry Sobers or WG mould.

That uniformly abused tag of icon may legitimately be applied, however bold the deeds of other heroes, to only two cricketers. In that cricket is transparently a cult, Grace and Bradman played the roles of founder and consolidator. Because of the initial momentum of cricket, WG, the creature of the railway, the steamship, the telegraph and the popular newspaper, has the wider distinction of being the father of modern sport at large, while the Don, although aided by the wireless, missed out on the expansion, engendered by air travel and satellite television, that has given sport a broader global spread.

WISDEN 2005

Gloucestershire v Middlesex
At Gloucester, June 9, 10, 11 and 12, 2004.

Middlesex 383 (Klusener 63; Shabbir Ahmed 4–96) and 358 (Shah 72; Fisher 4–110);
Gloucestershire 695-9 dec (Spearman 341; Peploe 4–199) and 47–0.
Gloucestershire won by ten wickets.

At 2.36pm on the sunny third afternoon, Craig Spearman pushed through midwicket to reach the highest score in Gloucestershire's 135-year first-class history. It was two and a half years after he was lured back from a planned career in the city, and 498 minutes after his epic innings began. Along the way he eclipsed two towering giants: the previous record-holder was W. G. Grace (318 not out against Yorkshire at Cheltenham in 1876); four balls earlier Spearman had passed Jack Hobbs's record for the biggest first-class innings against Middlesex (316 not out for Surrey at Lord's in 1926). "You are talking about the father of cricket as he is known the world over," said Spearman, who admitted targeting Grace's record, "so it is quite something." Even umpire Kitchen shared his pleasure. "Get rid of the old man," he said. "He used to pick up the bails and put them back on the stumps."

GLORY AT GLOUCESTER

Highest first-class innings for Gloucestershire:

341	C. M. Spearman v Middlesex at Gloucester (Archdeacon Meadow)	2004
318*	W. G. Grace v Yorkshire at Cheltenham	1876
317	W. R. Hammond v Nottinghamshire at Gloucester (Wagon Works)	1936
302*	W. R. Hammond v Glamorgan at Bristol	1934
302	W. R. Hammond v Glamorgan at Newport	1939
301	W. G. Grace v Sussex at Bristol	1896
290	W. R. Hammond v Kent at Tunbridge Wells	1934
288	W. G. Grace v Somerset at Bristol	1895
286	G. L. Jessop v Sussex at Hove	1903

WISDEN 2013

To celebrate the 150th edition of Wisden, *the editor, Lawrence Booth, picked "Ten Moments In Time". Remarkably, even though only the first three "moments" were in the first 100 years of* Wisden's *existence, W. G. Grace featured in two of the ten.*

WISDEN'S TEN MOMENTS IN TIME

And the game changed for ever

Which of W. G. Grace's feats was the most resounding? And which aspect of Twenty20's gold rush best captured its impact on the modern game? These were the kinds of questions to which *Wisden* hoped to find a convincing answer when it chose the ten most seminal moments in the years spanning the Almanack's 150 editions. The list that emerged contains some that will come as a surprise: among readers who entered our competition to guess the ten, no one managed more than six. But then consensus would have spoiled the fun.

… Who changed batting for ever: Grace in 1871 or Bradman in 1930? We went for Grace, who – as Ranjitsinhji explained – invented an entire methodology, of which Bradman would become the most ruthless exemplar…

1871: W. G. GRACE REWRITES THE RECORD BOOKS, BY STEVEN LYNCH

At first, bowlers held the upper hand in first-class cricket, helped by rough, almost unprepared pitches. Then came WG. He had hinted at exceptional talent, but in 1871, the year he turned 23, Grace reshaped the game. No one had previously made 2,000 runs in a season. Now he made 2,739, a record that stood for 25 years. The next-best was Harry Jupp's 1,068, and of the 17 first-class centuries that year, WG made ten. Batting was never quite the same again.

Grace buried the quaint notion that scoring on the leg side was ungentlemanly. He batted in a way we would recognise today: usually a decisive movement forward or back, bat close to pad, although he was also a master of what Ranjitsinhji called a "half-cock stroke", which we would probably term playing from the crease. In his *Jubilee Book of Cricket*, Ranji wrote: "He revolutionised cricket, turning it from an accomplishment into a science… He turned the old one-stringed instrument into a many-chorded lyre, a wand… Until his time, a man was either a back player like Carpenter or a forward player like Pilch, a hitter like E. H. Budd or a sticker like Harry Jupp. But W. G. Grace was each and all at once."

1882: THE ASHES ARE BORN, BY ANDREW MILLER

The history of England v Australia, the mother of all Test series, was first distilled into a minuscule urn-shaped vessel, then pressure-cooked to create a hyper-contest for the 21st century. But time and distance cannot diminish the role played in the creation myth by a single game. The Oval 1882 was a microcosm of the tension that has never left the Ashes.

Australia's indomitability was summed up by their first-day recovery from 30 for six and Fred Spofforth's demonic bowling – inspired, legend has it, by W. G. Grace's caddish run-out of Sammy Jones. More than 2,000 Tests have taken place since, but Australia's seven-run victory remains in the top ten tightest wins.

CHAPTER 7
STATISTICS: THE EXTRAORDINARY
ACHIEVEMENTS OF W. G. GRACE

WG had a very keen interest in the statistics of his career. In 1898 he declared an innings closed when he was on 93 not out, as 93 was the only score between nought and 100 on which he had never finished an innings. Most cricketers would not have a statistic such as that in their head.

The final statistics of WG's career are inevitably a source of some dispute and disagreement, but Wisden *has almost always taken the traditional line in assessing the numbers behind WG's brilliance, a tradition that began with F. S. Ashley-Cooper's ground-breaking statistical work at the turn of the last century. "Almost always" rather than "always", because in 1981,* Wisden's *new editor John Woodcock published a revised set of figures, based on the work of the Association of Cricket Statisticians, who had reclassified some matches previously thought of as first-class as not first-class, and some matches previously not thought of as first-class as first-class. The furore was immediate and great. In 1982, Woodcock reasserted the validity of the traditional WG statistics, and since then,* Wisden *has followed this line rather than the revised figures of the ACS.*

When we remember that Grace played for most of his career on wickets that were underprepared by modern standards, uncovered and overused, it is astonishing that he was able to score so many runs, and usually at a rapid rate. His superiority over all other cricketers of his time is proven by the statistics.

WISDEN 1903

The Editor asked the pioneering cricket statistician F. S. Ashley-Cooper to comment on WG's hundreds, in an attempt to clarify and classify the total.

MR W. G. GRACE'S HUNDREDS, BY F. S. ASHLEY-COOPER

The fact that during the course of the season Mr W. G. Grace accomplished the extraordinary feat of playing his 200th innings of 100 or more runs, provides one with an opportune time for placing before the readers of *Wisden's Almanack* details of all his three-figure scores, in first-class as well as minor matches. Whilst perusing the tables set forth below, the reader should remember that when WG was in his prime he was not only expected to make far more runs than anybody else on the side, but also to bear the brunt of the bowling. It says much for his physique and wonderful powers of endurance that he should have held the foremost position in the world of cricket for so many years, for even now, at the advanced age (for a cricketer) of 54, he is worth a place in almost any team in the world. As seven years ago, after the great batsman had enjoyed a most successful season, reminiscences of WG appeared in these pages from the pens of Lord Harris and Mr A. G. Steel, there is no necessity to refer again now to his wonderful feats during his long and eventful career... It will be observed that the champion has played as many as 124 three-figure innings in first-class cricket, and 79 in matches of less importance.

The list of hundreds in first-class matches includes some played against odds, of which his 152 for the Anglo-American XI against XV of MCC at Lord's in 1873 is the most bizarre.

Among the list of "Hundreds in Minor Matches" are his first two recorded, at the age of 15 or 16:

170 for South Wales v Gents of Sussex, 1864
126 for Clifton v Fowne's XI, 1864

The innings of 170 was compiled a few days before his 16th birthday.

Sixteen of the 79 hundreds listed in minor matches were scored for London County, and thirteen for Thornbury. At least 16 of them were against odds.

WISDEN 1907

Sydney Pardon, Wisden's editor, was fascinated by the statistics of WG's career.

W. G. Grace in Gentlemen v Players Matches

The fact that on July 18 – the day on which he completed his 58th year – W. G. Grace played an innings of 74 for the Gentlemen furnishes sufficient excuse, if any were needed, for giving in detail a record of his doings in Gentlemen v Players matches. The chances are that he will not again be seen in the Gentlemen's Eleven, and if this be so he made a worthy end. Alike as regards duration of time and magnitude of achievement, his record is without parallel and has never been even distantly approached. Playing first for the Gentlemen both at The Oval and Lord's in 1865, when a lad of just under 17, he has in the whole series of matches scored 6,008 runs with an average of 42, and taken 271 wickets for less than 19 runs apiece. The bowling figures go far to support the late Bob Thoms's contention, that if WG had not been the greatest batsman in the world he would have been the greatest slow bowler. Looking through the wonderful array of figures, one is perhaps struck most of all by the fact that the first and last of his seven hundreds for the Gentlemen at Lord's were divided by a period of 27 years. He made his 134 not out in 1868 before he was 20 and his 118 in 1895 within ten days of his 47th birthday. The two innings were as regards merit almost on an equality, WG in some mysterious way renewing in 1895 all the power of his youth. Since then his batting has naturally declined with the lapse of years, but even at The Oval last July there was something to suggest the brilliancy of former days. Happily the time has not yet come to review WG's career in the cricket field as a whole. He still enjoys the game of which he has been the greatest exponent, and though allowances have of necessity to be made for advancing age the public still like to see his familiar figure.

There then followed seven pages of statistics. The note to his 134 not out at Lord's in 1868 states:

Aged under 20. He went in first wicket down and carried out his bat. The next-highest score in the match was 29. WG has himself described this as one of the finest innings he ever played. He made his runs without a chance against Wootton, Silcock, Willsher, Grundy and James Lillywhite, jun., and hit a six, two fives and 11 fours.

His 215 at The Oval in 1870 provoked this comment:

In the second innings WG and J. W. Dale (55) made 164 together for the first wicket. WG scored his runs out of 329 obtained while he was in, hitting an eight (an on-drive with an overthrow for a single, off Wootton), three fives, and 14 fours. After passing 200, he gave a difficult chance of stumping, but he made no other mistake.

Of his 169 at Lord's in 1876, Wisden *wrote:*

He made his 169 out of 262, hitting a seven and a six (in the same over, off Emmett) and 11 fours, and giving but one chance (at 139).

The 1898 match at Lord's...

was played in honour of WG whose 50th birthday fell on the first day. At the end of the game WG and C. J. Kortright (46) added 78 together for the last wicket. Later in the season a medal, suitably inscribed, was presented to each cricketer who took part in the match.

The 1906 Oval match gave him his highest score of the season, in which he only played five first-class games.

He made his 74 on his 58th birthday, his success being hugely appreciated by all. With C. J. B. Wood (49) he made 94 for the first wicket, and with M. W. Payne (48) added 70 for the second. He was missed when 59. He captained the side and, it is of interest to note, appeared for the Gentlemen against the Players before any of the other 21 who took part in the match were born: he was, in fact, old enough to be the grandfather of half a dozen members of his own side.

Mr W. G. Grace's Performances in Gentlemen v Players' Matches Summarised

Matches Batted In	Innings	Times Not Out	Highest Score	Total	Average	GROUND AND DATE OF FIRST APPEARANCE	Matches bowled in	Balls	Runs	Wickets	Average
35	66	5	215	2,582	42.38	OVAL, 1865	34	5,831	2,403	110	21.84
35	62	3	169	2,398	40.64	LORD'S, 1865	29	4,867	1,863	108	17.25
1	2	0	217	217	108.50	BRIGHTON, 1871	1	324	123	7	17.57
5	8	0	110	281	35.12	PRINCE'S, 1873	5	1,322	473	39	12.12
1	1	0	174	174	174.00	SCARBOROUGH, 1885	1	159	60	3	20.00
7	12	2	131	356	35.60	HASTINGS, 1889	5	295	171	4	42.75
84	151	10	217	6,008	42.60	TOTALS	75	12,798	5,093	271	18.78

WISDEN 1982

The long-accepted career figures of W. G. Grace, largely compiled by F. S. Ashley-Cooper, were as follows:

Batting	Matches	Innings	Not out	Highest Score	Runs	Average	100s
	878	1,493	105	344	54,896	39.55	126

Bowling	Runs	Wickets	Average	5 wickets/inns	10 wickets/match
	51,545	2,876	17.92	246	66

The Association of Cricket Statisticians, for the reasons outlined in Michael Fordham's article which follows, felt that the correct figures for WG's career should be a little different.

Batting	Matches	Innings	Not out	Highest Score	Runs	Average	100s
	869	1,478	104	344	54,211	39.45	124

Bowling	Runs	Wickets	Average	5 wickets/inns	10 wickets/match
	50,980	2,809	18.14	240	64

The changes, published by Wisden *in the 1981 edition, caused a furore.*

THE CAREER FIGURES OF W. G. GRACE, BY JOHN WOODCOCK

There follows an article by Michael Fordham, *Wisden*'s chief statistician since 1979, in which he gives his reasons, and those of the Association of Cricket Statisticians, for wanting to change, quite significantly, the career record of W. G. Grace. While acknowledging the amount of work done by Mr Fordham and his fellow scrutineers, and though grateful for the pleasure they give us, I prefer to leave the great man's figures as they have been for as long as anyone cares to remember.

That they appeared in *Wisden 1981*, my first as editor, in their revised form was because Mr Fordham thought, mistakenly, that he had cleared them with me. In future, various books of reference, though not *Wisden*, will show WG as having scored not 126 but 124 hundreds. To avoid confusion, the figures now claimed by the Association of Cricket Statisticians are to be found in footnotes on pages 180 and 200.

No amount of research could, to my mind, justify changing a record so honoured by time and custom. If wrong decisions are thought to have been made, they should be altered reasonably soon or left to stand. That one-day games played more than a century ago should have been termed first-class need not surprise us: there were no regulations in those days stipulating the minimum time for a first-class match. Then, as now, contemporary opinion was the best criterion.

So, in *Wisden* at any rate, WG's 152 at Lord's for the England team that had toured North America in 1872 against Fourteen Gentlemen of MCC (with Rylott), survives, as does his 113 for Gloucestershire against Somerset at Clifton in 1879. To remove them, as the Association of Cricket Statisticians would have us do, would, I think, be presumptuous and sadly unromantic. The first of them, anyway, is referred to in *Wisden 1874* as having been one of the Doctor's superb lot of first-class triple-figure scores.

Who, too, would wish to invalidate such historic occasions as WG's 100th hundred, the origin, as *Wisden* put it at the time, of a national testimonial taken up with enthusiasm in many places far beyond the limits of the United Kingdom, or the great match at Taunton when Jack Hobbs first equalled Grace's total of hundreds and then passed it? In recognition of Hobbs's feat, *Wisden* wrote how "the match was rendered forever memorable by the triumph of Hobbs, who, playing innings of 101 and 101 not out, beat the 'Grand Old Man's' record. Circumstances generally combined to invest the occasion with exceptional excitement. Tremendous cheering greeted the accomplishment of the feat: indeed so pronounced was the enthusiasm that the progress of the game was delayed while at the end of the over all players in the field shook hands with Hobbs and the Surrey captain brought out a drink for the hero, who raised his glass high and bowed to the crowd before partaking of the refreshment!" Far be it from me to say that that might as well never have happened.

BY MICHAEL FORDHAM

Some surprise was caused last year when, in *Wisden*, I revised the career figures of W. G. Grace, for the figures that were compiled by F. S. Ashley-Cooper for the 1916 *Wisden* after Grace's death have come to be regarded as having an established niche in cricket records. However, many statisticians have been dissatisfied with the figures over the years and this article is an attempt to illustrate where the discrepancies arise.

They fall into two categories: (a) the inclusion in the past of a number of matches that cannot strictly be regarded as first-class, and, in the opinion of both myself and other statisticians, should never have been included in the first place; (b) the differences in scores in *Wisden* and *Scores and Biographies*.

Dealing with (a) first, Grace in 1871 made the outstanding and undisputed aggregate of 2,739 runs. Although well short of 2,000 runs in 1872, he was close to the target in 1873 in matches whose status is not in doubt. As far as can be ascertained many years afterwards, a journalist-cum-statistician proceeded to add his scores in four minor matches – MCC v Hertfordshire at Charleywood [*sic*], MCC v Staffordshire at Lord's, the 1872 North American XI v 14 Gentlemen of MCC with Rylott at Lord's (in which he scored 152), and a one-day match at The Oval between North and South after the main fixture finished in two days.

Neither Hertfordshire nor Staffordshire has ever had any claims to first-class status, nor to be classified among the leading counties before there was a clear-cut division of First-Class and Minor counties. The MCC side which opposed the North American XI was clearly a weak one, because it could not play on level terms and it was necessary for it to be strengthened by a professional, and the one-day match at The Oval was obviously a scratch game to fill the time available. However, the addition of these matches gave Grace an aggregate of 2,139 runs for the season, and in retrospect it is difficult to escape the conclusion that it was done deliberately, as his bowling figures in these matches were omitted. Although they did not have a significant effect on his figures, he was also credited with two similar matches in 1872 – MCC v Hertfordshire at Charleywood [*sic*] and another one-day South v North match at The Oval, to fill the time available after the main match had finished early.

There are four other matches which are perhaps slightly more open to doubt. Three of these were for Gloucestershire v Somerset, one in 1879, in which Grace scored 113, and two in 1881. Now the status of Somerset before it became a first-class county officially in 1891 has been open to conjecture over the years. However, the Association of Cricket Statisticians, which has researched 19th-century cricket in greater depth, through a group of statisticians working in unison, than any individual statistician in the past, has given in its booklet *British Isles First-Class Cricket Matches* contemporary evidence from both *Wisden* and *James Lillywhite's Cricketers Annual* (the "Red Lillywhite") that Somerset were regarded as first-class only from 1882 to 1885, after which they ceased to play matches against the recognised first-class counties until their reappearance in 1891. As modern *Wisdens* have stated this for some years under the heading Constitution of the County Championship, it is obviously inconsistent to credit Grace elsewhere in the Almanack with matches against Somerset before 1882.

The remaining match is Gloucestershire v MCC at Lord's in 1868. Here again there is contemporary evidence from *John Lillywhite's Cricketers Companion* (the "Green Lillywhite") that the match was not regarded as first-class, and the *Companion* does not grant Gloucestershire this recognition until they began playing against the leading counties in 1870.

In regard to the second category, there has been a tendency among statisticians in the past to regard *Wisden* in its early years as unreliable, and to work from *Scores and Biographies* until this ended in 1878, though this is due partly to *Wisden* not publishing bowling analyses until its 1870 issue and the difficulty and cost of obtaining the early issues before the facsimile editions were printed. However, the Association of Cricket Statisticians, which is in the process of publishing booklets of the first-class scores of this era, has consulted contemporary newspapers such as *Bell's Life* and also, where available, county scorebooks. These have shown the reverse to be true; i.e. that *Wisden* is more reliable. The discrepancies seen to arise only on bowling analyses, and result in adjustments to Grace's bowling figures for a number of seasons, nearly all in the early part of his career. His bowling figures are 67 runs more than those given in the 1981 *Wisden*, through the Association of Cricket Statisticians finding a further discrepancy in his figures and the more recent discovery of an unpublished analysis for the Gentlemen of England v Oxford University at Oxford in 1866.

As has already been stated, Ashley-Cooper compiled Grace's full career record in the 1916 *Wisden*, and, his stature as a statistician at that time being unquestioned, one feels that it was a great pity that he did not grasp the nettle firmly in the hand and delete the obvious minor matches. Even he himself, in the magazine *Cricket* in 1896, in making the first attempt to summarise Grace's career figures, had referred to the matches in 1873 as not being really first-class, though he had continued to include them.

The first public query that I can trace over these figures was in a letter to *The Cricketer* magazine for June 25, 1927 about the 1873 season. It was followed by letters in two subsequent issues, including the comment that it was unthinkable that anybody should wish to deprive the Old Man of the credit attaching to the feat of scoring 2,139 runs! The matter was again raised by E. L. Roberts in an article in *The Cricketer* for May 4, 1940, when he listed Grace's catches and queried the matches accepted as first-class. He suggested revised batting and bowling aggregates through the deletion of five matches. There was no follow-up in correspondence, possible because more serious matters at that time were occupying the minds of historians and statisticians.

The first real attempt to provide alternative figures for Grace came from the late Roy Webber in the February 1961 issue of *Playfair Cricket Monthly*. He gave season-by-season figures, indicating the matches he had omitted as well as certain bowling corrections. His findings were not identical with those of the Association of Cricket Statisticians, as he took a harsher view of what were and were not first-class matches in the 1870s and 1880s. He gave Grace lower totals than those quoted currently, though he did agree with 124 centuries.

Finally, in an article in *The Cricketer Winter Annual* (November) 1975, John I. Marder queried the inclusion of Grace's century against Somerset in 1879, giving detailed contemporary evidence that Somerset were not first-class at that time.

Upon this account rests my case for revising the long-established figures of W. G. Grace.

WISDEN 2014

The Cricket Records section of the 2014 edition still shows WG at or near the top of many of the lists.

Most Runs

	Career	Runs	Innings	Not Out	Highest Score	100s	Average
J. B. Hobbs	1905–1934	61,237	1,315	106	316*	197	50.65
F. E. Woolley	1906–1938	58,969	1,532	85	305*	145	40.75
E. H. Hendren	1907–1938	57,611	1,300	166	301*	170	50.80
C. P. Mead	1905–1936	55,061	1,340	185	280*	153	47.67
W. G. Grace	1865–1908	54,896	1,493	105	344	126	39.55
W. R. Hammond	1920–1951	50,551	1,005	104	336*	167	56.10
H. Sutcliffe	1919–1945	50,138	1,088	123	313	149	51.95
G. Boycott	1962–1986	48,426	1,014	162	261*	151	56.83
T. W. Graveney	1948–1972	47,793	1,223	159	258	122	44.91
G. A. Gooch	1973–2000	44,846	990	75	333	128	49.01

1,000 Runs in a Season Most Times

W. G. Grace	28
F. E. Woolley	28
M. C. Cowdrey	27
C. P. Mead	27
G. Boycott	26
J. B. Hobbs	26
E. H. Hendren	25
D. L. Amiss	24
W. G. Quaife	24
H. Sutcliffe	24

1,000 Runs In May

	Runs	Average
W. G. Grace, May 9 to May 30, 1895 (22 days)	1,016	112.88
Grace was 46 years old		
W. R. Hammond, May 7 to May 31, 1927 (25 days)	1,042	74.42
Hammond scored his 1,000th run on May 28, thus		
equalling Grace's record of 22 days		
C. Hallows, May 5 to May 31, 1928 (27 days)	1,000	125.00

2,000 Wickets

	Career	Wickets	Runs	Average
W. Rhodes	1898–1930	4,187	69,993	16.71
A. P. Freeman	1914–1936	3,776	69,577	18.42
C. W. L. Parker	1903–1935	3,278	63,817	19.46
J. T. Hearne	1888–1923	3,061	54,352	17.75
T. W. J. Goddard	1922–1952	2,979	59,116	19.84
W. G. Grace	1865–1908	2,876	51,545	17.92
A. S. Kennedy	1907–1936	2,874	61,034	21.23
D. Shackleton	1948–1969	2,857	53,303	18.65
G. A. R. Lock	1946–1971	2,844	54,709	19.23
F. J. Titmus	1949–1982	2,830	63,313	22.37

Remarkable All Round Matches

V. E. Walker	20*	108	10–74	4–17	England v Surrey at The Oval, 1859
W. G. Grace	104		2–60	10–49	MCC v Oxford University at Oxford, 1886
G. Giffen	271		9–96	7–70	South Australia v Victoria at Adelaide, 1891–92
B. J. T. Bosanquet	103	100*	3–75	8–53	Middlesex v Sussex at Lord's, 1905
G. H. Hirst	111	117*	6–70	5–45	Yorkshire v Somerset at Bath, 1906
F. D. Stephenson	111	117	4–105	7–117	Notts v Yorkshire at Nottingham, 1988

Note: E. M. Grace, for MCC v Gentlemen of Kent in a 12-a-side match at Canterbury in 1862, scored 192* and took 5–77 and 10–69

The Double – 1,000 Runs and 100 Wickets

W. Rhodes	16	M. S. Nichols	8
G. H. Hirst	14	A. E. Relf	8
V. W. C. Jupp	10	F. A. Tarrant	8
W. E. Astill	9	M. W. Tate	8
T. E. Bailey	8	F. J. Titmus	8
W. G. Grace	8		

750 Catches

		Career	Matches			Career	Matches
1,018	F. E. Woolley	1906–1938	979	784	J. G. Langridge	1928–1955	574
887	W. G. Grace	1865–1908	879	764	W. Rhodes	1898–1930	1,107
830	G. A. R. Lock	1946–1971	654	758	C. A. Milton	1948–1974	620
819	W. R. Hammond	1920–1951	634	754	E. H. Hendren	1907–1938	833
813	D. B. Close	1949–1986	786				

Only Frank Woolley (58,969 runs, 2,068 wickets and 1,018 catches) has all-round career figures that can compare with WG. But even he is not on the list of century-makers on Test debut, as WG is.

Acknowledgements

In compiling this anthology I have received help from many quarters. First of all, I must thank Charlotte Atyeo for seizing upon my idea of a Grace anthology so eagerly: I can now reveal to her that I thought up the idea about four seconds before I mentioned it to her, and I was thrilled if also amazed by her immediate enthusiasm for what was not much more than a title back up by several glasses of wine.

At Wisden I have had tremendous help from the usual suspects – Jane Lawes, who has managed the book through to publication; Steven Lynch who not only had the daunting task of copy-editing, but also helped significantly with some of the statistical issues that arose; and Chris Lane for his general enthusiasm. I must also thank Philip Bailey for coming up with some hard to come by facts about WG's career, and Howard Milton and David Robertson at Kent CCC, who confirmed several facts about Grace's Canterbury Weeks for me. Robert Winder, author of "The Little Wonder – The Remarkable History of Wisden" was also very kind in sharing his views on Wisden's treatment of W.G., which helped crystallize my views on that slightly equivocal relationship. I also referred regularly to Simon Rae's brilliant biography of W.G., which gave me several leads in my searches through Wisden for some of W.G.'s more recondite feats.

My wife Jan has as ever been long-suffering and uncomplaining even though I have shut myself away at my desk and ignored requests to join in with the rest of humanity in getting a life. I have promised not to do it again until the next time.

Jonathan Rice
August 2014

INDEX